D0501494

Talking
Trees
&
Singing
Whales

Talking Trees & Singing Whales

Charles C. Case

This book is published in collaboration
with the Youth Department as an enrichment of
the Morning Watch devotional plan.

REVIEW AND HERALD PUBLISHING ASSOCIATION

Washington, DC 20039-0555
Hagerstown, MD 21740

Copyright © 1985 by
Review and Herald Publishing Association

This book was
Designed by Richard Steadham
Cover photos by Animals Animals/Richard Kolar (whale); Com-
  stock, Inc. (tree)
Printed in U.S.A.

Library of Congress Cataloging in Publication Data

Case, Charles C., 1931-
    Talking trees and singing whales.

    "Published in collaboration with the Youth Department
as an enrichment of the Morning Watch devotional plan."
    Includes index.
    1. Youth—Prayer books and devotions—English.
2. Devotional calendars—Seventh-day Adventist. I. Title.
BV4850.C37   1985   248.4'8673202   85-8249

ISBN 0-8280-0285-1

MEET THE AUTHOR

Charles C. Case was born in Oakland, California, and went to elementary school in Pennsylvania, Colorado, and California. He graduated from Fresno Union Academy in 1949, from La Sierra College in 1954. He entered the ministry in the Southeastern California Conference as a temperance and communications intern in 1954. In 1955 he was married to Mildred Mattison. In August, 1956, they went to the North Brazil Union, where he served as home missionary, Sabbath school, and radio director. From 1959 to 1967 he served in Peru, part of the time as president of the Upper Amazon Mission. During the time spent in the Amazon he saw the church membership double and started the first denominationally-approved airplane program.

In 1967 he returned to the United States and began working as director of university relations at Loma Linda University. In 1970 he was chosen as youth, education, and temperance director of the Kansas Conference, where he built the youth camp, Broken Arrow Ranch. In 1975 he moved to the Southern New England Conference as youth and temperance director. While there he received his doctorate in education from Boston University. In 1980 he was called to the Lake Union, where he presently serves as communication director. He is also the camping and outdoor specialist for North American Youth Ministries. His wife, Millie, teaches at Andrews University in the Department of Nursing. They have two children, Charles, Jr., and Jacquelyn Bragaw, both born in Brazil, and three grandchildren.

DEDICATED

To my wife, Millie,
for her encouragement and love;
To my daughter, Jackie,
for her faithful typing of this manuscript;
To my son, Charlie,
for his encouragement;
To my father, Asa,
for instilling in me a love for the outdoors.

Bible texts credited to Amplified are from *The Amplified Bible and New Testament.* Copyright 1965 by The Lockman Foundation. Used by permission.

Scripture quotations marked N.A.S.B. are from the *New American Standard Bible,* © The Lockman Foundation 1960, 1962, 1963, 1968, 1971, 1972, 1973, 1975, 1977.

Texts credited to N.E.B. are from *The New English Bible.* © The Delegates of the Oxford University Press and the Syndics of the Cambridge University Press 1961, 1970. Reprinted by permission.

Texts credited to N.I.V. are from *The Holy Bible: New International Version.* Copyright © 1978 by the International Bible Society. Used by permission of Zondervan Bible Publishers.

Scripture quotations marked R.S.V. are from the Revised Standard Version of the Bible, copyrighted 1946, 1952 © 1971, 1973.

Verses marked T.L.B. are taken from *The Living Bible,* copyright 1971 by Tyndale House Publishers, Wheaton, Ill. Used by permission.

A MESSAGE FOR MY YOUNG READERS

As we begin this new year I want to turn your attention each morning to the marvelous things that God created for you and me to enjoy. After He created everything, I'm sure that He must have looked back and admired the beauty and perfection. What a scene that must have been! Although now marred by sin, the beauty of these things still shines forth.

As God created Adam and Eve He carefully thought out every little detail; He equipped them to see, hear, taste, touch, and smell. As descendants of Adam and Eve, we have also received the blessings of the senses. If we didn't have them, we would miss out on a lot in life because "nature speaks to their [men's] senses, declaring that there is a living God, the Creator, the Supreme Ruler of all."—*Patriarchs and Prophets,* p. 48.

We will be studying the different objects of nature because "there is a simplicity and purity in these lessons direct from nature that makes them of the highest value. . . . The children and youth, all classes of students, need the lessons to be derived from this source. In itself the beauty of nature leads the soul away from sin and worldly attractions, and toward purity, peace, and God."—*Counsels to Parents and Teachers,* p. 186.

It is my hope and prayer that we will see that "the character and power of God are revealed by the works of His hands. In the natural world are to be seen evidences of God's love and goodness. These tokens are given to call attention from nature to nature's God, that His 'eternal power and Godhead' may be understood."—*Medical Ministry,* p. 103.

Charles C. Case

LAMP OF THE BODY

The eye is the lamp of the body. Matthew 6:22, R.S.V.

Our eyes are a marvelous part of our body. The eye is made up of different parts called the cornea, iris, pupil, lens, retina, and optic nerve. These parts, all functioning in harmony, allow us to see in living color what God created. The light waves that the eye receives are transmitted to the brain along the optic nerve, and the brain quickly translates them into images. It is impossible for us to comprehend the great thought and care that God took in creating man, and especially our sense of sight.

The ability to see is one of the greatest physical gifts God has given us. It is sad to think that the presence of sin has ruined sight for so many people to the extent that they are totally blind. Others are partially blind or need glasses to see well. Some people are color-blind—they cannot distinguish certain colors. God's world is a beautiful world; He spoke and it all came forth in living color.

Through our eyes pass images that are stored in the brain like a computer. After you have returned from a vacation trip to the mountains, you may say, "I can still see those tall mountains with all those evergreen trees. It was beautiful." You are recalling what your eyes had seen and was recorded in your brain on that trip.

Scientists tell us we remember about 85 percent of what we see. Satan knows that the eyes are one of the most important organs of the body, so he puts scenes on television, in books and magazines, and on billboards, that will capture our attention. We put them into our computer—the brain. In this way he gets to our mind. "If he [Satan] can control minds so that doubt and unbelief and darkness shall compose the experience of those who claim to be the children of God, he can overcome them with temptation."—*Gospel Workers,* p 161. Satan wants to pervert our sight, captivate our minds, and take over in our lives. Are you going to let him?

Reconsecrate yourself to God at the beginning of this new year and ask Him to help you today to overcome Satan and his deceitfulness.

11

THE SENSE OF HEARING

He that hath an ear, let him hear. Revelation 2:7.

A second important sense that God has given us is hearing. The system of hearing that God created in the human body is fantastic. Man has tried to imitate this system for receiving messages by radio, telephone, television, and satellite.

The human hearing system has three major areas: the outer ear, the middle ear, and the inner ear. The part we see is the outer ear, which picks up the sound waves and sends them through the ear canal to the middle ear. In the middle ear the sound waves first hit against the eardrum and then against the three little bones called the hammer, anvil, and stirrup. As the sound travels from the outer ear funnel to the eardrum, the hammer hits the anvil, which passes the sound through the stirrup. The different vibrations send different impulses through to the inner ear where the semicircular canals and cochlea are situated. These pass the sound vibrations on to the brain by means of sensitive nerve endings that unite to form the auditory nerve. The brain then helps us identify what we hear.

Sounds are measured in loudness by a term called *decibels*. Absolute silence is 0 decibels. A whisper is about 20 decibels, an automobile horn about 85 decibels, a jackhammer about 118 decibels, and an airplane engine about 130 decibels. Music has regular vibrations whereas noise has irregular vibrations. Rock music is usually played so loud that it is more like noise.

God gave us the sense of hearing so we could hear the pleasant and melodious songs of the birds and other animals, as well as to listen to one another. Isn't it great to be able to hear what your parents and friends are saying? Satan will try to divert your sense of hearing from the good things. He will also try to captivate your hearing by immoral talk, unkind words, and unhealthful music.

What we hear, like what we see, is put into our mind and recorded there. Although we don't remember as much of what we hear as of what we see, still much of what we hear can be recalled by the brain. God wants us to hear all of the nice sounds of creation.

TASTE AND SMELL

Gods, the work of men's hands, wood and stone, which neither see, nor hear, nor eat, nor smell. Deuteronomy 4:28.

Idols of wood and stone cannot use any senses, as God gave these only to *His* created beings. Taste and smell are two of God's gifts. These gifts are very closely related. Here is an experiment that you might want to try. It will demonstrate the close relationship.

Hold your nose with one hand, then put some food that you really like into your mouth with the other hand. Notice that it is almost impossible to taste it. Why? Because taste and smell go together. The sense of smell has saved many lives, as people have smelled smoke, gasoline, and other harmful substances. God wanted us to enjoy the sweet aromas from the blossoms and flowers, so the sense of smell was made to be very sensitive. Most animals also have a keen sense of smell.

Taste is a different sense, but it is definitely related to smell, as we have seen above. On the tongue are the taste buds that tell us if the substance is sweet, sour, salty, or bitter. The taste buds on the tip of the tongue detect saltiness and sweetness; at the side is sourness and at the back, bitterness. Try another experiment. Put a few granules of sugar in the palm of your hand and lick them with your tongue. Now try a few grains of salt. Notice how quickly the taste buds notified the brain? It didn't take long, did it? Taste varies, of course, from one person to the other, so not everyone likes the same thing. For that matter, not everyone likes the same smells. Some like one kind of perfume and some another, so life is different for everyone.

Satan tries to pervert the senses that God has given us. Those who smoke a lot cannot smell or taste as well as they might. Satan tries to get us to taste and eat things that are harmful to our bodies. God has given us these senses as gifts so that we can more fully enjoy life. Thank God today for the senses of taste and smell.

THE POWER OF TOUCH

They brought young children to him, that he should touch them. Mark 10:13.

Touch is another sense given to us that God desired we should use to enjoy His creation. The sense of touch or feeling involves the use of our nerve endings in the skin, especially at the extremities of our bodies. As we touch an object, nerve impulses are sent to the brain. The brain immediately tells us that the object we are feeling is hot or cold, prickly or soft, wet or dry, smooth or rough, and so on.

God gave man the sense of touch so that he could enjoy nature to its fullest. I'm sure you have gone to a beach and let the sand fall through your fingers. Or perhaps you've enjoyed getting your hands into mud and liked that gooey feeling. Maybe you enjoy taking off your shoes and letting your toes feel the coolness of a small stream of water, or perhaps you have touched a beautiful rose and felt the softness of the petals. When a woman sees a nice fur coat, what is the first thing she wants to do? You're right! She wants to run her fingers over the soft fur to feel it.

There is a real emotion that one experiences in touching. The sensation of touching the bark of a tree doesn't give us the same emotion as the softness of the grass in the yard. The itchy feeling from peach fuzz on the arm doesn't give the same feeling as the soft stroke of a human hand on the arm.

Touch, perhaps more than any other sense, gives us an emotion. It can even give us the sense of belonging. The mothers in Jesus' day brought their children to Jesus for Him to "touch them" and give them a blessing. The sick woman wanted to touch Jesus' garment, and she knew she would be healed.

Jesus again demonstrates His love for us in the importance of the power of touch. He wants us to enjoy life as much as possible, so He gave us the sense of touch. Thank God today for the feelings you receive in the power of touch.

On this first Sabbath of the new year, maybe the touch of your hand on the hand of a sick or elderly person in your family, church, or neighborhood would bring the love of Jesus to them through you. Touch someone today with your life for Jesus.

"LET THERE BE LIGHT"

God said, "Let there be light;" and there was light. Genesis 1:3, R.S.V.

As God began to create the world on the very first day, He spoke the words, "Let there be light," and the Bible story of Creation reports, "There was light." God just spoke and there it was—light.

Light is composed of all the color rays coming together. If you have access to a prism, which is a three-sided glass object, you can see the different colors that are in white light because the prism separates the light into its different colors. The reason for the different colors is that God created each color with a different wavelength as it travels through space.

Light travels at 186,282 miles in one second. That is really traveling! If we multiply that by sixty seconds, we find light travels over 11 million miles in one minute or 670,615,200 miles an hour. Because of the tremendous distances of space, scientists do not measure it in miles but in "light-years," the distance light travels in one year.

The expanse of the heavens is so vast—and we'll talk about that tomorrow—that if God shut off the light rays from the sun, we would still have the light for about eight and one-third minutes, as it takes about 500 seconds for the light to travel from the sun to the earth. Light travels nearly 6 trillion miles in one year, and that is difficult for us to comprehend.

Light is very important to all life living here on this earth. Without light most vegetation cannot grow. Man has created artificial light in light bulbs, candles, kerosene lamps, and matches, but only God could create the light that lights up the universe.

We cannot understand how, but God spoke, and the light was there with all of the color waves. God had an orderly plan in His creation, so the light came first. Aren't you glad that as a God of love, He thought ahead about how to have His children enjoy the outdoors. He gave them light to see by. I thank Him for this light, what about you? Thank Him this morning.

HE CREATED THE SKY

And God said, "Let there be a firmament in the midst of the waters." Genesis 1:6, R.S.V.

On God's second day of Creation He spoke and commanded the firmament to separate from the waters. The firmament has no shape to it, but it is all around us. This is the space above us that we sometimes call atmosphere, or sky. The sky was put there by God for a specific purpose. It contains the weather system, and helps keep the temperature in balance.

As you look up into the sky on a clear day, you see the color blue. There have been many different ideas or theories as to why the color of the sky is blue. Some people said that the atmosphere was made up of tiny water bubbles and the light passing through these thin bubbles caused the blue color. The most commonly accepted theory is that the atmosphere, up to about 100 miles above the earth's surface, is composed of oxygen, nitrogen, carbon dioxide, several other gases, water vapor, and suspended particles. As the light rays pass through this atmosphere, these various molecules scatter the light. The shorter the wavelength of the color, the more it is scattered. As blue color wavelengths are the shortest, and therefore are scattered more, they cause the blue-sky effect. The sky may appear bluer overhead and lighter toward the horizon because of the angle at which you are looking at it.

When the sun sets, the color waves must pass through more atmosphere than when the sun is overhead. With the dust particles in the atmosphere and the longer color wavelengths (red being longer) the deep red, yellow, and orange sunsets are produced.

Astronauts tell us that where there is no atmosphere to reflect the color waves, such as in outer space, there is no color and all one sees is black.

God created the atmosphere that made possible the blue sky. Have you ever stopped to think what this earth would be like if that blue sky was not above us? God not only created the atmosphere with a purpose, but He created it in such a way that it would be beautiful, too.

FOOD AND BEAUTY

And God said,... "Let the dry land appear.... [and] put forth vegetation." Genesis 1:9–11, R.S.V.

As God started His third day of Creation, He told the waters to divide and let the dry land appear. He called the dry land earth, and the waters He called seas.

After the waters parted and the earth appeared God told the earth to grow all types of vegetation such as trees, shrubs, flowers, grains, grass, and vegetables. The Bible story says that as all of these different kinds of vegetation sprang forth, there was to be seed in each one so they would continue to reproduce.

Can you imagine what a thrill it must have been for God to speak, and all the many varieties of flowers were made? My mind just goes wild as I think of all the lovely flowers that I have seen in different parts of the world. They are all so different.

And what about the trees? All of the fruit trees, palm trees, nut trees, evergreen trees, and others. Can you imagine God speaking, and all of a sudden there are trees everywhere? He didn't have to wait for them to grow. We wait for years for trees to grow from seeds or small plants, but not God. He spoke, and all the varieties of trees were there. What a powerful God!

God created the grass as a covering for the earth to make it beautiful and provide a soft, carpetlike effect. He created the wheat, barley, oats, corn, and other grains. And also springing forth from the earth were the vegetables and all other vegetation.

It must have been very exciting for God to see all of the vegetation spring forth and cover the soil and make the earth colorful. God was demonstrating His love in a magnificent way on the third day of Creation. He was preparing the earth for something else. He had in His master plan the creation of creatures that would need vegetation for food, so on this third day all the food that would be necessary for these creatures was created.

God will provide for all your needs today, if you trust Him, because "my God shall supply all your need according to his riches in glory by Christ Jesus" (Phil. 4:19). Thank God today for His provisions for your physical needs.

GOD'S LIGHTS

And God said, "Let there be lights in the firmament of the heavens to separate the day from the night." Genesis 1:14, R.S.V.

Light, sky, vegetation, and now lights in the heavens. God knew what He was doing, and He did it in perfect order. In living color God had beautified the earth. Then God made two great lights, the greater light to rule the day—that's the sun, and the lesser light to rule the night—that's the moon. The Bible adds, "He made the stars also."

The sun gives light and heat, and its rays are very beneficial, because it is impossible for most vegetation to exist without sunlight. The sun's rays cause the plants to produce food for the plant to stay alive, and the plants provide food for humans and animals to live on. Sunlight is also very necessary for the human body to produce in a natural way vitamin D. This vitamin is essential for the human body to function properly.

The object of the moon was to light up the night and influence plant growth and produce tides in the oceans. The moon is called the lesser light; it receives its light from the sun, acting as a reflector of the sunlight. Thus it provides the moonlight for the growth of plants at night.

I'm sure you have gone outside at night and looked up into the sky and noticed all the stars. Yes, there are stars, stars, and more stars. It makes a person wonder how God could create so many stars, but He spoke, and there they were.

Physicists and astronomers have studied the stars for centuries. They have made telescopes of high magnification, enabling them to study the stars. These men have learned much about the stars, but they really know very little compared to God's knowledge of how it all works.

If God could do such marvelous things at the time of Creation, and create them in harmony, don't you think He could do some great things in your life if you'll just let Him try? Ask Him to help you with any problem you have, and He will help you overcome it.

FISH AND BIRDS

And God said, "Let the waters bring forth swarms of living creatures, and let birds fly above the earth." Genesis 1:20, R.S.V.

On the fifth day of Creation God broke the silence of His world when He created all of the sea creatures and the birds of the sky.

Sea creatures of every description came forth at God's command. Picture yourself standing there by God's side and hear Him say, "Mammals of the sea, come forth," and the whales and porpoises began to splash around. "Now I want fish"; then the sharks, angel fish, guppies, goldfish, trout, salmon, bat rays, bass, yellowtails, marlins, barracudas, cods, halibuts, swordfish, and others churned the water. Next, "Come forth, other sea creatures," so the octopuses, starfish, sea horses, crabs, lobsters, shrimps, and all the other kinds of moving creatures began to swim in the water. "I want some more beautiful things in the water," and the sea anemone, sand dollars, sea urchins, corals, mollusks, and other sea creatures appeared. I would suppose by this time your eyes would be really bulging as you heard God speak and saw all these creatures come to life and the waters swarming with this new life.

He spoke again, and birds began to appear in the sky, such as eagles, hawks, vultures, crows, ravens, macaws. Strutting around on the earth, the ostriches, emus, peacocks, and flamingos spread their wings. Ground birds such as the quail, grouse, pheasants, chickens, and turkeys began scratching the earth's surface. Singing birds including the robins, sparrows, meadowlarks, whippoorwills, and bobwhites began their songs. Paddling around in the water and flapping their wings were the many varieties of ducks, swans, coots, and geese. Little birds such as the hummingbirds, chickadees, wrens, titmice, and nuthatches floated through the air from tree to tree.

As these newly created birds came forth from the Creator's hand, they were perfect and tame. Fear did not exist, and they had nothing to be afraid of. God in His love had created them without fear. Thank God this morning for the wildlife in your world.

19

ANIMALS AND MAN

And God said, "Let the earth bring forth living creatures according to their kinds. . . . Let us make man in our image, after our likeness." Genesis 1:24-26, R.S.V.

Five full days of Creation, and God must have had a great time. It would have been fun to see all of the different things and creatures on the face of the earth. Now God was beginning to start the sixth day. Only God was wise enough to decide what to create on this day. According to His master plan, He would create land animals. God spoke, and the massive elephants, rhinoceroses, and hippopotamuses came forth. The lions, tigers, giraffes, deer, antelope, zebras, horses, cattle, baboons, monkeys, and many other animals responded to His voice.

God wanted other creatures, so the amphibians (such as frogs, toads, and salamanders), the reptiles (such as alligators, crocodiles, lizards, snakes, and turtles), and many others came forth. Smaller insects (such as flies, katydids, locusts, and grasshoppers) and thousands of other tiny creatures crawled forth at the Creator's voice. As God looked over the earth, it was covered with moving and flying creatures. He knew that one thing was yet lacking, but His master plan was about to be completed.

God saved the best for last. He formed man out of the dust of the earth and breathed into his nostrils the breath of life. Then God saw that it was not good that man should be alone, so He caused Adam to fall asleep, and He performed the first surgery. He opened up Adam's side, took out a rib, and made Adam's side like new. He formed Eve from that rib. Then God performed the first marriage. Now His creation was complete. The earth was full, and God had someone to take care of things for Him. He had some new friends in the Garden of Eden.

Now as God looked over all that He had made, He saw that it was very good. He gave man the opportunity to name all the creatures. He turned over His creation for man to take care of, and that demonstrates to me that God is a loving, caring, and trusting God. Thank God this morning that He trusts us with this world, and ask Him to trust you today and help you in your opportunities to tell others what a great God He is.

GOD'S DAY

And on the seventh day God finished his work which he had done, and he rested on the seventh day from all his work which he had done. So God blessed the seventh day and hallowed it. Genesis 2:2, 3, R.S.V.

God had a very eventful six days in creating this world; it had been a busy week. He had ended His work with the creation of man, and His master plan was complete—well almost, anyway. After He had finished His work and made the Sabbath, the Bible says He rested on the Sabbath day. He blessed it and hallowed it. He set this day apart for a special purpose.

God set the seventh day of the Creation week aside for rest. Even though God had been busy during Creation week, He was not resting because He was tired. He was resting because He had accomplished His goal of Creation. If God blessed and hallowed the seventh day of the week, to me that means it is sacred.

God set an example for us. He worked during the six days of Creation, then rested on the Sabbath day from His labors. In the fourth of the Ten Commandments He has told us to do the same. During His ministry on earth Jesus went about healing, teaching, and visiting people on the Sabbath. He went into the synagogues and read. He, too, worshiped on the Sabbath.

Jesus created the Sabbath to be a blessing to man; a day to rest from all his labors and a day to worship God and show love for his Creator. God has never changed that day.

I'm glad God loved man enough that He didn't expect him to work all the time. He set the Sabbath aside to be a special and happy day. It is to be a day of worship, a day of helping those who need help, a day for sharing our faith with others, and a day of real enjoyment. How about starting this new year off right and make this a special day. Thank God for the Sabbath and ask Him to help you have a good day today and always.

21

STOP! LOOK! LISTEN!

Make me to understand the way of thy precepts: so shall I talk of thy wondrous works. Psalm 119:27.

Two men were walking down a busy street in New York City. One of the men stopped and said, "Did you hear that?" "Hear what?" replied his friend. The first man said, "Listen." Again the noise came. He led his friend down a couple of stairs. Over between two bricks was a cricket singing his song. The second man said to the first, "How did you hear that?" "Watch," replied his friend. He went back up onto the sidewalk and dropped a coin. Many people stopped walking to look for the fallen coin.

There are people today whose ears are tuned to the sound of money but are not tuned to the sound of a cricket. There are also people whose ears are tuned to the many sounds of nature. I have suggested to boys and girls that they sit down outdoors and cover their eyes with a blindfold and just listen to the sounds of nature. Try it yourself sometime.

God's world has so much going on in it that we sometimes hear or see very little because we are caught up in the busy life we are living. There are many sounds that when listened for are very melodious. There are many beautiful sights to be seen if we will just take time to do so. We have a porch on the back of our house that faces west. We stop many evenings and watch the beautiful sunsets take place. From our bedroom window we see many beautiful sunrises. So many people miss these beautiful sights because they refuse to take time to look. They are too busy!

God wants us to take time for both of His books—the Bible and nature. We can learn many lessons from God's Word, and we can learn many lessons from God's world. God can teach us spiritual lessons from His physical world.

Ask God to impress you to take time to stop, look, and listen to His Word and His world.

MIKE WAS MY MACAW

A merry heart maketh a cheerful countenance: but by sorrow of the heart the spirit is broken. Proverbs 15:13.

One day as I was walking with another missionary at the outdoor marketplace in Iquitos, Peru, I saw a large red macaw that called to us. The vendor called to us, too, and we stopped. As I came close to this macaw he put up his foot to take my arm. Knowing that these birds have a strong beak that could clip off a finger in one bite, I refrained from putting my arm too close. The owner said, "Go ahead, he won't hurt you." Hesitantly and cautiously I put my arm over toward this big, beautiful bird, and he put out his big foot and climbed onto my arm. He shuffled sideways up my arm until he could put his head and body against my chest. Then he began to move his head back and forth. I rubbed the feathers on the side of his head, and it seemed that he and I struck up a special friendship. I had always wanted a macaw; now was my opportunity. I gave the man the $7.50 he was asking for the bird and carried him home on my arm. I named him Mike. Mike was my bird; however, he loved my children, too. He would go to them just like he did to me.

If I was home on Sabbath I'd take Mike out after church and walk around the mission compound with him on my arm. He liked that! Once I had been traveling for two weeks and arrived home late on Friday. On Sabbath I had a full day with church duties and went by the cage only to say "Hi" to Mike. My wife, Millie, said Mike seemed sick; he hadn't been acting like he usually did. On Sunday I had to leave again, so I didn't take Mike out of his cage. Tuesday I called home and Millie informed me that Mike had died on Monday. I talked to a veterinarian and asked why Mike died. He said, "One reason could be that Mike died of a broken heart because he missed you, and you showed him little attention while home that last time." Do birds really die of a broken heart? I don't really know, but I doubt it.

Jesus died of a broken heart on the cross. He didn't want sin to separate you from Him; He loved you. He died for your sins. Thank Him today for His great love toward you.

WHITE AS SNOW

Come now, and let us reason together, saith the Lord: though your sins be as scarlet, they shall be as white as snow. Isaiah 1:18.

I like snow. I like to wake up in the morning and see everything covered with snow; it is so beautiful. I don't like to see the beautiful snow-covered landscape marred by animal or human tracks, but once it is, I enjoy being in it myself.

I'm sure many of you have had the privilege of waking up and seeing the ground covered with snow. You may have gone outside and played in the snow, and even watched the snow get dirty. Then you may have watched it snow once more, and as the snow covered everything it was clean and white again. The old dirt cannot be seen; all is a beautiful and picturesque scene—white and clean.

In our text today God is speaking through the prophet Isaiah. He says, "You have sinned. I know you have sinned. You have been disobedient to Me, but I still love you. Sit down and let's talk about it." Have you ever had your mother or father say that to you? I'm sure you have, and so you and your parent talk things out. That is exactly what God is saying: "Let's talk about it." Since sin entered this world, we cannot talk to God face to face, so we use the method of prayer. We tell God our troubles, our joys, and confess our sins. John writes, "If we confess our sins, he is faithful and just to forgive us our sins, and to cleanse us from all unrighteousness" (1 John 1:9).

We have all made our lives ugly with sin. Jesus accepts our confession of sin, and with His robe of righteousness He covers up those ugly sins and makes our lives clean again. We are cleansed from sin. That is exactly the way God's plan of salvation works for you and me. We mess it up! God cleans it up! As long as God cleans up our lives we have nothing to fear because He has cleansed us from all sin.

That is the promise that is spoken about in our text today, "Though your sins be as scarlet, they shall be as white as snow." Claim that promise today in your prayers.

BABOONS

Out of the mouth of babes and sucklings hast thou ordained strength because of thine enemies, that thou mightest still the enemy and the avenger. Psalm 8:2.

Animals that are amusing to me include the baboons. These creatures from Africa and India are so different, funny looking, and almost human, that it makes one stop and think about them and their lifestyle.

Baboons usually live on the ground during the daytime and sleep up in the trees at night to avoid danger from the lions and leopards that prowl around looking for food. After a night's sleep the baboons will come down from the trees and begin to look for breakfast. It is not easy to find the roots and other vegetable matter that they eat, such as fruits and grass seed, so many times they have to search around for food. Once in a while they will pounce on an insect, but their diet is largely vegetarian.

After breakfast they will sit down in pairs and begin to clean each other's fur by picking off the pests and dirt. This is called grooming. They spend a great deal of time in grooming, probably more than in doing any other thing. The babies are carried around on the backs of their mothers, or like a swinging bundle underneath the mother's chest. The "teenagers" run and chase each other around, screaming and yelling. They may chase each other up a tree, clear out to the end of the branch. Then the one being chased will have to drop to the ground to get away.

Baboon babies have to stay with their mothers for a long time to "grow up." Scientists have said this is one of the reasons why they believe humans evolved from other primates. I wouldn't like a God that would make me evolve from an animal. I like it that He created me and gave me strength to overcome the devil, with His help. Thank Him this morning that He indeed did create you, and that you didn't evolve from the baboon, and that He gives you strength to overcome Satan.

REFLECTIONS

Remember the sabbath day, to keep it holy. Six days shalt thou labour, and do all thy work: but the seventh day is the sabbath of the Lord thy God: in it thou shalt not do any work, thou, nor thy son, nor thy daughter, thy manservant, nor thy maidservant, nor thy cattle, nor thy stranger that is within thy gates: for in six days the Lord made heaven and earth, the sea, and all that in them is, and rested the seventh day: wherefore the Lord blessed the sabbath day, and hallowed it. Exodus 20:8–11.

Reflections in nature are so beautiful. I enjoy going out beside a beautiful lake and just sitting there and watching the beautiful reflections. As I notice the beautiful mountains or trees or grass or wildlife in the reflections of the lake, it naturally makes me think of a mirror, and that helps me to remember many things.

As a teenager I used to go up to Yosemite National Park with my parents. We enjoyed camping, so we went often. Several times during our camping trip, I would hike up to Mirror Lake to see if I could see famous Half Dome mirrored in the lake, as well as some of the other rock formations. I would hope for a smooth lake, and many times got what I had hoped for. The reflection reminded me of the Rock, Jesus.

Then I would remember what He said in many places in the Bible, and I would reflect on His Word. The only commandment where He said to "remember," to reflect back on His creation and what He had done, was the fourth commandment. Jesus said to reflect back, to remember what had been done on that day and what was not to be done on that day. It is difficult for a Christian to look at a reflection of some object of nature and not think of God's creation.

I enjoy going to one of our youth camps. From a seat on a bench in the campfire bowl I can sit and watch the sun go down and reflect on God's love. He wants to keep our lives alight with His word and love until Jesus comes. Ask God this morning to continually allow you to reflect back on what He has done for you.

RAINBOW

I do set my bow in the cloud, and it shall be for a token of a covenant between me and the earth. Genesis 9:13.

If you have the sun at your back just after a rainstorm, many times you can see a beautiful rainbow. We can see only half of it because of the earth's surface. As seen from an airplane a rainbow has no end; it is a complete circle. Rainbows are caused by drops of moisture in the air, each drop acting like a tiny prism when a ray of light strikes it. As these droplets refract—bend and separate—the white light that God created on the first day, the beautiful colors are seen. You probably learned in first grade that the seven colors of the rainbow are violet, indigo, blue, green, yellow, orange, and red.

You have perhaps seen rainbows as you were watering your lawn or playing in the sprinkler. Rainbows can be seen around waterfalls. I was flying over a cloud bank one day and all of a sudden I saw the shadow of our plane completely encircled by a beautiful rainbow.

It is interesting to note what others have believed about the rainbow. The ancient Greeks thought the rainbow was the bridge of Iris, a goddess-messenger who carried news of war and discord. Africans saw it as a great serpent that came out to eat after a storm, and ate anyone under either end of the bow. Some Europeans also thought it was a snake and sucked up the water from the lakes and rivers and then redistributed it as rain. A Germanic myth said that God was using the rainbow as the bowl of colors to paint the birds. When I was a child I was told that at the end of the rainbow was a pot of gold. I looked for it but someone always must have beat me to it.

Strange what different people think about different things, but the rainbow is not something we have to speculate about. God promised His people that He would never destroy the earth again with a flood, and the rainbow was the memorial of His promise. To me it is comforting, as I see the beautiful rainbow, to know that God will keep His promise. Thank God today that He keeps His promises.

LEOPARD OR PANTHER

Can the Ethiopian change his skin, or the leopard his spots? then may ye also do good, that are accustomed to do evil. Jeremiah 13:23.

One of the keenest, smartest, and most patient hunters in African countries is the leopard. The leopard is probably the most adaptable of all the cat family. It can survive in grasslands, arid areas, thornbush, scrublands, rain forests, in semidesert zones along the coasts, and on mountains.

Little is known about leopards because they are loners and sly. They do not rush to make a kill in a hurry. They may wait for up to a couple of hours until the right moment to make a kill. They are known to be nocturnal creatures, but away from the business of life, they have been observed quite a bit in daylight.

The pigmentation of their hide that is seen as markings is called *melanism*. It is a phenomenon that man does not fully understand, but the leopard's usual light background coloring seems to have been dyed black or brown in spots.

The "black panther" is a leopard that has not colored out. A female leopard may give birth to four or five cubs, one of which may be black. Scientists speculate that in some areas of dense rain forests the lack of daylight may give advantage to the black leopards and allow them to be more abundant.

The leopard cannot change his spots and you and I cannot effectively change our lifestyle alone. We need help to change our lives and put them in harmony with God's plan for us. We can't do it alone no matter how hard we may try. Only God can change a life through the power of the Holy Spirit. I know people who have held a grudge against someone for years, but then their lives changed and they learned to love that person. What made the difference? The Holy Spirit was allowed to work in their life.

You have the opportunity this morning to ask God to perform a miracle in your life and make you a different but lovable person.

SEEDS TELL THE TRUTH

The seed is the word of God. Luke 8:11.

Seeds are very interesting little things. Did you know that seeds tell us a very important story? Suppose you plant some seeds and you don't know what they are. When they produce plants, you can tell what kind of seeds they were. Seeds come in all sizes. The Bible talks about the mustard seed (see Mark 4:31, 32) as being the smallest of the seeds, yet it grows into a big plant.

I remember when I was a boy my grandmother asked me to help her plant some seeds in our garden. I said OK, so she gave me a package of squash seeds and asked me to plant these seeds in hills, three seeds in a hill. Then I was to cover them lightly with soil. I started down the row. I would mound up the dirt, then dig a hole in it, put in three seeds, cover them up lightly, and then go on to the next one. It was a long row. By the time I reached the end of the row I was tired of bending over. I still had quite a few seeds and should have started another row, but instead I just dumped the rest of the seeds into the hole and covered them up, thinking, Grandma will never know.

Days went by, and with Grandmother's watering and the sunshine, the seeds began to sprout. You can imagine my surprise when she asked me to come to the garden and showed me that hill where I dumped the last of the seeds. There were not just three little plants but a whole bunch. She scolded me and told me that these little plants told her the whole story. She knew what I had done.

God's Word is like seeds. If we put only a little of it into our lives people will be able to tell because only a little will show. But if we put a lot of God's Word into our lives much will show, and people will know that we spend time with God and His Word. God's promises in His Word and other great truths and counsels are to help us on the path toward heaven. We'll know which path to take. Pray today that God's Word will grow in your life, and you will know which path to take—the one that leads to heaven.

SYRUP TREES

The trees of the Lord are full of sap. Psalm 104:16.

God made trees full of sap because sap is the life of the tree, just as blood is life to the human body.

Through experimentation, man has found out that the sap of some trees is sweet and can therefore be used for food. Sugar maple trees are best known throughout the United States and Canada as the syrup-producing trees. Long before white settlers arrived, the Indians of the Great Lakes and St. Lawrence region were extracting the "sap" (sweet water) from the sugar maple trees. Black maples also have this sweet water, but it is not as commonly used as the sugar maple's sap. You might think that extracting this sap from the sugar maple would kill it. Apparently, the sweet water that is extracted from the sugar maple is different from sap that makes the tree grow.

When the right time arrives, January to April, depending on the area, the sap starts to flow up the tree. It flows the greatest when a thawing spell follows a freezing spell. Holes are drilled into the trees and the sweet water will flow out of the holes through pipes placed in the tree and into awaiting buckets. The sap is then taken and boiled to evaporate the water. Normally, 30 to 50 gallons of sap will produce about one gallon of maple syrup. Ever wonder why the price of pure maple syrup is so high? Now you know. If the syrup continues to boil, it becomes maple sugar.

As God made all trees with life-giving sap, He made us with life-giving blood. However, He also has given to us a life that doesn't require blood, and that is the spiritual life. It requires power from Jesus to live it correctly. Don't let Satan tap into your life. Ask Jesus to guard your life so that Satan cannot tap into you for that spiritual "sweet water," because as he takes this from you, your life will be nothing.

SAFETY IN NUMBERS?

For many are called, but few are chosen. Matthew 22:14.

There are more than 3,000 species of aphids in the world; they are considered to be the highest reproducers of all insects. They may even be the most abundant creatures on earth.

Aphids reproduce at a very rapid rate. A French biologist estimated that if all the offspring lived, the amount produced from one aphid and its offspring in one summer would amount to more than 6 billion.

To explain how the aphid lives and reproduces, let's use an example. One species is called the green peach aphid; it lives exclusively on peach trees. The offspring from the green peach aphid may live on some 70 types of plants and ferns. There may be more than 15 generations of offspring in one year from a single female.

There are enemies and friends of aphids, besides humans. The ladybird beetle known as the "ladybug" will devour aphids. She may lay up to 400 eggs and the larvae from these could eat more than 140,000 aphids. Parasitic wasps will sting the aphid and lay an egg inside it. When the egg hatches, the larva eats the aphid from the inside out. That kills the aphid, naturally, and the larva uses the body shell of the aphid as a shelter. The aphid has a real friend in some kinds of ants. The ant protects the aphid because the aphid produces a "honeydew" substance that is part of the ant's diet. The ant strokes the aphid with its antennae. This causes the "honeydew" to flow and the ant eats it. The aphid is known as the "ants' cow." Like cattle, the aphid is more productive when continually "milked."

There is a saying, "There is safety in numbers," but that isn't true concerning salvation. It would be wonderful if Christians numbered more than non-Christians, but that isn't the situation. We should thank God that we are numbered among those Christians who "know" Him.

PRECIOUS PEARLS

The kingdom of heaven is like unto a merchant man, seeking goodly pearls: who, when he had found one pearl of great price, went and sold all that he had, and bought it. Matthew 13:45, 46.

As far back as history goes, pearls have been precious items. Pearls are in short supply, and that is evidently part of the reason their value is so high.

Pearls are made by mollusks, which are water creatures that have shells, such as the clams and oysters. Even though we generally think of saltwater mollusks making pearls, some of the most expensive and beautiful pearls have been made by freshwater mollusks, but this is rare. The most famous freshwater American pearl was found near Patterson, New Jersey, in 1857. It is called the "queen pearl."

Pearls are begun when a foreign object (grain of sand) is introduced into the shell. The mollusk feels the irritation and tries to eliminate the irritation by coating it with a pearl secretion that helps to smooth it out in the shell. If the object is in the inner part of the body of the mollusk, then it produces a round or pear-shaped pearl. If it is attached to the inner wall of the shell, then it produces a flat-bottomed pearl. If it is in the muscle of the mollusk the muscle cannot accommodate it correctly so the pearl will be odd-shaped.

"We are to seek for the pearl of great price, but not in the worldly marts or in worldly ways.... There are some who seem to be always seeking for the heavenly pearl. But they do not make an entire surrender of their wrong habits. They do not die to self that Christ may live in them. Therefore they do not find the precious pearl. They have not overcome unholy ambition and their love for worldly attractions.... But Christ as the precious pearl, and our privilege of possessing this heavenly treasure, is the theme on which we most need to dwell."—*Christ's Object Lessons,* pp. 117, 118.

Ask God to help you find Jesus, the precious "Pearl," today. You must want Him and be willing to pay the cost, which may mean giving up some pleasures you like. Are you willing to do that this morning? If so, ask God to help you today to accomplish that in your life.

PACIFIC SALMON

Fear none of those things which thou shalt suffer: behold, the devil shall cast some of you into prison, that ye may be tried; and ye shall have tribulation ten days: be thou faithful unto death, and I will give thee a crown of life. Revelation 2:10.

One of the most fascinating and yet saddest stories is the life story of the Pacific salmon. There are five species of Pacific salmon—chinook, sockeye, coho, pink, and chum, and their life story is about the same.

The word *salmon* comes from a Greek word meaning "hooked snout," which the male salmon develop when they go to spawn. Spawning actively involves both the male and the female salmon. Let's look at spawning and the life of the Pacific salmon.

These salmon are all born in little streams or lakes along the Pacific Coast of the United States and Canada. When they have grown to be about five or six inches long, they leave their homes and head downstream toward the ocean. At the ocean they go into deeper waters, eating and growing. After being in the ocean for several years, the "spawning instinct" comes and they swim toward their "home." They usually find their home stream and head upstream. They will sometimes have to thrash their way upstream, and maybe even "climb" the salmon ladders built on the face of dams. Many of them die in the attempt to "go home." Arriving home, the female will swish her tail around in the sand and gravel and make her redd (nest). There she will lay up to 10,000 eggs. The male will come along and secrete from his body a milky solution called milt, which fertilizes the eggs. After about five months the baby "alevins" hatch, and the lifecycle begins again. The adults swim downstream and die.

Jesus gave His life for us and He promises us a crown of life if we are faithful. The faithful salmon should be a good lesson for us—to be faithful unto death. Pray this morning that Jesus will help you be faithful to Him, regardless of what happens in your life.

NEW TAILS

And he that sat upon the throne said, Behold, I make all things new. And he said unto me, Write: for these words are true and faithful. Revelation 21:5.

Some little creatures that crawl around on the ground are boys' favorites. I am speaking of lizards. All but two species in the world are nonpoisonous, so some boys and girls have fun with them. I don't think that there is a reasonably warm place in the world where there are no lizards. Scientists have identified more than 3,000 species to date. Lizards are cold-blooded reptiles that adapt to the temperature around them. They have a dry, scaly skin.

When I was a boy I delighted in catching and raising horned toads. At times I had cans, boxes, and cages with my "friends" in them, all over our yard. When I was told the fable that these "toads" caused warts on the skin, I dropped the horned toad I had in my hand and went running into the house crying. I asked my mother if it were so. She told me that it wasn't true; I had been handling toads and I didn't have any warts. I felt better and went out and picked up my "friend" again. Did you know that horned toads are not toads, but short-tailed lizards? When I learned that it surprised me.

Lizards do not have a built-in temperature control like many other animals, so they have to live in ground where it doesn't freeze. When the desert and dry areas become too hot for them, they hunt up shady areas or burrow into the sand to escape the heat. Most lizards are about four to six inches long, but there are a few even smaller. There are also large ones that are found in Indonesia; they may be up to nine or ten feet long and weigh 300 pounds. Big ones, huh? These are called Komodo dragons. We'll talk about those another day.

Most lizards have a defense mechanism that helps them escape their enemy. As the enemy grabs their tail they are able to detach it and let the predator have it. Many lizards' tails will continue to wiggle after they have been separated from the body. The lizards can grow new ones. In our lives, we may be detached from sin, and Jesus can make us new creatures. Pray that Jesus will help you to be separated from sin and be a new creature today.

GREAT BUSTARDS

Consider the ravens: for they neither sow nor reap; which neither have storehouse nor barn; and God feedeth them: how much more are ye better than the fowls? Luke 12:24.

The great bustards are birds that live in the country of Hungary, on the famous Great Plain. A bustard looks like a miniature ostrich, or as someone described it, "a cross between an ostrich and a vulture." The feathers on the body and wings are speckled brown, white, and gray, and a solid tan on the neck. A bustard's cry is eerie—like a subdued whistling moan.

There are 23 species of bustards that live in Southern Europe, Africa, Asia, and Australia. They prefer running to flying, but they can fly when necessary. Bustards have been observed at altitudes of 10,000 feet, over mountains on a migration flight. They are about three to four feet long, weigh as much as 30 pounds, and are about as large as a good-sized turkey. The female is about half the size of the male.

Bustards prefer dry, hot climates, although there are exceptions. Some can be found living in a variety of habitats—dry flatlands, prairies, wooded pastures, and meadows—but prefer open savannas and arid plains. They are also extremely shy toward humans.

The nest of the bustard is basically a depression in the ground, scratched out primarily by the female. She lays her one to five eggs and incubates them for 25 to 28 days. When the babies start to hatch, it will take them 12 to 36 hours to break out of the shell. Because the bustards were hunted so much, the Hungarian Government set up a special game reserve for their protection. The country of Poland is following the same program as Hungary.

God provides for His created creatures out in the wilds, for He loves them. But He loves us so much more that He not only provides for our needs but He gave His Son Jesus to die on the cross for each one of us. Thank God again this morning for His love and watch care toward you.

PETE AND THE ANTS

Go to the ant, O sluggard, observe her ways and be wise.
Proverbs 6:6, N.A.S.B.

Pete had been at camp for a week. It seemed he was always showing off. While he and some of his friends were out on the ball field, Pete noticed an anthill. He pulled back his leg and with one mighty kick he sent sand and ants flying for a short distance.

Back in the cabin after campfire that night, the boys in Pete's cabin, along with their counselor, were having their "talk-over" time, telling what they did during the day. Pete couldn't wait to tell how he had kicked the anthill and how the sand and ants flew all over the place. Pete's counselor had studied about ants in a biology class, and as soon as Pete stopped talking his counselor started telling the boys about ants.

"Have you ever seen an ant give up when it couldn't get over an object?" he asked the boys. "Have you ever seen an ant carry something larger than itself? Have you seen an ant helping another ant? Ants will help each other. They do not give up easily. They keep trying until they either get over the obstacle or around it, but they rarely give up. They are very persistent and energetic."

After Pete's counselor stopped talking, Pete said, "I didn't know all that. I am really sorry for the way I treated those ants. I just didn't think about them other than as pests." The next morning when the counselor got up and went outside the cabin, he looked over to the ball field. There was Pete on his hands and knees putting the sand back into the anthill for the ants.

As Pete's counselor mentioned, when an ant comes to an obstacle, he doesn't say, "I can't do it! I can't get over it!" God has given the ant an instinct that says, Keep trying and you can get over the obstacle.

With God's grace, we can overcome the obstacles of sin that Satan puts in our way. Never give up and say it is too hard. If you ask God to help you, He will show you the way to overcome.

PEAT HEAT

If then God so clothe the grass, which is today in the field, and tomorrow is cast into the oven; how much more will he clothe you, O ye of little faith? Luke 12:28.

Some years ago our family was traveling along the country roads of Ireland. We saw interesting fields that had been cut like steps. Other fields had straight up-and-down cuts like a knife cut. That night as we stopped at a tourist house we found that they were burning a sweet-smelling, bricklike substance called "peat" in their fireplace.

We found out that peat is formed when plants such as mosses and sedges are partially decomposed in water. For about $7 a year, the Irish lease from the government the space they need in a bog. They go there and cut out the peat bricks to burn. The peat bricks are cut with an L-shaped tool called a slave, which is sharp on the bottom. This part is pushed down into the bog like a shovel or spade. As it is pushed down, it cuts.

The peat bricks, which weigh about 15 pounds each, are taken to the owner's house and put out to dry. A dry brick weighs from four to five pounds. When dry, a process that takes about two months, the bricks are stacked against the house on the end that has no gable. The peat acts like insulation, helping to keep the heat in. A family may cut several thousand peat bricks in a week. Many households will use up to 15 tons of dried peat a winter, so 50 or 60 tons of wet peat must be cut.

Peat bricks are used for heating and cooking. Food that is cooked with peat bricks has a special sweet odor, similar to the way frying potatoes over a hickory fire picks up a special flavor. Water is also heated for bathing and washing clothes by burning peat bricks.

God takes care of all our needs if we will just trust Him. For years H. M. S. Richards used to end his radiobroadcasts of the Voice of Prophecy with "the longest unfinished poem": "Have faith, dear friend, in God." We must have faith in God. Tell Him in your prayer about how much faith you have in Him as your God.

LIGHTNING

For as the lightning cometh out of the east, and shineth even unto the west; so shall also the coming of the Son of man be. Matthew 24:27.

Lightning is all around us in this world. The National Weather Service reports that there are more than 4,000 electrical storms in the world at any one time. That may be hard to believe, but if you have done much traveling by airplane you may have seen the weather changing every little while. It is also reported that 100 to 300 bolts of lightning strike the earth somewhere every second of the day.

The distance you are away from lightning can be estimated by the number of seconds it takes from the time you see the flash of lightning until you hear the thunder roll. Since sound travels at about 1,088 feet a second at sea level, if you count the seconds between the flash of lightning and the clap of thunder and find it to be five seconds, you know you are about 5,000 feet away, or almost a mile.

Lightning is not a trifling matter. It can be very dangerous. My father tells the story of when he was in a violent thunder and lightning storm. The wind was so strong that it blew down the high power lines. Over the radio, authorities told everyone who was in a car to stay in their cars and not touch anything metal on the car. He saw the power lines come crashing down upon a car with a young woman in it. Several cars immediately stopped and shouted at her to stay in her car and away from all metal. Dad said she stayed there until the power company men arrived and cut the power. Then they were able to remove the high-tension power lines and set her free. The rubber tires saved her life. She was insulated or she might have been killed.

The coming of Jesus is not a trifling matter, either. Jesus has told us that He will be coming when we least expect Him. We don't know when that will be. We should be ready today and every day so as not to be caught unawares. Ask Jesus to help you today to be ready for His lightninglike appearance, and that you will not be afraid on that day but will be ready and waiting to meet Him.

GOOD NEWS AND BAD NEWS

Like cold water to the throat when it is dry is good news from a distant land. Proverbs 25:25, N.E.B.

This morning we introduce you to some interesting animals that live in Africa. They are called gnus or wildebeests. They are very large animals that resemble moose, except they do not have large horns. Wildebeests' horns are relatively short and curl over the head. Actually, wildebeests are antelope. They roam the African countryside in larger herds now than ever before.

It is estimated that in one national park reserve there are more than 300,000 wildebeests. The government leases the land for them to roam on for their protection. But the landowners are somewhat unhappy with the wildebeests, because they eat everything in sight, including the grass for the landowners' own cattle.

The largest herds of wildebeests at present are in Tanzania and Kenya, in reserves called Serengeti and Tsavo, respectively. It is estimated that there are more than 1.5 million wildebeests in this national park area. One of the dangers to the wildebeests is that the human population is expanding, and that is threatening their grazing land. The wildebeest is very particular in its eating; it likes only a few kinds of grasses. When these types of grasses run out it moves on to another area.

The male wildebeests have a very interesting ritual for claiming their territory. They will square off, then run at each other. Just before hitting heads they will drop to their knees and hit their heads and tussle. They seem to like the eyeball-to-eyeball tussle. After a few minutes they will do it again. It seems that about ten minutes is long enough for them to tussle, then one of them gets up and walks away, and the territory belongs to the winner.

Just as there is good news from a distant land about the flourishing of the wildebeest, so there is good news from a distant land that God loves you. Thank Him for His love and care this morning.

DRAGONFLIES

Surely he shall deliver thee from the snare of the fowler, and from the noisome pestilence. Psalm 91:3.

Dragonflies are very interesting and helpful to us. They have four crystal-clear wings that have veins running through them. As tiny as these veins in the wings are, there is a blood supply in each. (Remember, blood brings life.) With these four wings the dragonfly can move along at speeds of up to 50 miles per hour. It can climb straight up, dive straight down, and hover like a helicopter. Each dragonfly has its own territory. It flies back and forth to protect its territory and keep other dragonflies from entering its domain. Mosquitoes are the dragonfly's favorite food, and that is the reason it is so beneficial to man. It keeps down the number of mosquitoes.

Dragonflies have two large eyes and the threadlike neck permits the head great freedom of movement. These two eyes take up almost the entire head. Each eye has from 10,000 to 25,000 facets (small seeing units). No wonder it is difficult to catch a dragonfly. However, if you can sneak up on it directly from the back, and if it doesn't turn its head, it cannot see you. It has a blind spot in the back of its head. From the front to the sides it can see everything.

Satan knows that each of us has at least one "blind spot" or weakness. It is through this blind spot that he tries to tempt us. With some people it is music, comic books, novels, mystery stories, or other things. With others it might be movies, T.V., clothes, jewelry, or appetite. David stated that God would deliver us from the snares of the devil.

Pray today that God will take charge of your "blind spot," whatever that may be, so that you will not fall into temptation during this day. Without His help, we might think we can do it ourselves, but when Satan tempts us we may fall. God will watch our "blind spot" for us if we ask Him to do it.

KILLER WHALES

And God created great whales, and every living creature that moveth, which the waters brought forth abundantly, after their kind. Genesis 1:21.

Killer whales, also known as orcas, are the largest members of the dolphin family. They grow to a length of about 30 feet and weigh about nine tons. Their dorsal fin can grow to about six feet in height. Like the dolphins, they have a sonar system that helps them in their navigation and in communication with each other.

These whales are said to be very sociable. When one pod (group of whales) meets another pod, they will swim directly toward each other. When about 30 feet away they will stop, regroup, dive down deeper into the water, and swim toward each other, touching as many as possible as they swim past. One researcher said that he had observed this ritual on nine different occasions. It happened the same way each time. Female killer whales who do not have calves (baby whales) of their own will help take care of the other calves in the pod.

Researchers who have studied killer whales for the past decade have come to the conclusion that they are playful and gentle creatures.

A group of them were observed taking bunches of seaweed down into the deep water. The whales released the seaweed, and the air bubbles that were on the seaweed would bring it rushing to the surface. It would pop out of the water, making a sound and turn the water to foam. The whales seemed to think that was fun.

You may have seen a killer whale at a marine park. These whales are black with white trim (back and fins). It is fascinating to find out that God gave to seemingly every creature He created a desire to play. God certainly is a God of love, and He thought of everything.

It will be great to get to heaven and find out more of what God created in every one of His creatures.

I want to thank God today that He filled this world with so many interesting creatures that I can learn about—that it never gets boring. If you feel like I do, thank Him today in your prayers that He created this world to be so interesting.

41

HORNBILLS

And seek not ye what ye shall eat, or what ye shall drink, neither be ye of doubtful mind. Luke 12:29.

The question is asked, "What sounds like a locomotive, sports a bizarre beak, and seals itself up to hatch its eggs?" Yes, it is the hornbill. There are 44 different species of this peculiar-looking bird, ranging from Africa to the Solomon Islands in the Pacific Ocean.

These birds have black feathers on the top side of the body and wings, and white cottonlike feathers on the underside. They have long beaks like the toucan. On the top side of the beak is a casque (helmetlike growth) that is differently shaped according to the species. Some researchers agree that the casque helps the bird dissipate the heat from the body, while other researchers think that the casque is strictly an adornment for attracting females. The casque consists of a honeycomblike tissue with numerous blood vessels running through it, which does help in the release of heat, thus keeping the bird comfortable in the hot tropical forests it inhabits.

The helmeted hornbill is the only species with a solid casque on its beak. This characteristic has caused Chinese artisans to hunt the birds for the casque. They carve it into very beautiful artifacts such as belt buckles, pen holders, decorative miniatures, and snuff bottles.

Hornbills live principally on fruits. During the nesting period the female will seal herself in the nest, using a mixture of mud, droppings, and saliva, leaving only a small opening through which the male will bring her food. One male was observed making 18 trips to his mate in one day, and another male was observed bringing a total of 24,000 pieces of fruit to his mate.

We are admonished by Scripture to not be concerned about the food and drink we need. If we trust in God He will provide, like the male hornbill provides for the female. Thank God this morning for His provisions for you, and tell Him again today that you trust in Him. He'll love to hear that from you.

NEW ANTLERS EVERY YEAR

Put on the new man, which after God is created in righteous-ness and true holiness. Ephesians 4:24.

There are more than 50 kinds of deer, elk, moose, caribou, and other wild animals that grow antlers. Each of these animals has a different kind of antler. Some of the antlers grow straight up above the head; others have many branches called tines or prongs and may spread as much as six feet across as in the moose.

The antlers of the "deer" family are grown new each year. You may have seen antlers that looked like they had velvet on them. They do! In the early stages of growth the antlers are covered with a soft brown-haired skin called "velvet." Just under the surface of the velvet on the antlers is a network of tiny blood vessels and nerve fibers that provide the necessary elements to help them grow. During the velvet season the antlers are tender. If the animal hits a tree limb or some other object and scratches off some of the velvet, it is similar to when you scrape your skin—it bleeds.

The antlers are used for protection, but the principal use seems to be for mating. As the velvet sloughs off the antlers they get tough and hard. Then the bucks or bulls each sets up his domain; any other animal coming into that domain is consid-ered an intruder. As they fight for the females, they use their antlers, and the bigger, stronger animal is usually the winner.

After the mating season is over, the males shed their antlers. In the spring the procedure starts all over again. You may wonder why you rarely see antlers lying around in the forests and mountains. It seems that the antlers contain a great deal of calcium, phosphorus, and other minerals needed in the diet of many animals. Therefore mice, chipmunks, porcupines, squirrels, and others gnaw away on the antlers.

As the animals grow more antlers, they once again become like new creatures. God has promised to help us become new creatures. Ask Him to help you to be a new creature today; He will not let you down.

43

TUBE WORMS

Behold, he spreadeth his light upon it, and covereth the bottom of the sea. Job 36:30.

It wasn't until 1977, when two men went down into the ocean near the Galápagos Islands off the coast of South America, that the first deep-sea tube worms were discovered. The scientists were looking for thermal vents. When the temperature shot up on the thermometer of their research instruments, they got inside their little minisubmarine named *Alvin* and went down almost 9,000 feet. There they saw a whole community of life. Tube worms and other creatures lived all around the thermal vents.

Deep-sea tube worms had never been seen before, and marine biologists were not even aware that there was such a creature. This opened up some new theories and speculations. It was first thought that this was the only area where they lived. Since that time they have been located in six or seven areas. In March of 1984 *Alvin* took a crew of two to the bottom of the Gulf of Mexico. There they sighted tube worms that were not living near a thermal vent. This led marine biologists to speculate that there may be tube worms living all over the world at the bottom of the sea.

How do they eat and stay alive, you ask? Scientists have discovered that there are bacteria that live in the tube worms. They provide the food for the tube worm. The bacteria, in turn, by utilizing certain properties in the blood of the tube worm, can manufacture food for themselves from chemicals in the water. So they help each other.

Just as scientists are still discovering new creatures in nature, so there are many that are discovering new truths in God's Word. God has not hidden anything from us; it is just that we haven't found many things, both in His natural world and His spiritual world. I am constantly looking for new things, and I hope you are, too. Ask God to help you find some new truths in His Word today, and that He will help you believe them when you find them.

PENNSYLVANIA INFERNO

Where their worm dieth not, and the fire is not quenched.
Mark 9:44.

In the Pennsylvania town of Centralia there is an uneasiness among the townspeople because there has been a coal-burning fire underneath their town for a long time. Some of the townspeople think that the fire started in the coal mines back in the 1930s, and others think that it may have started in 1961 when a burning trash heap ignited an abandoned mine. Whatever the date of the fire, there is a hot spot in Centralia.

On Valentine's Day in 1981, a 12-year-old boy was running across his grandmother's yard when a 100-foot pit opened up in the ground and the boy fell in. Fortunately for him, a tree root stopped his fall and he was rescued. It is estimated that the temperature of the burning coal reaches 1,000°F. With that intense heat, no system of pumping water can be effective enough to quench the fire, so it has continued to burn. For 21 years the townspeople have tried to put it out. At present it is burning over a 195-acre area, and they expect it to soon go to another 350-acre area. There is a lot of coal in this place.

God has told us about a hell that will have a very hot fire. This is not the type of hell that we commonly hear people talk about today—that will keep burning forever and ever. When the wicked are destroyed on this earth at the end of the thousand years, it will be a hot fire. I can imagine that the fire will be so hot it won't take long for the wicked to be burned to ashes.

God has given us the opportunity to escape that hot fire. He has told us that if we are faithful we will receive a crown of glory and be with Him in heaven. I'd like to be there and escape that hot fire, wouldn't you? Make your decision to follow Jesus today, and ask Him once more to take control of your life. The life submitted to Him will be with Him throughout all eternity.

TINY FOOD FACTORIES

I will meditate also of all thy work, and talk of thy doings.
Psalm 77:12.

I am amazed at the numerous varieties of shapes and sizes of leaves. Leaf shapes resemble such objects as sewing needles, human hands, arrows, and feathers. One of the smallest leaves known is about one sixteenth of an inch long and belongs to the walffia plant that grows in ponds. While traveling in South America, I saw the large *Victoria regia,* a giant water lily that has floating leaves six feet across. Some banana plants have leaves up to ten feet long and two feet wide. The *gunnera* herb tree has an umbrellalike leaf about eight to ten feet across, and a large palm tree with leaves 26 feet long and five feet wide. The African raffia palm tree has leaves up to 40 feet long.

All leaves have one thing in common. They are all food factories for the plant. As the Creator made the trees with their leaves, He put into each leaf a small food factory. Even the pine needle has a small food factory inside it. The leaves take carbon dioxide and water to make food for the plant. This provides energy for seeds to sprout, flowers to blossom, and the fruits to form. These food factories are operated by solar energy, using the sun and chlorophyll to form sugars from the water and carbon dioxide.

God created in man a small "factory" to provide energy for the human body. The brain produces impulses for the nerves, which stimulate the muscles, which in turn allow us to perform all the many things we do. God gave us minds to use, and a sure way to keep the mind useful is to expose it to the great objects in God's natural world and meditate on the lessons we can learn from nature. E. G. White wrote, "In itself, the beauty of nature leads the soul (mind) away from sin and worldly attractions, and toward purity, peace, and God."—*Counsels to Parents and Teachers,* p. 186.

If the light of God's Word penetrates our minds and fills them with good things, we will have the opportunity of living forever. Let us pray that God will help us meditate upon good things that will prepare us for eternity.

LIGHT FOR GROWTH

Seek ye first the kingdom of God, and his righteousness. Matthew 6:33.

Yesterday we discussed leaves and the importance of the leaf to the life of the plant, due to the small food factories within each leaf. Did you know that it takes about 50 apple leaves to make one apple, about 30 peach leaves to make a peach, about 15 grape leaves to make a bunch of grapes, and about 12 large banana leaves to make a bunch of bananas? That is why there are so many leaves on the different fruit trees!

Most leaves have three parts: (1) the blade, (2) the petiole, and (3) the stipules, although some leaves do not have stipules. The blade is the part that houses the food factory that we call the leaf. The petiole is known as the stem. This stem plays a very important part in the life of the tree. If the leaf blade did not have the stem to attach it to the limb of the plant, it would not be possible for the food manufactured in the leaf to be absorbed into the plant. The stem is made up of many tiny tubes that, when viewed under a microscope, resemble a handful of drinking straws.

The purpose of the stem is to help the blade to manufacture food and to always ensure sunlight for the blade. If the leaf is shaded, the stem will grow longer to allow the blade to take in the sunlight that is needed for energy. As you look up in a tree you will notice that all leaves have some sunlight during the day. The stem allows the sugars manufactured by the blade to enter the plant and the water from the plant to enter the blade. Thus, the stem is the connecting link between the plant and the leaf.

Jesus is our connecting link to God the Father. Jesus said, "I am come that they might have life, and that they might have it more abundantly" (John 10:10). He is interested in each of us having the light from heaven through His Word, that we might have life through Him. As the stem pushes the blade up to receive the maximum sunlight possible, His Holy Spirit will put you in the light of heaven so you will live forever. Ask God to send the Holy Spirit into your life today.

47

WHISTLING SLEEPER

Watch therefore: for ye know not what hour your Lord doth come. Matthew 24:42.

Have you ever felt like you'd like to just sleep and sleep, but someone made you get out of bed when you didn't want to? How about seven months? Does that sound good? Maybe that is too long for you to enjoy sleeping, and I'm sure it is, but the marmot is a five- to seven-month sleeper.

Marmots, of which there are five species in North America, are the largest of the squirrel family. They spend their time in the ground or among rocks. In the Eastern and Midwestern United States they are commonly known as woodchucks. They have a body about 20 inches long and weigh up to about 20 pounds. The marmots are vegetarians. They eat only grasses, herbs, and grains. They have a long, furry tail, and some people have even mistaken them for beavers.

The creatures will go into a hibernating sleep in late September or early October when there is still vegetation and grains around, and wake up from their sleep when there may be snow on the ground. Marmots in the Northwestern States and southwestern Canada have a short mating season, from 40 to 60 days.

Marmots are great lovers of community living. They always have a watchman looking for enemies when the colony is out eating or playing. As soon as an enemy is spotted the guard will make a whistling noise and all the other marmots will scamper into holes. A coyote approached a colony of marmots and the signal was given. Down the holes all the marmots went. The coyote began to dig in one hole when from another hole a marmot stuck up its head and whistled. The coyote ran over there and began to dig, and another marmot stuck its head out of another hole and whistled, and so on. The poor coyote was so confused that it finally left, defeated and hungry.

We have been told by God that we are to watch and be ready for Jesus' second coming, as it will come as a thief in the night. We don't know when Jesus will return, so we need to be prepared everyday. Ask God to help you be ready from today forward, so that as you watch you will see Jesus come in the clouds of heaven and will be ready to meet Him and go home to heaven with Him.

48

SUCCESSION

For I am the Lord, I change not. Malachi 3:6.

God has worked things in such a marvelous way that the natural world pretty well takes care of itself through God's sustaining power, if man will let it alone. God had planned that all be perfect, but as sin entered the world God needed to make some adjustments to take care of this sinful state.

The world in its natural state has ways by which it continues to live on and exist that men cannot understand. There are times that a swamp or small lake just disappears. We have also seen, especially in desert areas, where there have been large lakes, but they are no more.

There are times when plants do interesting things that we call succession. As the plants grow and the atmosphere, climate, and soil change, the plants change too. Eventually the soil and climate may become unsuitable for some plants and so they die out. As they do, there are usually other plants that will take root and fill the void, and a whole new group of plants dominate the area. As the plant world changes, so the animal world changes, because certain animals live on specific plants, and as these plants die out the animals move on to "greener pastures." Succession in nature is an orderly process, a series of changes. These changes occur until there is a stability of plant life. This is called a "climax community," meaning that they have arrived.

After a fire, volcano, or flood, there are plants that come in and seem to grow immediately. These are called pioneer plants. They have to accommodate the hot sun, the infertile, and sparse soil. The beautiful pink fireweed grow after the volcanoes erupt in Hawaii, and the willow herb blankets the earth where there has been a fire and all vegetation has been destroyed.

Although the earth's vegetation changes because of the circumstances, God says that He never changes. He is always the same. What He said and promised you can count on, because God never changes. Thank Him this morning, because He is a changeless God.

LEUCAENA TREES

My God shall supply all your need according to his riches in glory by Christ Jesus. Philippians 4:19.

The leucaena tree is called "the tree that does everything." A very rare find was made about twenty years ago when a crop specialist from Hawaii went to Guatemala and El Salvador. He noticed trees that resembled a Hawaiian bush. He took some seeds back to Hawaii and watched these trees in the first year grow higher than a two-story building. In two years they were 60 feet high. The wood was as hard as oak. This tree not only grows fast but also improves the soil, needs little water, and resists fires and winds.

What makes this tree so fantastic? Twelve reasons: (1) the tree yields more lumber than most trees; (2) the wood fiber makes excellent paper; (3) animals can use the nutritious leaves, which are high in protein, as food; (4) small pods and leaves are also good food for humans; (5) it is good for firewood; (6) it adapts well to many environments and fixes nitrogen in the soil; (7) it has a deep taproot, which helps to control soil erosion; (8) it is a good umbrella tree for other crops; (9) it shades undergrowth to where it dies and cuts fire hazards and it has frilly leaves that make it nice for landscaping, (10) its seeds, pods, and bark are used for yellow, red, brown, and black dyes; (11) it makes excellent charcoal; and (12) it is excellent for reforestation because of its rapid growth.

The Hawaiian crop specialist and those working with the leucaena are afraid people may expect too much from this tree, because it does have shortcomings. Frost kills it and it grows poorly in high altitudes and in acid soils.

Many people depend on the leucaena trees to answer many of their needs, but we can depend on Jesus who never fails. He has no shortcomings and will really be the answer to all our needs. Present your needs to Jesus, who created the leucaena tree. He will take care of them. Ask Him today.

MONARCHS AND MILKWEED

And they were helped against them, and the Hagarites were delivered into their hand, and all that were with them: for they cried to God in the battle, and he was intreated of them; because they put their trust in him. 1 Chronicles 5:20.

Monarch butterflies are probably the most popular and most populous butterflies in the world, especially in the United States.

The milkweed plant produces a sweet nectar from its flowers. Native Americans made a brown sugar from this nectar. The monarch butterflies also discovered this sweet nectar and they flock to the milkweed plants to suck up this natural sweetness. One might think that as these black-and-orange creatures suck this nectar they would attract predators, but most birds have learned that monarchs are not good tasting, but bitter.

Adult female monarchs usually deposit their eggs on the underside of the milkweed leaf. When the caterpillars come out of the eggs, they begin to eat the milkweed plant. If all the milkweed plants are consumed, many monarchs will perish. The monarch caterpillar turns this milkweed-plant food into a "heart drug" called cardiac gylcosides or carenolides, which gives any creature that eats it violent stomach upsets.

Once the caterpillar gets through its growing stage it spins a cocoon, also attached to the milkweed plant. From the cocoon it emerges as a full-fledged monarch butterfly. As winter approaches the monarchs migrate by the thousands to the Southern United States and Mexico.

While the milkweed plant will survive on its own, the monarch butterfly cannot survive without the milkweed plant.

There are many people in the world today who are living without Jesus, but one of these days they will lose their lives because they will not be able to live without a relationship with Jesus. Those who ignore Him and say they don't need Him will be sorry one day soon.

As the monarch trusts for life in the ever-present flow of sweet nectar from the milkweed, you and I must trust in Jesus for life today and forever. Tell Jesus this morning that you want to trust in Him.

BLACK GOLD

And every living substance was destroyed which was upon the face of the ground. Genesis 7:23.

God caused a great flood to come upon this earth. The water came with such force that the mountains and hills were moved, and the large majestic trees, along with other living things, were buried under the dirt and rocks. These large trees, forests of them, have fossilized, forming large deposits of coal. Oil and natural gas are also products of the fossilization process.

These large deposits of coal, gas, and oil have been used to meet the needs of humanity for heat and fuel. Refined oil has many uses, such as gasoline for automobiles and airplanes; heating oil and kerosene; diesel for trains, trucks, and ships; fuel for power plants; lubricants, waxes, asphalt, plastics, synthetic rubber, paints, perfumes, dyes, vitamins, medicines, detergents, fertilizers, insecticides, film, photographic chemicals, inks, and numerous other items. As you see, much of our life depends on oil that is pumped from the earth, which is a result of the Flood.

Natural gas was discovered under the property of Union Springs Academy in New York State. It is used to heat the academy buildings and houses. Another Christian church group found themselves heirs to a deposit of oil under their property. The royalties from the sale of this oil are used to help the needy and handicapped people in their church, provide education for the children in their church school, and pay for the upkeep on their buildings and property. If there are any funds left over, they are used in community services outreach. To this church the oil is considered "black gold" to help them meet their needs. They say, "God is taking care of us."

As you think about what God has done, thank Him that He cared enough about you, that He was willing to make provision for you, so that many of your present day needs would be taken care of by the oil that is in the earth. He is a loving God and takes care of His children. Thank Him for that today.

PHYTOPLANKTON

And the peace of God, which passeth all understanding, shall keep your hearts and minds through Christ Jesus. Philippians 4:7.

The oceans that cover about two thirds of our earth teem with tiny microscopic plants called phytoplankton and microscopic animals called zooplankton. These plankton are very important to life in the seas as well as to life outside the seas.

Scientists estimate that the phytoplankton are responsible for producing about 80 percent of earth's oxygen, and that they also produce as much new plant material as do land plants. Each of these phytoplankton is a "masterpiece" of engineering. It was not until the 1960s when the electron microscope was introduced that scientists were able to really see the intricate and interesting forms of the phytoplankton.

One phytoplankton resembles a ball composed of pineapple slices with holes in the center, all wedged together. Another one looks like a miniature pillbox. These phytoplankton are mined in masses, and the shells are used in swimming-pool filters and highway lane stripes to give them the reflecting sparkle. Others add red color to the water and are very toxic. Some early Indian settlers saw in the water some mussels and clams that had a red glow and cooked them and ate them. They became sick from the toxic poison. Many shellfish that are contaminated by the "red tides" are toxic when eaten by humans.

One scientist speculated that a humpback whale could have 5,000 herring in its stomach and that there may be up to 7,000 larval shrimp in the stomachs of each herring, and each shrimp may have up to 130,000 phytoplankton. Many scientists are predicting that plankton may soon be a very vital source of food for humans also.

I am thankful I don't have to worry about the future. It is in God's hands and as I confide and trust Him, I have peace that only He can give. Thank God this morning for His provisions and peace that you receive from Him, and ask Him to give you peace through this day.

CAN ANIMALS REASON?

How think ye? if a man have an hundred sheep, and one of them be gone astray, doth he not leave the ninety and nine, and goeth into the mountains, and seeketh that which is gone astray? Matthew 18:12.

How does a person think? Right, with the mind. Our minds have been given to us by our Creator. Then how does an animal think? Or does it? Scientists are studying much into animal behavior today, and there is confusion as to whether an animal thinks.

God may have given many of His created creatures the possibility of thought, but it is not the human mind. That is one difference that humans have from other creatures. Now let's look at some things other creatures do.

A German horse named Clever Hans was said to understand arithmetic. His owner could write $2 + 5 = ?$ and the horse would tap its foot seven times. It was later discovered that the horse did not actually know arithmetic but it was nevertheless intelligent. It watched the owner, and when it noticed a relaxing on his part, which indicated to the horse that it had tapped the correct number of times, it would stop tapping. A pigeon was taught to look at slides; when the ones with people in them appeared, it was to peck for food. At one time the pigeon was shown 1,200 unfamiliar slides and it pecked for food only at the slides with people in them.

A story that really is interesting is the one of scientists who were working with bees, trying to coax them to go a farther distance from their hive than they were used to going. They used a bowl of sweet water that they would move about five feet at a time. After a while the bees seemed to sense what was going to happen and they would go on ahead. When the men got there with the bowl of sugar water, the bees were there waiting for them.

I know that all of this sounds strange, but I am sure that God gave some degree of intelligence to His creatures. He saved the best for last; the human brain for mankind. Let's thank God today that He created this particular brain for us, the "crowning act" of His creation.

54

LIZARD DEFENSES

*My defence is of God, which saveth the upright in heart.
Psalm 7:10.*

Lizards have many defenses against their enemies. One is
the letting go (autotomy) of the tail, which in some cases
wiggles, distracting the enemy and allowing the lizard to get
away. I don't know if the lizard feels pain when it loses its tail,
but it doesn't seem to.

The glass snake is a prime example of this type of defense.
The glass snake looks like a snake but it is a lizard. It doesn't
have any feet to walk on but slithers around on its belly like a
snake. One difference between the glass snake and a real snake
is that it has a tail twice as long as its body. When in danger the
glass snake lets part of its tail go. The tail will grow back but
not as long as before. When let go, the tail may flop around for
three or four minutes. This often distracts the enemy and the
lizard can escape.

Other lizards use different methods of defense. The horned
toad will squirt a fine stream of blood out of the eyes for a
distance of about three feet. Some lizards can change their color
for protection. Some lizards just bluff their way through life—
that is their defense. The Australian frilled lizard will stand up
like a frog and blow out from each side of its neck a roll of skin
that looks like an umbrella draped around the back of the head.
It will open its mouth wide and hiss. This makes it look and
sound bigger than it really is, and most predators will leave it
alone.

I am glad that we don't have to worry about fighting the
enemy in our own power. We can give him the knockout blow by
calling on the power of Jesus. David realized that he needed
God for his protection. Call upon Jesus and His angels this
morning to look after you today, to defend you against the old
devil, Satan. God will defend you if you ask Him to do it. Now is
your opportunity.

SANDHILL CRANES

And be ye kind one to another, tenderhearted, forgiving one another, even as God for Christ's sake hath forgiven you. Ephesians 4:32.

In the early 1900s the sandhill crane almost became extinct. Several reserves were set up to offer protection to these birds, and today the sandhill cranes are making a slow but positive return.

I live in Michigan where there are several wildlife reserves for the protection of the sandhill crane; conservationists count about 200 breeding pairs.

There are six sub-species of sandhill cranes, three of which are migratory. The migrating birds go to the Southern United States and northern Mexico. They are the lesser sandhill crane, the cavallion sandhill crane and the greater sandhill crane. The other three species are the Mississippi sandhill crane, the Florida sandhill crane, and the Cuban sandhill crane.

Sandhill cranes grow to be three to four feet tall. Where I live the most common ones have a bare, red, wrinkled-skin forehead with a few scattered black hairlike feathers. In the fall the birds molt their feathers and turn a beautiful gray. However, when they return from migration they have a reddish-brown or deep-brown plummage.

Both birds of a mated pair participate in the raising of the young. The female will lay one egg and about two days later will lay a second egg. The male and female will tend the nest during the daylight hours but the female only, during the night. The male roosts close by during the night by standing on one leg in shallow water. After 29 to 32 days the clutch of eggs hatch. The chicks stand eight to ten inches high and weigh three to four ounces at the time of hatching. The chicks cannot fly for 75 to 90 days, so the family spends time together in the water in a remote area.

God intended for us to do things as a family and do things for one another's good. Sometimes, like the sandhill chicks, you may not get along with your brother or sister, but ask God to help you love, be kind, and be able to get along with your brother or sister today. He will help you.

SOLAR ECLIPSE

And the sun stood still, and the moon stayed, until the people had avenged themselves upon their enemies. Joshua 10:13.

An interesting natural phenomenon that physicists and astronomers will fly all over the world to see and study is a solar eclipse. This is when the moon passes between the sun and the earth. It happens during the daytime, and for a few minutes the sun is darkened out by the moon. Strangely enough, the moon, which is in orbit about 240,000 miles from the earth, appears to be the same size as the sun, which is about 93 million miles away from the earth.

Most of the time the moon misses the eclipse position as it passes around the earth. Every 18 years or so, however, the moon passes directly between the earth and the sun, causing the solar eclipse. On June 11, 1983, the longest solar eclipse of this decade was best seen across the Indonesian islands, and hundreds of scientists spent millions of dollars to go see this natural phenomenon and study it for five to seven short minutes.

The rays from the sun that can be seen around the edges of the moon at the total eclipse stage is what intrigues scientists because this "corona," as it is called, is lost when the sun is not shielded. Scientists are studying the corona, trying to understand the nature of natural gases. Scientists keep studying to understand the nature, causes, and effects of God's natural world.

Our Creator, no doubt, created some things that we as humans may never understand. God made the sun stand still in Joshua's day. He allowed the dark day of May 19, 1780. Science will never understand how God did this. Ask God today in your prayer to help you radiate the light of God's love to your friends instead of blocking it.

A HAND FOR DADS

As a father has compassion on his children, so has the Lord compassion on all who fear him. Psalm 103:13, N.E.B.

There is a great disparity among animals and birds as to what the males of the various species may do, but there are many species in which the "daddy" spends more time with the "kids" than "mama" does. Let's look at a few this morning.

The male plover will risk its life when a fox comes along. It will flutter along the ground, pretending to be injured, to lure the fox away from the nest. Small seahorse dads carry the eggs laid by the female until the young are born. Male giant waterbugs may have up to 150 eggs "glued" to their back with a waterproof glue by the female. They will carry these until they hatch. Male ostriches will spend up to two years with their offspring, teaching them about life.

Among more than 90 percent of all birds, the fathers are involved in raising the babies. Only about 10 percent of the mammals but a surprising number of fish and amphibians have fathers involved in "baby-sitting." Some of these fathers prepare the "home" for the family, while others are actively involved in child rearing.

The male pipefish has a pouch on the abdomen. The eggs are put into this pouch, where, after hatching, a blood supply provides fresh oxygen and food for the young. After three weeks the young leave the pouch and are on their own.

In the case of the marine catfish, the dad carries the eggs in his mouth. After they are hatched, the father will still gather them into his mouth for safety.

Mongoose males protect the family from snakes and other predators while the female is out getting food.

The behavior of males among God's creatures may or may not demonstrate the role of the human father, but one thing is sure, there is a heavenly Father who will protect, feed, and help His children mature with His love. God loved this world so much that He gave His Son to save it. He longs to have His children in His heavenly home.

Thank God for His fatherly care and love today, and tell Him how much that love means to you.

PEST OR FRIEND

If we confess our sins, he is faithful and just to forgive us our sins, and to cleanse us from all unrighteousness. 1 John 1:9.

While it may be beautiful to behold, some people call it a pest, others a plague, and some even a friend. South Africans call it the "Florida devil," and in India it is known as the "Bengal terror." How could one thing have so many bad names yet possibly be useful?

The water hyacinth is a native plant of tropical America. Because of its beauty and rapid growth, tourists have carried it to more than 80 countries around the globe. Now many millions of dollars are spent every year to eradicate this pest from lakes and waterways. Just the three States of Florida, Louisiana, and Texas spend more than $11 million a year to control this pest.

The water hyacinth has what is termed an "explosive-growth" pattern. Under normal growing conditions, ten hyacinth plants can multiply to more than 600,000 plants and take more than an acre of water in about eight months. As these plants grow, they mesh their root systems into a thick mat. In Indonesia a few years ago, the water hyacinths were so thick that they actually dammed up a waterway and caused flooding throughout the province of Kota Bharu.

Water hyacinths take their nutrients from the water and have been found to be very biologically beneficial to polluted waterways and lakes. The nutrients that they absorb for life are the nitrates, phosphates, and potassium that are the common pollutants. Hyacinths are also being credited with absorbing toxic wastes, pesticides, and heavy metals from the water.

Jesus has promised to be our filtering system. He has said that He will take our sins from our lives and make us clean and new creatures. He wants a pure and holy people.

Ask Jesus to come into your life today and filter out the pollutants of sin, cleansing you in preparation for heaven. He has promised He will do that if we ask Him.

TSUNAMI WAVES

Thou art a God ready to pardon, gracious and merciful, slow to anger, and of great kindness, and forsookest them not. Nehemiah 9:17.

The word *tsunami* comes from the Japanese word meaning "harbor wave." These large waves are sometimes called seismic waves or tidal waves. Tsunamis are the result of submarine earthquakes or volcanic eruptions, and there is no way of stopping them. When a quake is deep beneath the floor of the ocean, these tsunami waves move very rapidly—up to about 450 miles per hour. Where the water is deep the height of the wave is not very high, but as the waves reach the beach where the water is shallow, the waves may reach up to 100 feet high, but with much slower speed.

On May 26, 1982, a Japanese fisherman was tying up his little fishing boat when he felt the water beneath him recede quickly and then begin to rise. He knew the sign and ran for high ground. As he did, he noticed a group of school children having a picnic on the beach. The wave came and washed them all out to sea. As soon as the wave receded, the fisherman ran to his boat, untied it, and went to rescue the children. He was able to rescue ten, and others clung to floating wood and offshore rocks. Thirteen of the 43 children drowned. They had no warning or idea that this 30-foot wave was soon to sweep upon them. There had been a quake about fifty miles away, and within seven minutes from the time of the quake the large wave hit the beach where the children were picnicking.

In our lives, some of us set off tsunamis. When something doesn't go our way, we have an "earthquake" in our lives and "let go" with our temper and words. Usually someone else, often someone who is innocent, gets the brunt of our rampage. Should our lives cause tsunamis?

Right now, why not get down on your knees and ask God to help you not to "lose your cool" today, fly off the handle, or say anything unkind to anyone? If you want to be a good person today, ask Jesus to help you. He will, I know, because He gave me victory over my temper. He will help you if you ask Him.

TERMITES

And they said, Go to, let us build us a city and a tower, whose top may reach unto heaven; and let us make us a name, lest we be scattered abroad upon the face of the whole earth. Genesis 11:4.

The Tower of Babel was a tremendous engineering feat. The closest that we find to this feat in the animal kingdom is with the termites. I did not know much about termites until I went to South America and lived in the jungles of Brazil and Peru. There we had many termites; they are extremely plentiful in the tropical regions of the earth.

In the termite colony there are three castes or social levels. The largest caste, about 95 percent of the million or more insects in one colony, are workers. These workers are blind, wingless, and move around by touch, taste, and smell. They build the large colony homes. The second caste are the soldiers, it is their job to protect the colony. Some are also blind and wingless. The third caste in the colony are the reproductives. Each termite colony has a king and a queen, and it is their job to continually reproduce more termites. A queen may lay up to 30,000 eggs a day. In Africa, one species has a queen that is 2,000 times larger than the other termites. She is huge!

Termite nests can be quite large, some look like a chimney that towers up to 30 feet in the air. They may be built like pyramids, or dome-shaped; some have pinnacles. The outside of the nest is built with soil and a cementlike substance that the termites produce, so as to make a hard shell. An inner lining is made of softer fiber that is called *carton,* which is a compound of chewed-up plant material mixed with saliva and other substances.

As at the Tower of Babel, men have tried to outdo God and surpass what the Creator had intended for them to do. God is patient and will let men go only so far, then He calls a stop to evil. He did it at the Tower of Babel and He will do it again, soon, for the whole world. Ask God to help you understand His will and help you put your life in harmony with His will.

FOSSILIZED WOOD IN INDIANA

Study to shew thyself approved unto God, a workman that needeth not to be ashamed, rightly dividing the word of truth. 2 Timothy 2:15.

Many types of plant fossils have been found by geologists, miners, and hobbyists. Such fossils range from a small microscopic size to about 15 feet in diameter. In the State of Indiana, an area has been discovered that has tree fossils from one to two feet across in size. The geologists have found only tree trunks with no traces of bark, branches, or leaves. It is interesting to note that apparently these trees never grew in Indiana. None of the trunks have been found in an upright position. They have all been lying down.

Scientists say that these trees "floated" into Indiana from New England or southern Canada where their species are found growing today. These scientists say that these trees came to Indiana during a 50-million-year period called the Devonian period.

We, of course, know from the Bible that God caused a great flood to cover this earth and everything was destroyed. The large trees were uprooted, deposited, and covered with soil. They fossilized and some turned into what we know today as coal. Have you ever wondered why coal burns so well in a stove? It has many of the same properties as wood.

Scientists are somewhat puzzled about how all was done in the past. We as Bible-reading Christians know what happened in the past. Someone once said, "It takes more faith to be an evolutionist than a creationist."

I am happy I have God's Book to help me understand what happened in the past and what will happen in the future. We have a God who loves us and gave us a "Guidebook" to guide us in this life here on earth.

Pray today that God will guide your mind as you open His Word to help you live a Christlike life—one that will not lead to destruction but to eternal life.

SALT

Ye are the salt of the earth: but if the salt have lost his savour, wherewith shall it be salted? it is thenceforth good for nothing, but to be cast out, and to be trodden under foot of men. Matthew 5:13.

Salt is a very precious commodity in the world, and our lives depend on it. Some problems do present themselves when we use too much of it, but some of it is necessary for survival.

Salt is obtained in several ways. There are large salt deposits under the ground that are mined by miners. There are salt wells, where a hole is drilled into the salt deposit and fresh water is pumped in under pressure, dissolving the salt, which is then pumped out in liquid form. A third method is to allow sea water to come into specially prepared holding tanks or evaporating beds. When the water evaporates, salt is left. Most of the salt for the United States comes from salt wells.

Someone has estimated that there are 140,000 uses for salt. Less than five pounds out of every 100 pounds of salt is used for food seasoning. Salt and its by-products are used by meat packers to preserve meat, by chemical companies to make chemicals, by tanners for the tanning of hides for leather. Fisheries use salt to preserve fresh fish; food and dairy processors use it in their processing. Millions of tons of salt are used in making soda ash, which is used in making soap, glass, and washing compounds.

When salt is broken down by passing an electric current through salt water—a process called electrolysis—caustic soda, chlorine, and chlorine products are made. Salt is fed to cattle in their feed or in blocks set out for them to lick. Salt is used to melt snow and ice on the highways to ensure safety, and because of the lower freezing point of salt water, salt is used in the ice-cream freezer to melt the ice and freeze the cream.

Jesus told us that we are the salt of the earth. This means that we are here to put seasoning into the world. We are to make it a better place, but sin has put a real damper to this. Jesus will help us to be the "salt of the earth" if we will allow Him to do such. Pray this morning, asking Jesus to help you flavor someone else's life today.

THE OTTER

And when her days to be delivered were fulfilled, behold, there were twins in her womb. Genesis 25:24.

A water creature that we seldom hear about today is the otter. There are two kinds, river otters and sea otters. There are many similarities between the two kinds but some differences. For instance, the river otters are about four feet long. The sea otters are from four to five feet long. The female river otter usually gives birth to one to five young (usually two or three), whereas the sea otter gives birth to only one pup. The river otter eats a lot of fish and some crayfish, snails, frogs, and insects. The sea otter does not eat fish but lives on octopuses, squid, sea urchins, abalone, and other shellfish.

Both species of otter have a tapering tail, a large flat head, strong teeth, large nostrils, and small ears and eyes. They have webbed toes and a flexible body, which allow them to have great speed in the water.

Otters have a very valuable fur, the sea otter's being more valuable. It is used for coats, cuffs, and collars. The sea otters' fur varies in color but is usually brownish black and has some silvery hair mixed in. Otters are very intelligent creatures and have even been trained by the fishermen in China and Bengal to fish for them.

We have described two creatures from the same family that are somewhat alike, but yet different. Maybe you have brothers or sisters, or both, in your family, and you've probably been told you are each different.

When God made each of you He "threw away the mold," as no two people are alike, even though they come from the same family. Each person has his or her own characteristics.

Esau and Jacob were twins from the same family but they were very different. Thank God for your uniqueness. You are who you are because God made you to be who you are. Thank Him for that today.

LOONS

And ye said, Behold, the Lord our God hath shewed us his glory and his greatness, and we have heard his voice out of the midst of the fire: we have seen this day that God doth talk with man, and he liveth. Deuteronomy 5:24.

Loons live in the lakes of the North and winter in the South. Both males and females look alike, shiny black with white spots. There are only so many loons in a specific area, due to their territorial claims. The males stake out their territorial claim, then the females move in. There are three species that live in the United States and Canada.

The common loon is the most numerous. Different from most birds, the loons do not have hollow leg bones, but solid bones. Their legs are toward the back of the body, which helps them in their diving for food. They may dive to depths of 160 feet, following fish or searching for aquatic organisms, their main foods. Loons have dense body feathers, well lubricated during the preening process. This keeps the body dry and insulated from the cold waters of the north.

Loons have interesting calls; once heard they are never forgotten. They can yodel, laugh, talk, and tremolo (8 to 10 notes repeated loudly). Each sound has a significance. Tremolos are produced when the loon is excited or threatened. Yodels are sounded when a male loon encounters another male. Laughs are used to locate other loons or the young, and the "talking" is used to communicate between pairs or flocks.

Both parents take an interest in raising the young. They incubate their eggs on a nest of heaped-up vegetation that may be used year after year. The one or two eggs hatch in about 28 to 30 days. The young will either swim or ride on the backs of their parents. In order to fly, a loon must flap its wings and run along on top of the water until it is airborne.

Loons have different methods of communication, and so does God. He tries to communicate with us in many ways under differing circumstances. Allow God to communicate with you today. Invite Him to speak to you today and He will, in His own way, and you will understand.

LIFE UNDERGROUND

He that saith he is in light, and hateth his brother, is in darkness even until now. 1 John 2:9.

Although we don't pay much attention to it, the underground world is a world all of its own, and it is quite interesting. There is much activity that goes on under our feet everyday. Most of us are not aware of this, because we are so engrossed in our own little world of activities and don't take time to look.

Many animals make their homes in the ground. There are the ants, prairie dogs, chipmunks, ground squirrels, badgers, earthworms, turtles, toads, some bees and wasps, lizards, salamanders, moles, and many insects. However, there are millions of little creatures that we cannot see without a microscope that live in the soil under our feet. Just a single spoonful of soil could produce thousands of these microscopic protozoans, minute spiderlike mites, tiny nematodes, roundworms, hookworms, and many other creatures. They creep and crawl among the grains of dirt or sand and spend their time eating decaying plants and animals, and sometimes each other.

Many of the creatures that live in the ground have been equipped with legs that are capable of digging. Some, like the chipmunk, are not necessarily equipped for digging. Yet the chipmunk is an example of those that loosen and pull the dirt with the front feet and then kick it out with the back feet. Some of these animals can throw the dirt quite a distance with their hind feet.

The spadefoot toad digs backward into the ground to build its home. It will remain underground during the day and hunt for food at night. Earthworms, all 2,000 species of them, do much to enrich our soil. Of course, the ants are probably the ones that we notice most.

Many of us are not aware of all of this life that goes on in total darkness, and some of us are not even aware that some of our friends and relatives are living in total darkness. Jesus doesn't want any to live in darkness, and He expects us to help those who do live in darkness. Pray, asking God this morning to help you find someone in "darkness" today and give him the "light" of the gospel.

66

VICUÑA

And all they that were about them strengthened their hands with vessels of silver, with gold, with goods, and with beasts, and with precious things, beside all that was willingly offered. Ezra 1:6.

One of the most beautiful animals in the world is the vicuña. It has lovely soft, dense wool that protects it from the harsh, Andean cold. Vicuñas used to roam the highlands of Peru, Bolivia, and Chile by the millions, but they were hunted for their meat and soft fur. About 95 percent of the vicuñas were killed.

The vicuña is the national animal of Peru. A picture of the vicuña is on most of the Peruvian coins, and in much of the national art. The vicuña is one of the species of South American camels, but it does not have a hump. It looks a lot like the llama (YAH-ma) and the alpaca (al-PAK-ca).

In Peru, and all over the world, the vicuña is protected. It is against the law to buy or sell vicuña fur. The Peruvian Government has several herds of vicuñas. Occasionally some have to be killed to preserve the others, due to the lack of grazing land. Even though the government has the skins in their warehouses, they cannot sell them for fur coats and other items due to the conservation agreement to protect them.

It is now estimated that there are about 45,000 again in Peru, guarded by about 70 guards. Vicuña wool is so expensive that on the black market it is sold for about $600 a kilo (2.2 pounds). Cashmere wool sells for only about $100 a kilo.

The vicuñas were around when the early Inca Indians roamed the mountains of Peru. The vicuña can be seen on ancient pottery and other art treasures that have been found.

The Peruvians and others want to have that precious wool because it is so valuable. We should want to have Jesus in our lives because He is precious. He will bring to us the opportunity of eternal life. Thank Him this morning for the life eternal that He provides.

EARTHQUAKES

And, behold, the veil of the temple was rent in twain from the top to the bottom; and the earth did quake, and the rocks rent. Matthew 27:51.

At the time of the crucifixion of Christ, the earth quaked and opened up. Quite an event! I'm sure that the earthquake at the death of Jesus was the same type as we feel today. Some scientists estimate that some of the large quakes release energy equivalent to about 200 million tons of TNT or 10,000 times more energy than the first atomic bomb. The rocks in the outer layer of the earth are continually being squeezed and stretched by forces within the earth. When this force is more than the rocks and elements can stand, the rocks rupture and are displaced causing an earthquake.

Have you ever experienced an earthquake? One time I was walking down a street in southern California when the asphalt began to roll under my feet like sea waves. Another time, I was in our Inca Union Conference office in Lima, Peru, when a large earthquake struck. Our building leaned and rocked. People ran to the streets and cried and yelled. At the moment the quake hit I was meeting with fellow workers in a Welfare Services committee, known as SAWS. I immediately went to work with my staff, and we went to the north of Lima, where the center of the quake had been. More than 60,000 people were left without homes there. Many were taking their "siestas" (naps) and were either hurt or killed.

Earthquakes produce much damage. While the Bible does not tell us about all the damage that happened at Christ's death, the earth did open up and some damage was done. The shock waves must have been felt for a long distance. Think of it, even the earth quaked at the death of the Creator!

I suggest that you think about the importance of the death of Jesus today. As you pray, ask God to help you understand the significance of that event when, with His death, Jesus paid the price for sin, even though He had never sinned. He died for you and me. Let's be thankful today to Jesus.

POLLINATION

I am the vine, ye are the branches: He that abideth in me, and I in him, the same bringeth forth much fruit: for without me ye can do nothing. John 15:5.

God planned everything just right when He created this earth. If you had been the creator would you have thought that pollination would be a good idea? You and I probably wouldn't have even thought about it, let alone thought it was a good idea, but God did.

Pollination is what keeps this world going. If it were not for pollination there would not be so many types of plants producing new plants and there would not be a lot of the insects necessary to maintain life. Believe it or not, there would probably be no hay fever, either! Many of you might rejoice for that.

Pollination is mostly for the reproduction of plant life. There are several ways of pollination. A few plants depend on the wind to spread the pollen from one plant to the other. Most plants depend on insect pollination.

In some plants, the insects have to dig down with their tongues or probe to get the nectar and pollen, while in others the insects are sprinkled by the plant with the pollen the moment they touch the plant. One single catkin on a birch tree, which depends on wind pollination, may send out 5.5 million grains of pollen to other birch trees, and there may be hundreds of catkins on a single tree. In some places you may see pollen all over the ground. That comes from a tree that usually spreads its pollen by the wind.

Jesus said that it was impossible to do anything without Him. Just as reproduction in most plants cannot take place without pollination, so a new spiritual life cannot take place without Jesus. We need to have a close relationship like the vine and branch, if we are to succeed spiritually. If we fail in doing things, it is because we try to do them ourselves. Let's rely on Jesus today. Ask Him for His help this morning.

69

ANIMAL REMEDIES

Go up into Gilead, and take balm, O virgin, the daughter of Egypt: in vain shalt thou use many medicines; for thou shalt not be cured. Jeremiah 46:11.

Some years ago a shipyard fire in Singapore claimed the lives of 70 men. It left one man alive but badly burned. When Western medical methods failed to alleviate his pain, the family took him to a Chinese doctor. He prescribed powdered cyst from a porcupine brain. One hundredth of an ounce cost $500. The man drank the concoction and took two other treatments and claimed his suffering was gone.

Witch doctors have been using different concoctions for years. Today there is a tremendous market for animal parts to be used in the treatment of physical ills. Crocodile scales cooked in butter is said to cure toothaches and boils. Pieces of tortoise tied on the head is supposed to relieve malaria. Monkey bones are boiled for ten days to make a tonic to improve circulation and cure severe cases of rheumatism. Scales of pangolin are used for many skin disorders. Whiskers of golden cats are burned and mixed with opium to relieve pain from snakebites.

Parts of the tiger are used for many ills. Just to name a few: The bone from the tail is ground and mixed with soap to make an ointment for skin diseases. The leg bone is to be added to wine to make a healthful tonic. Tying the small foot bones to a child's wrist is said to prevent convulsions. Sitting on a tiger skin is supposed to reduce fevers caused by ghosts. (If this treatment is used too often, it is said, the patient may turn into a tiger.) Mix the brain with oil, rub it on the body, and it is a "cure" for laziness and acne. Roll the eyeballs into rolls and take to avoid convulsions. Wear a claw on a bracelet or carry it in the pocket to give courage and protect from sudden fright. Eat the heart to give strength, carry a rib for good luck, and add honey to ground-up gallstones for a cure for abscesses on hands and feet.

Many people will try many remedies but will not be healed. Jesus is the only remedy that will "cure all." Try Jesus; ask Him this morning to give you health and strength for today.

COMET DUST

Immediately after the tribulation of those days shall the sun be darkened, and the moon shall not give her light, and the stars shall fall from heaven, and the powers of the heavens shall be shaken. Matthew 24:29.

Scientists are still trying to explain the why of some things. They do not understand the "falling stars." They do not understand how the meteorites—falling or shooting stars—are formed, and why they are floating around in outer space. Scientists are asking many questions concerning these stars.

Researchers are trying to find answers to comets. Where do they come from and where do they go? In about October of 1985, scientists from France, Japan, the Soviet Union, and several European nations were starting their search for Halley's comet. They expected it to pass earth again in early 1986. The purpose of all of this is to scrutinize the material that the comet's tail is made up of, such as the type of gas, the type of dust particles, and the icy head.

Some years ago, the United States Space Agency attached onto the ends of the wings of two U-2 spy planes, which can go to extremely high altitudes, little plates that the pilot could project out that would catch particles of comet dust. On the first flight they got one speck of dust. The second flight they got nine. But these particles really couldn't tell them much. Other methods were tried, such as attaching a vacuum cleanerlike object to a balloon, but none of their methods have proven effective.

Men continually try to figure out what God has done. One researcher said, "Only God can tell us more. And God ain't talking." God is talking through His Word, and we only have to read and believe. No, God hasn't told us all the details, but He did say He made this world, and that is good enough for me. Tell God this morning that you believe His Word, and that you will trust Him.

NATURAL ANTIFREEZE

O Lord, thou art my God; I will exalt thee, I will praise thy name; for thou hast done wonderful things; thy counsels of old are faithfulness and truth. Isaiah 25:1.

There are 15 species of poplar trees in North America. Many of these are well known, usually by other names, such as quaking aspen, lombardy poplar, white poplar, bigtooth aspen, eastern cottonwood, swamp cottonwood, and balsam poplar. Interestingly, all poplars belong to the willow family.

Some of these trees, such as quaking aspen and eastern cottonwood, have long leafstalks that are flat or twisted, so that the leaves are able to flutter. In the breeze they look green and flutter as they shiver back and forth.

Poplars are very fast-growing trees—some of them grow up to eight feet a year. The wood is good for making paper and for firewood.

Poplars can live in areas where the winter temperatures go down to −40°F. They can even survive in −100°F. How? Through what is called the freeze-dry process. In the fall the trees draw out most of the water from the living cells and it freezes between the cells. This moisture that freezes contains sugar, which acts as an antifreeze. In the spring, when the warmer weather comes, the ice melts and the moisture is absorbed back into the cells.

Poplars provide food for more than 40 species of animals. Rabbits and beavers depend on the poplar trees for more than 50 percent of their diet. Where poplars grow, worms abound, so the base of poplars is a good spot for many animals and fishermen.

Yes, God is a wonderful God and He has done so many wonderful things that it is amazing all that scientists are finding out about His creation. Thank God this morning because He is a wonderful God and has done so many wonderful things for you.

GOLDEN-EYED LACEWING

Ye shall eat, and not be satisfied. Leviticus 26:26.

Perhaps one of the greediest of all creatures is the lacewing. These creatures eat all of the time and never seem to get full. They will continue to eat as long as there is food.

The golden-eyed lacewing is a beautiful creature. It has golden eyes and four light-green transparent wings that allow the ribs in the wings to be seen. These insects are about one inch long and very beneficial to those who raise flowers and gardens.

The female lacewing will usually go to a plant that is full of aphids. There, from her abdomen, she will begin to expel a string-like substance onto the leaf. She will wait a few seconds until it dries, then she will lay an egg on the end of it. She continues on until she has many eggs on the end of these little "sticks."

After six to 14 days these eggs mature and out of each will come a small, pale creature with hair all over its body. It has pinchers out front to eat with. As this larval lacewing crawls down the leaf or stem of the plant, it will begin to suck the body liquids out of the aphids, scale insects, leafhoppers, thrips, mites, and other plant pests. The larval lacewing has been named the "aphis lion," because it is constantly eating them. As this aphis lion grows, the skin becomes tight, cracks, and is cast off. This happens four times in the larval stage of the lacewing. After about ten days the full-grown larva spins a golden cocoon around itself. It passes two weeks in this stage. Finally it comes out the beautiful and graceful lacewing. The females then begin the process all over again, and there are more lacewings. If you see lacewings, don't hurt them because they will not hurt you and they will help kill many insects that bother and injure or kill plants.

Jesus told the people of Israel what would happen if they disobeyed. He assured them that they would eat and not be satisfied. They were just like the lacewings. Today there are people in the world who are so hungry for the Word of God that they constantly are reading it, so that they can become more familiar with God's promises to His people. Ask God to give you that desire for His Word so you will be spiritually satisfied.

FISH WITH THE GOLDEN EGG

To whom God would make known what is the riches of the glory of this mystery among the Gentiles; which is Christ in you, the hope of glory. Colossians 1:27.

The sturgeon fish that live in the Great Lakes of the United States and Canada, and in Russia, were exploited to the point that they were almost extinct. But modern technology in Russia and laws to regulate the catching of these fish in the Great Lakes has started the sturgeon on the comeback trail.

Sturgeon grow to about eight to twelve feet in length and weigh up to 300 pounds. They are the largest fish in the Great Lakes. They live near the bottom and eat insect larvae, snails, and clams. These fish have slender bodies covered with rows of bony plates that the early settlers used as rasps and graters.

Russians and Eastern Europeans have regarded the sturgeon of more value than the early settlers in the United States because they discovered that the eggs tasted good. Thus the Russian caviar industry was born and became a great business.

Sturgeon are very slow in growing. It takes the male 15 to 20 years to mature and the female 24 to 26 years before she begins to spawn (lay eggs). The females spawn only once in four to six years, so their laying of eggs is not very frequent. Now, according to the laws in the Great Lakes area, the sturgeon has to be a certain size before it can be kept when caught. The sturgeon takes about 25 years to grow to that size.

The Russians have learned how to raise these fish in fisheries so they can gather the eggs for their caviar. Caviar is very expensive. In some stores a two-ounce bottle of caviar sells for $15.25. When people realized the importance of the sturgeon, they immediately began to protect them.

Many people in the world do not realize the importance of Jesus. He is the most valuable treasure, but many have not found that out. Some will find it out too late, others in time to go to heaven with Him. Tell Jesus how much He means to you as you pray this morning.

PETRIFIED

Yea, they made their hearts as an adamant stone, lest they should hear the law, and the words which the Lord of hosts hath sent in his spirit by the former prophets. Zechariah 7:12.

What does it mean to be petrified? It means to be turned to stone. The children of Israel turned their hearts into stone because they didn't want to do what God wanted them to do. Figuratively they became petrified, although the petrifaction that we talk about this morning is a real physical change.

Trees are known to have become rock through the process of petrifaction. These can be seen in the Petrified Forest in the Arizona desert. It is interesting to see the trees now turned to rock.

Scientists say that in order for petrifaction to happen several things must occur. It begins when water that is bearing some minerals circulates through buried fresh wood and combines with oxygen so that no microorganisms such as fungi or bacteria, capable of digesting and rotting the organic material, can get into the wood pores. The moving water carries dissolved calcium carbonate or silica that infiltrates and surrounds the woody tissues. As the water moves out it leaves the minute particles of calcium carbonate or silica that infiltrate any cavities in the wood cells and replaces them. That is the process of petrifaction.

Some scientists talk about the billions of years that it took to do this, but we understand and believe that this is largely a result of the Flood. As you look at petrified wood you see different colors. Iron oxides produced the fiery reds, yellows, and browns. Researchers tell us that there are more than 40 minerals that are petrifying agents, but only four are common.

As the children of Israel hardened their hearts to God's word, so we, through sin, harden our hearts to the Saviour. He wants to come in, but if we allow sin to penetrate our lives our hearts will petrify and Jesus cannot get in. Pray this morning, asking God to send Jesus into your life so your heart will not become hardened and petrified by sin.

WORKERS OF DARKNESS

Rejoice not against me, O mine enemy: when I fall, I shall arise; when I sit in darkness, the Lord shall be a light unto me. Micah 7:8.

Moles live almost exclusively in total darkness underground. They do have eyes, but they are not very good. Moles are not found in Africa or in Central and South America.

These tunneling creatures have front legs and feet suited for digging, and they can dig up to about 100 yards of tunnel a day. They have a very soft, short, and extremely thick fur that helps reduce friction as they run through the tunnels.

I remember several years ago when I was in the youth tent at the southern Illinois camp meeting, a mole decided that it wanted to burrow through the tent. The song leader was directing the music. Those of us who sat up front watched the mole lift up the sod as it made its tunnel. It passed within a foot of the music leader's foot. When the music stopped, the mole turned its course and went out of the tent.

Moles do not have external ears, no doubt because of the dirt that they go through, but they are very sensitive to vibrations. If you see a mole digging and try to sneak up on it, you'll have to do so very slowly and cautiously or it will feel the vibrations and escape through its tunnel system.

There are seven species of moles; one of them is called the star-nosed mole. It has about 22 soft-skin projections on its nose that make it resemble a star. Snakes and water that floods their tunnels are real threats to moles. Even though we may not like them (and I don't, as they tunnel my yard every spring) they are beneficial to us as they control many insect grubs and other soil-inhabiting invertebrates by eating them.

God does not want us to live or work in darkness. His Word will be a light unto our path (See Ps. 119:105), and Jesus will bring light into our life (see John 1:9). Ask Him this morning to bring His light into your life, so you are no longer in spiritual darkness.

CARRIER PIGEONS

And, behold, one came and said unto him, Good Master, what good thing shall I do, that I may have eternal life? Matthew 19:16.

There are many experiences wherein animals and birds help humans. This morning I want to talk about the carrier, or homing, pigeon. This is a special breed of pigeon that has been used effectively over the years to carry messages.

When I was a boy growing up I had many pigeons that I raised, but I never had a homing pigeon. I had friends that did, and what fun we would have. We would put them in cages and take them miles away. We would then open the cages and let the pigeons out, and then we would return home. Most of the time the pigeons beat us home.

Carrier pigeons were used a lot in World Wars I and II to get messages from one place to another. The report is that in World War II the Germans strapped small automatic cameras to pigeons. These cameras were triggered by timing devices as the pigeons flew over the countryside. Thus the Germans could learn the whereabouts of the French.

Probably the most famous pigeon was named Cher Ami. She was a British racing pigeon. In World War I an American battalion had gotten ahead of its own army and was surrounded by the enemy. The men sent a call for help by means of carrier pigeons. Several birds were intimidated by the shelling, but Cher Ami had determination. She was hit by shrapnel (flying metal) and one leg was shot off. She continued to fly for 25 minutes and got the message to headquarters in time to save the battalion. Today, Cher Ami's stuffed body rests in the Smithsonian Institution in Washington, D.C. She was a real hero.

Jesus was asked what good thing was needed to be done, and He gave the instructions. Oh, that we might heed the instructions we receive, just like the carrier pigeons do. Ask Jesus this morning to help you heed His instructions today, so you can be a "hero" of the day and come through victorious like Cher Ami.

ANIMALS DO GOOD

And he saith unto them, Is it lawful to do good on the sabbath days, or to do evil? to save life, or to kill? But they held their peace. Mark 3:4.

Yesterday we talked about carrier pigeons and how they have helped man. Today we will consider other animals that help.

Many different types of animals have been taught to do many things, and many lives have been saved as the result. Peoples' lives have been made happier by animals. Robert Foster, of Boston, Massachusetts, was in an automobile accident that left him paralyzed from the neck down. Hellion is a capuchin monkey, the type that organ-grinders use. She was trained to help Foster around his house. Hellion unlocks doors, turns on the lights, puts cassettes into a tape recorder, retrieves food from the refrigerator, and feeds Robert. Hellion also takes a container of juice, sticks a straw in it, and gives it to Robert.

Hellion fetches objects for Robert, or moves them at his request. How does she understand? Hellion was trained, and when Robert holds a light device between his lips, he will flash it onto an object and Hellion will obediently do her chore. Robert rewards Hellion for her good work by feeding her banana-flavored pellets that are released from a dispenser on the back of his wheelchair.

In California the United States Navy is using porpoises to carry tools to the men who are working in a laboratory in about 200 feet of water. It is much easier than sending a diver down, and a lot faster. Sea lions have been trained to go down and hook "grabbers" to the tail of rockets that have fallen to the ocean floor, so that they can be raised. In southern Thailand, the macaque monkeys help the villagers harvest their coconuts from the tallest palm trees.

Animals have been taught how to relate to their master in obedience. Most of the time they do what they have been taught. Jesus has taught us through His Word, and He hopes we will respond positively. There are lives to be saved, both physically and spiritually. Ask Jesus to help you today to respond to a needy call, whether it be a physical saving or spiritual saving.

COEVOLUTION

That they all may be one; as thou, Father, art in me, and I in thee, that they also may be one in us: that the world may believe that thou hast sent me. John 17:21.

Plants and animals adapt to pressures from each other in a process called coevolution. A biologist was walking along a road in Veracruz, Mexico, when he saw a beetle land on a bush. As soon as the beetle landed on the bush, it was driven away by ants. The biologist discovered that the bush was an ants' acacia bush. The ants were protecting their domain; they live on nectar from the acacia.

It appears that the ants also protect these acacias. They make a hole in the thorns of the acacia, then hollow the inside of the thorn. There they make their home. The queen ant controls her colony from inside these hollow thorns. The hollowing out of the thorns of the acacia plant does not hurt it. The ants keep away other insects and herbivores that might eat parts of the acacia for food. They defend the acacia plant and as a result the plant continues to live and survive. Thus the ants and the acacia are good for each other.

The biologist took a colony of ants away from some acacia bushes in Mexico. He discovered that the ants didn't like any other vegetation and died off. They liked only the thick syrupy nectar that they harvested from the acacia's leaf tips. Also, the acacia trees died because they were destroyed by various insects and other animals.

You and I need Jesus, and He needs us. We can go to Him for comfort and shelter when we encounter the storms of life. He needs us to spread His love to others, so they might know about His ever-present protection. We need each other, and as we have that close relationship with Jesus, we will have life and safety.

Ask Jesus this morning to help you keep close to Him today. When your friends want you to do something that you know you ought not do, just whisper a prayer and Jesus will give you the courage to say No.

CAPTIVE FREEDOM

*My God hath sent his angel, and hath shut the lions' mouths,
that they have not hurt me. Daniel 6:22.*

In many places in the world there are wild animal parks
where visitors can ride in their cars and view the animals in a
natural, uncaged environment. I had the privilege of driving
through "Lion Safari Country" in southern California. As we
entered the park we were told to stay in our cars and keep our
windows rolled up for safety. Driving slowly, we observed the
animals as they roamed in "captive freedom" and as they mingled with many other animals. They were not fighting with one
another—just mingling.

There were ostriches, emus, varieties of deer and antelope,
wildebeests, llamas, giraffes, zebras, and some varieties of ducks
and geese, all in one area. Then we entered a high-fenced area
that had guards by each gate. Here the African lions were
housed. Interestingly enough, there were no other animals in
with the lions. Two of the ostriches decided they wanted to get
close to the lion area. Immediately a jeep appeared. On the
other side of the wire fence an African lion was walking close to
the wire, eyeing the ostriches. Finally the ostriches were driven
off, the lion was driven away from the fence, and all was at
peace.

At two-thirty in the afternoon a jeep pulling a trailer came
into the first two areas and poured feed in the center of the
paved road. All the "wild animals" ran to the road and ate. They
stood side by side. I marveled as I saw so many animals come
together. I immediately thought of heaven and of how the lamb
and the lion will lie down together and eat. At the park the lions
and lambs were separated. God wants all His creatures to be in
unity, and heaven will be the only place for that to happen.
Lions won't be caged, and humans won't be locked in cars.

As the guards kept the lions from the other animals, so God
will keep Satan from us. He protected Daniel from the lions, so
He will protect you. Ask Him for His protection from Satan
today.

PLANTS FOR LIVING

And God said, Behold, I have given you every herb bearing seed, which is upon the face of all the earth, and every tree, in the which is the fruit of a tree yielding seed; to you it shall be for meat. Genesis 1:29.

In the beginning God gave man many wonderful things to eat, but then the Flood came along and destroyed all of the vegetation. Immediately after the Flood man had to eat the clean animals. When vegetation started to grow, the descendants of Noah had some vegetables and fruits again to eat.

Since that time, man has grown many kinds of plants for food. Botanists and other scientists have experimented with many kinds. They have tried to improve upon them and have tried to develop better seeds for growing bigger and better vegetables.

If you had a garden, what would you plant in it? What would grow that you really like? I might plant some things I really didn't care for, but because my wife likes them. Okay, let's plant our garden this morning. I would plant some corn, a nice sweet corn that would melt right in your mouth off of the cob. Then we have to have some spinach, Swiss chard, carrots, beets, cabbage, celery, string beans, lima beans, radishes, onions, peas, cauliflower, lettuce, rhubarb, asparagus, squash, cantaloupe, watermelon, cucumbers, and there must be some other things I have left out. Oh, yes, tomatoes, potatoes, and lentils.

I thank God that He created all of these things for my body to enjoy. God knew what was best for man to eat, so He created these neat things. Scientists are finding out that when we eat lots of leafy vegetables we don't gain weight so readily, our blood pressure stays normal, and we feel good all over. Did you ever notice that cattle eat green grass and other plants, including corn, to keep healthy; then they are killed to be eaten? You and I should get our good food firsthand from the plants like the cow does. Thank God this morning that He created this good food for you to eat.

STARS

And He [God] took him [Abram] outside and said, "Now look toward the heavens, and count the stars, if you are able to count them." Genesis 15:5, N.A.S.B.

Perhaps many nights you have gone out and looked up at the starry heavens and said, "Wow! Look at all the stars! I can't even begin to count them." God told Abraham to look up and try to count the stars. It is humanly impossible!

Astronomers have made many studies of the sky and, by using mathematical formulas, they try to come up with some type of count, but who knows how accurate they are. Astronomers tell us that there are more than one octillion stars in the universe. Can you understand that figure? I can't. What it really is, is a "one" followed by 27 zeros. Still can't understand it? I can't, either!

James Snelling, a naturalist friend of mine from Battle Creek, Michigan, says that if the sky began raining green peas, and the lakes, rivers, and oceans froze over so that the peas would stack up, you would need 250,000 planets the size of our earth all covered with green peas four feet deep in order to have one octillion peas. That is a lot of green peas! But that's how many stars there are. It is hard for our minds to comprehend the greatness of our God and the universe He has created.

There is a God who created all the heavens and the earth. Psalm 147:4 says: "He [God] determines the number of the stars, he gives to all of them their names" (R.S.V.). On this earth we will not understand all about the heavens, but we can spend eternity learning about them from the Creator.

I want to have that opportunity, don't you? Let's pray today that God will help us on our road to heaven, to trust and believe in Him as the Creator. We see evidences of God's Creation all around us. Trust in His Word, the Holy Scriptures.

HIMALAYA MOUNTAINS

How beautiful upon the mountains are the feet of him that bringeth good tidings, that publisheth peace; that bringeth good tidings of good, that publisheth salvation; that saith unto Zion, Thy God reigneth! Isaiah 52:7.

The Himalaya Mountains are wedged between Tibet and India and are known as the most inhospitable mountains in the world. Many peaks are more than 20,000 feet high. This vast complex of stone and ice extends about 1,500 miles from Pakistan to Assam and is from 100 to 200 miles wide.

Naturally, the climate will vary in these mountains, depending on the altitude. Temperatures range from the subtropical with lush plants, to the alpine, where few or no plants grow. In the western sector, forests flourish between 3,000 and 10,000 feet elevation. They include oaks and magnolias, with an undergrowth of bamboo. These give way to fir, hemlocks, and pines at higher elevations.

In these mountains, especially in Tibet, there is a variety of game animals. Most are from the goat and sheep families, with antelope, buffalo, and donkeys thrown in. Of course, they do not go by these names, and we would probably not recognize most of their names. Since most of these animals are unusual to us, we will spend the next four mornings describing eleven of them, so you will understand what the young people of Tibet and the Himalayas see.

Tibet is an arid desert, windblown and struggling with low vegetation, with an average altitude of more than 15,000 feet. It sits atop Asia like an elevated island. Temperatures range from 100° to −45°F. Even though the land may seem uninviting, the people are very hospitable.

There are God-fearing people in this high land who love the Lord Jesus and bear good tidings to those about them of His great love. Thank God this morning that God is known in this part of the world and that you, too, know Him and love Him as your God.

HIMALAYAN HIGH WALKERS

The range of the mountains is his pasture, and he searcheth after every green thing. Job 39:8.

The text this morning certainly fits perfectly the three Himalayan animals we'll discuss today. The yak, chiru and ibex live from 12,000 feet to 20,000 feet elevation. The yak lives at the highest altitude, where green food is scarce.

The yak looks similar to the American bison. Someone said that it is "an ungainly mass of black-brown hair." It is also called the "grunting ox" because it makes a grunting sound as it moves along. Grown yaks are about six feet high at the shoulder and weigh about 1,200 pounds; they are quick, surefooted, and agile climbers. They are easily domesticated and used as the only means of transportation in the region. They can cope with deep snow and swim icy rivers with a load on their back. They provide milk and meat, and their droppings are used for heating and cooking fuel.

The next creature, the chiru, belongs to the antelope family. It has two horns that protrude about 27 inches straight up from the head. As one looks from the side, they look like one horn so the animal has also been called a "unicorn" in legends. These animals usually segregate into herds of males or females; they mix only when mating. They stand about 32 inches high and weigh about 100 pounds each. To some they are sacred; to others they are hunted for meat and blood.

The third animal is the ibex, an agile climber on the precipices. It is a true goat. Ibex have long recurved horns, up to 50 inches, and are one of the most favorite "game" animals for hunters. Hunters have found that they must be above them on the mountainside in order to hunt them. They say that when the ibex is in danger it will use its long horns to cushion the bounce as it leaps downhill in long leaps.

The animals that we've talked about from the Himalaya Mountains in Tibet live so high up that there is very little food, and they have to hunt for it. God has given us much food to sustain us. Thank Him today for His blessings to you.

HIMALAYAN VALLEY SEEKERS

He sendeth the springs into the valleys, which run among the hills. Psalm 104:10.

There are three Himalayan animals that prefer the valleys among the mountains, at an elevation of from 10,000 to 17,000 feet. Two of these animals, the argali and the bharal, belong to the sheep family; the third, kiang, is a donkey.

The argali is the world's most desired big game species because of its tremendously large horns. There are three varieties of these animals, which are considered to be the world's largest wild sheep. They weigh up to about 400 pounds. Their horns may reach a length of about 75 inches around the curl. From these horns the shepherds make large bowls to eat from, and they use the horns to set up a night corral for the animals. Hunters pay up to $16,500 for a ten-day argali hunt in Mongolia.

Number-two animal from the Himalayan valleys this morning is the bharal, or "blue sheep." Zoologists have not yet determined whether the bharal is a sheep or goat. It does have curved horns like a goat; the horns are about 35 inches around and curl backward over the head. The males reach a weight of about 150 pounds and are about the size of the Rocky Mountain sheep. Bharal prefer the grasslands and run in large herds.

The kiang is totally different from all of the other animals. The kiang is a donkey that becomes very tame. Kiangs are usually found in herds and are real pests, especially to the hunters. They are extremely curious and inquisitive. They have been known to go right into the hunters' camp and scare the cooks.

Water from springs runs down through valleys, which become beautiful and green. When the love of Jesus runs into our lives it will water our lives with truth, which will bring eternal life to our souls. Thank God that His love flows into our hearts, when we let it. Let His love flow into your heart this morning, and throughout the day.

HIMALAYAN CLIFF CLIMBERS

The voice of my beloved! behold, he cometh leaping upon the mountains, skipping upon the hills. Song of Solomon 2:8.

Three of the Himalayan animals that we discuss this morning are high jumpers and live from 7,000 to 14,000 feet elevation. These animals are goats or related to the goat family, and are called the tahr, takin, and markhor.

The tahr is a champion among high jumpers. From a standing position, it can jump over a six-foot-high obstacle. It is a cousin to the goat and similar to the Rocky Mountain goat in body shape. The animals are reddish brown in color and have a shaggy mane around the neck and shoulders. Their horns are only about 14 inches long. People hunt them for meat because it is believed that this meat cures fever and rheumatism.

Takin are among the most unusual and least-known animals in the Himalayas. They look clumsy and are heavily built in the front. They stand about three and a half feet at the shoulder and have bulging shoulder muscles. Their horns are about 24 inches long. They emerge from the center of the head then abruptly turn outward, then backward, then upward. Takin inhabit steep terrain and like to be in thickets of bamboo or rhododendrons. In the summer they form into small herds but in the winter the herds are very large.

Probably no animal has such distinguished horns as the markhor. Their horns are snakelike and may extend to about five feet in length. Markhor is a Persian word meaning snake eater, but some people think the name really should have been markhar, or snake-donkey, meaning a donkey with snakelike horns. Because of their horns, they have accidentally hanged themselves in trees while reaching for leaves. These goats weigh up to about 200 pounds and are very surefooted.

As these animals come leaping along the mountains, so Jesus, when He comes, will come quickly. Jesus will return, so thank Him for that certainty this morning.

HIMALAYAN PRECIPICE LOVERS

The Lord is my rock, and my fortress, and my deliverer; my God, my strength, in whom I will trust; my buckler, and the horn of my salvation, and my high tower. Psalm 18:2.

The last two of the Himalayan creatures that we will talk about are the goral and the serow. These two animals enjoy the rocky ledges and precipices, but they like the areas where there is some vegetation. Both of these animals are very surefooted and can climb very fast on the ledges. They live in a wide range of altitudes, from 3,000 to 12,000 feet. Since the animals that we have discussed the past few mornings live at such different altitudes they do not get in each other's way and there generally is food for all.

The smallest of the eleven Himalayan animals we are studying is the goral. A goral stands about 28 inches tall and weighs about 60 pounds. It has horns that extend only about eight inches, and has a long, coarse, shaggy-hair appearance. The males have a semierect mane. Gorals are buffy gray to rufous brown in color, have a black streak that extends from the neck to the tail, and a whitish patch of color on the chin and throat. They never wander far from vegetation cover and when in danger sound an alarm—a hissing sound.

The most interesting of all of the creatures is the serow. It looks like the Creator took parts from the cow, the pig, the donkey, and the goat to make it. Serows are about 38 inches high and weigh from 200 to 300 pounds each. They have long, shaggy brown hair and ten-inch horns. They are very stocky in body size, have long, pointed ears, and a short, hairy tail. When they are frightened they utter a loud call, a combination between a snort and a screaming whistle.

These animals trust in the rocks for their safety. The psalmist trusted in God for his salvation. We should be happy this morning that we can trust in God. Thank Him this morning for His trustworthiness.

DRIFTWOOD

But let him ask in faith, nothing wavering. For he that wavereth is like a wave of the sea driven with the wind and tossed. James 1:6.

In the forests around the world there are many trees. Most of these, when they die, will lie on the forest floor and rot. Others are cut up by man and used for firewood, or made into houses or objects that are useful or decorative.

When some trees die they fall into or are washed into a body of water. Most of the time a river will carry the tree downstream to a lake or the ocean. As the tree bobs along, occasionally getting stuck on a sand or mud bar or in shallow water, some of the branches may break off. These go their own direction.

As these smaller pieces of wood break from the tree they begin to bob with the ripples of the current in the river. They are also rolled along, perhaps over islands of dirt and rocks. Bumping along, they become smooth, the bark and rough edges are worn off. This we call driftwood.

As they float along, these pieces of wood are not able to do anything about how or where they float. They just go along with the current, carried where it goes. They are also blown about by the wind. Driftwood is good for nothing but burning, unless a skilled person picks it up, works it over, and makes it into a useful article.

Many of us are like driftwood. We just drift along with the crowd. Where they go, we go, because we have no purpose. However, we can find a purpose for our lives if we will put them in the hands of the Master Craftsman. Jesus is waiting for us to quit our drifting and put our lives into His hands so He can make something beautiful out of them.

I invite you this morning to put your life in the hands of Jesus. Ask Him to take your life and give it a purpose and make something beautiful out of you today.

GYPSY MOTHS

My little children, these things write I unto you, that ye sin not. And if any man sin, we have an advocate with the Father, Jesus Christ the righteous. 1 John 2:1.

Gypsy moths first came to the shores of the United States from France in 1869. They were brought to Massachusetts to help in the production of silk, but that experiment failed and some of the adult moths escaped.

Even though called "gypsy moths," they do not travel very fast. The migration of gypsy moths is about one mile per year. Sailing on their silk threads, they are carried by the wind to different areas.

Gypsy moths lay their eggs in wood piles, doghouses, building supplies, bricks, flowerpots, and fenceposts. As these items are moved, the moths spread. You may have seen a gypsy moth. The female is creamy white and does not fly. She may not go more than a few yards in her lifetime. Her eggs hatch into caterpillars. Each larval stage of life is called an *instar* (first, second, etc.). The caterpillar is grayish brown and has rows of red and blue spots.

The male gypsy moth is smaller than the 1½- to 2½-inch female, but he can fly.

Gypsy moth caterpillars attach themselves to trees and, if undisturbed, could eat all of the leaves off of a tree. Fortunately they do not kill the tree, at least, not at once. Most trees cannot be destroyed unless more than 50 percent of the leaves are stripped for two years in succession. Gypsy moths are a pest and will probably be with us for a long, long time. As one science writer said, "We'll have to live with them as we try to understand nature and its ways."

Unfortunately we have to live with sin in the world, too. Sin will conquer us if we let it. Jesus will help us conquer sin if we ask Him. Pray this morning that God will help you conquer sin in your life.

SPRING

In whose hand is the soul of every living thing, and the breath of all mankind. Job 12:10.

Today is the first day of spring in the Northern Hemisphere, and we begin to see new life. Those trees and bushes that lost their leaves in the fall are beginning to bloom again. The flowers that lie dormant will soon be in full bloom, and many people will be planting other flowers, trees, shrubs, and grass.

Fawns will be born, and butterflies will be flying around after coming out of the cocoon. Bears and some other animals will be coming out of hibernation. The snow season will be over in some areas. It is a time for all life to say, "This is spring, and I want to enjoy it." I also know that when spring comes many boys and girls, who know that it won't be long until school is out, will jump up and down, wanting summer to come.

Spring is a beautiful time to be alive. As the buds begin to open up, many sweet aromas will scent the air, a joy to the senses. This is also the time the farmers go into their fields and prepare them for planting. Yes, spring gives us great promises of the beautiful summer that is soon to arrive.

Have you ever noticed that spring is a time when people go out and really enjoy nature? They are able to get outdoors long enough to really see what is going on in God's world. There are many young people that plan at this time of the year for a marriage in the summer. Spring is a delightful time of the year.

In His planning, God didn't leave anything out. He shows us what new life is all about in the spring, and says to us through His creation, This, My child, is what I have for you when I come again—a new life in Christ Jesus. Thank Him for spring and life today. It is your life, and Jesus will give you a new life when He comes the second time.

ARMORED NIGHT HUNTER

Wherefore take unto you the whole armour of God, that ye may be able to withstand in the evil day, and having done all, to stand. Ephesians 6:13.

Lobsters are animals that live on the bottom of the ocean and have a full armor that covers their body. A lobster's body has 19 parts: the head has five, the thorax eight, and the abdomen six. There is a soft place between the shells so it can bend the body. A lobster has ten legs, eight of which are used to walk with; the other two, which are out front, have claws on them. With these, lobsters grab and break up their food.

Ranging from 12 to 24 inches in length, and from one to 20 pounds, lobsters hide under rocks or in holes during the day. They have antennae that feel for food or enemies. Lobsters naturally are dark green or blue, and they turn red when boiled for eating.

The male lobster is called a cock, and the female a hen or chicken. The hen will lay eggs only every two years. She lays from 5,000 to nearly 100,000 eggs and carries them under her tail for a period of 11 or 12 months. When they are ready to hatch she will shake the young out of their eggshells. These little baby lobsters, which are less than one third of an inch long, float to the surface of the ocean. There they are prey for birds and fish for about three to five weeks. Those that survive sink back down to the bottom of the ocean.

Two days after hatching they will molt (shed the shell) the first time. Then they will molt three more times during the first month. During this soft-shell time they have no protection. If they are not caught by man or other sea life, their average life span is about 15 years.

We are told that we should put on the "whole armour" of God, not just part of it. As the lobster needs its whole armor, so do we, to protect us from our enemy. God has promised to be with us, so let us depend on Him to help fit us up with His armor of protection from sin. Thank God for His interest today, and ask Him to help suit you with a suit of armor that fits just you.

TOKI

For it is written, He shall give his angels charge over thee, to keep thee. Luke 4:10.

On the Japanese island of Sado lives one of the world's rarest birds. In English it is called the crested ibis, but in Japanese it is the toki. These heron-like birds are found only on this island, and in 1981 there were only six of them in existence. Ornithologists (bird scientists) from Japan are trying to save these birds. They captured five in the wild, and with a sixth one already in captivity, they are hoping to reinstate the beautiful and magnificent bird.

These birds are one of 28 species of ibis in the world. They are about 22 inches long and have beautiful white feathers with a pink tint to them. They have a long, black beak with a red tip, and orange legs. Both sexes have the ornate head crest, which has feathers that form a narrow mane down the back of the neck. They have become almost extinct due to hunting them for their beautiful plumage, and from pesticides in their natural food.

An all-out effort is being made by the Japanese, assisted by the World Wildlife Fund, to save these birds. Broken eggs have been found in nests on Sado Island. Ornithologists believe they were broken by crows or by the older ibis because they are getting too old to produce families.

Following the success that ornithologists in other parts of the world have had with ibis in captivity, the Japanese have brought in a colony of Indian white ibis and put them in cages beside the crested ibis. The scientists hope that, with the use of mirrors, they can make the crested ibis think they are in a large colony, and possibly breed in captivity.

While man is doing all he can to save the crested ibis in Japan, God is working with His angels all over this earth to save boys and girls from eternal extinction. Thank God this morning for His loving care and interest in you and ask Him for His angel protection today. Angels will be by your side all day, if you ask.

EARTHWORMS

But I am a worm, and no man; a reproach of men, and despised of the people. Psalm 22:6.

The earthworm has been used as a symbol of lowliness because it moves around under the ground. When someone doesn't have a very good feeling about oneself, one may say, "I feel like a worm today." Have you ever heard that little song that goes, "Nobody loves me, everybody hates me, I'm going out and eat worms. Big, fat, juicy ones; little, round, gooey ones; I'm going out and eat worms"?

It is interesting how we as humans see our feelings or behavior in comparison with other creatures: "blind as a bat," "sly as a fox," "slow as a turtle," "low as a worm."

I have asked the question Why did God create the earthworm? Of what good is it? When I was a boy on a small farm in Colorado I would dig up worms to fish with. My dad would say, "Chuck, don't dig up too many in one place. Go to several places to dig up your worms. Worms are valuable to our garden."

"Valuable to our garden?" I asked.

"Yes," he would reply, "valuable to our garden." Obedient to my dad's wishes, I would dig my worms in different places, but I couldn't understand why. Years later, I did.

As a freshman in college, taking a zoology class, I learned that the earthworm has no eyes but has sensory cells on each segment. These make the worm sensitive to light and touch. The earthworm has ten "hearts" or aortic arches.

We learned that the earthworm pushes through soft soils and eats its way through the harder soils. It eats decayed vegetation. This material passes through the body of the earthworm. The fecal matter is called *castings* and is brought to the surface of the soil. These castings are very good fertilizer, and the soil turnover makes the soil richer and produces better crops. The holes and tunnels the worms make are good for the soil, too.

When you have your prayer this morning, you can ask God to help you stay humble today. Although the earthworm is important for good soil, you are more important to God. He cares for you. Jesus died for you!

BEAKED WHALES

I pray not that thou shouldest take them out of the world, but that thou shouldest keep them from the evil. John 17:15.

There are about 14 species of beaked whales. Many of the species vary in size, and they are somewhat different in appearance. They all seem to have one thing in common. The bottom jaw sticks out farther than the top jaw and has from two to four teeth in it. The beaked whales differ from whales that have no teeth but have large fibrous plates sticking down in the mouth. The teethed whales, of which the beaked are only a few, have large throats, big enough that a person could pass through. Those without teeth have very small throats.

Some of the beaked whale species are rare; in fact, they are so rare that they have not been seen by man in the water, only when they have for some reason died or been killed and have washed up onto the beach. The largest of the beaked whales is the Baird's beaked whale. These grow to about 42 feet long; exceeded in length, in the toothed class, only by the sperm whales. There are larger whales but they are in the nontoothed or baleen whale category.

Probably the most common of the beaked whales is the Cuvier or goose-beaked whale. They are globe-trotters and received the name Cuvier from a nineteenth-century French naturalist. The other name was given for their tapered profile. They are found in both the northern and southern hemispheres and are quite plentiful. They like to swim in groups of 30 to 40. They will spout for about ten minutes then dive down and stay under for at least half an hour. Most of the beaked whales are gray, lighter on the bottom and darker gray to black on the top.

God has put these whales in the ocean, and He has put us in this world. He doesn't want us to be a part of the world, but that we should be in the world. We should be different, but work with the people of the world to complete the mission that we are here for, to save lost souls who do not know Jesus. Ask God this morning to help you complete Jesus' prayer, that you will be in this world to help wandering souls but that you will not become part of the world with all of its sinful ways.

DOWN

But what went ye out for to see? A man clothed in soft raiment? behold, they that wear soft clothing are in kings' houses. Matthew 11:8.

Just west of the main island of Iceland is a tiny island called Vigur. On this small island, which has about one square mile of surface, lives only one family, the Baldur Bjarnason family. They share this tiny island with about 4,000 pairs of eider ducks.

These ducks come to the island of Vigur to nest and raise their young. They do not like humans but they will tolerate them. The Bjarnason family go out into the nesting area during the summer and gather up the fine down feathers that the eiders use to make their nests. These islanders are very careful not to disturb the setting ducks more than once each year. Since the weather is cold, even in the summertime, they leave enough down feathers so that the eggs will be protected and hatch.

The Bjarnarsons gather this down in about a six-week period of time. About 35 nests will yield about a pound, and there are about 4,000 nests to gather from each summer. They take the down and let it dry in piles. After a short time they will put it into a special drum and dry it further, ready for shipment. They clean the down of grass and debris, but they can clean only about two pounds a day per person. Eiderdown sells for about $300 per pound.

Many of you have down jackets and other clothes, and some of you have a down pillow, nice and soft. Jesus talked to the people about looking for a person in soft clothing. I don't think He was referring to down, but it is very soft. Jesus wants us to look for and find the truth in Him and His Word. Ask God to help you as you search for truth in His Word today.

USEFUL PLANTS

For, lo, the winter is past, the rain is over and gone; the flowers appear on the earth; the time of the singing of birds is come, and the voice of the turtle is heard in our land; the fig tree putteth forth her green figs, and the vines with the tender grape give a good smell. Song of Solomon 2:11-13.

There are many useful plants and trees that God created for man. In the warmer climates of the world, including the Southern United States, a large amount of cotton is grown. The early settlers on this planet soon discovered the cotton plant, and they took the fiber from the cotton boll and began to twirl it and make it into thread. From the thread they wove cloth. I have watched the Indian girls and women in Brazil and Peru as they spin the cotton and make their thread. They make very beautiful garments and other things from the cotton that they spin.

What would we do without rubber? The rubber trees in Central and South America, Southeast Asia, and Africa, do much to improve our world. In South America the trees are sliced with a sharp knife and the liquid latex runs down the cut channels into containers. To take this latex does not hurt the tree. It is evidently a substance that protects the tree from injury. After the latex is gathered it is wrapped onto a stick and "barbecued" like meat over an open fire until it becomes a large ball. These balls are carried by men to the riverbank, and from there they are taken by canoe or boat to the rubber peddlers, who ship them to rubber products companies.

Another kind of latex that many of you enjoy is the chewing gum latex, which is gathered just like the rubber latex. After the chewing gum latex is gathered it is brought into the processing plant, cleaned, formed into large blocks, and shipped to the chewing gum manufacturers. Raw latex has no taste.

I thank God that He gave us so many interesting plants to get products from, and that He gave man the intelligence to be able to develop these products. Thank God this morning for your brain and the ability to think.

TALL AND MAJESTIC

The cedars of Lebanon, that are high and lifted up. Isaiah 2:13.

In the time of Christ, the largest trees growing in the Middle East were the cedars of Lebanon. There are many Bible verses referring to these large trees. However, neither Christ nor the people at that time had seen the large redwoods that are found in the United States. Two species are found on the coast of California and in the national parks of Yosemite and Sequoia, also in California. There is one other species found in China, but it is not an evergreen and not as large a tree.

The redwoods along the California coast are the tallest trees—the tallest being 368.6 feet high. The sequoias are not as tall but are much bigger around. The largest tree known today is the General Sherman Tree in Sequoia National Park in California. This tree measures 272.4 feet high and 101.6 feet in circumference. It is estimated that the tree would yield more than 600,000 board feet of lumber. Naturalists estimate this tree to be about 3,500 years old, which would mean that it would have started growing some 1,500 years before Christ.

Redwoods have an extensive root system. Because of this and the great strength in their trunks, strong winds can scarcely uproot them.

In Psalm 1:3, faithful and loyal people are likened to trees. But He wants us to beware lest we fall. God wants us to hold our heads up because we are Christians, but not to be proud of what we have accomplished. As Jesus said, "Without me ye can do nothing" (John 15:5).

Tell God in prayer this morning that you want His help to hold your head high as a Christian, and to represent Him today to your friends.

POWER PLAY

For the word of God is quick, and powerful, and sharper than any twoedged sword, piercing even to the dividing asunder of soul and spirit, and of the joints and marrow, and is a discerner of the thoughts and intents of the heart. Hebrews 4:12.

One of the common displays of a power struggle is the rutting behavior of the Rocky Mountain bighorn sheep. The method they use in declaring their domain and exercising their dominance is mind-boggling. The bighorn rams will back up a distance, rear up on their hind legs, and lunge forward until they collide with each other, head on. Observers say that when two bighorn rams collide they are going at a speed of about 30 miles per hour.

The creatures will keep this up until one or the other yields to the superiority of the other. This might be accomplished in one collision or it may take hours. One observer saw a battle continue for 25 hours and 20 minutes, until one of the rams surrendered. During these confrontations the rams will not only clash with their horns but they will shove with their chests or shoulders, growl, flicker their tongues, and use a variety of kicks. When two bighorn rams clash in the mountains, the resounding noise can be heard for a long distance.

These rams have a double-layered skull. The outer skull is like a helmet. Between the two skulls is about an inch of space, honeycombed with sturdy bone struts. Topping this off is a thick layer of skin. With all of this headgear, the blows are somewhat neutralized, and injuries are not too common.

God's word is stronger and more powerful than anything else. God gave us the Bible to help guide in our life. As long as we follow this guidebook and put our lives in His hands, they will be calmer and more peaceful because we can depend on Him.

Ask Jesus this morning to overpower the devil and sin in your life. He, with His power, will be the victor in your life.

MOUNT ST. HELENS

What manner of persons ought ye to be in all holy conversation and godliness, looking for and hasting unto the coming of the day of God, wherein the heavens being on fire shall be dissolved, and the elements shall melt with fervent heat? 2 Peter 3:11, 12.

It was a tragic day, the fateful day that Mount St. Helens blew its top. Scientists had been watching and recording the tremors of that beautiful mountain. Gases were spewing out of the top. Then, with a mighty blow, it exploded and hot ashes and all kinds of materials were sent flying into the sky.

As the hot lava flowed down the sides of Mount St. Helens it covered many beautiful lakes and rivers, thousands of acres of trees, and millions of wild creatures. The National Forest Service took a census after the first eruption and found more than 67,052 game animals dead. After the ash finished falling, they counted more than 1,483,900 game animals dead and more than 11 million salmon and other fish destroyed. It is estimated that more than one and a half million birds lost their lives as well as unnumbered nongame animals, amphibians, reptiles, and insects.

Twenty-six lakes were totally destroyed and twenty-four others partially ruined. More than a thousand miles of streams were ruined in that they were made inaccessible because of the lava flow.

In some areas around the mountain, the ash piled up from three to four feet deep. Forestry officials hoped that the rain would not make this ash like cement, which would completely eliminate any future use of the land. As one ranger said, "Nature has a way of taking care of herself."

God gave this world some marvelous methods of taking care of itself, of repairing what has been partially or totally destroyed. I thank God that He has given this earth this power, and that many ugly places, destroyed either through natural processes or by man, have somehow acquired some vegetation and eventually covered up the scars. Thank God that He will cover up those scars in your sinful life with the robe of His righteousness. He has promised, and He will do it.

FEATHER ZIPPERS

Fear ye not therefore, ye are of more value than many sparrows.
Matthew 10:31.

Bird feathers are a very fascinating example of God's creative ability and thought. Feathers not only cover the body of the bird but are also used in many different ways. Feathers serve two primary functions: flight, and thermoregulation. Flightless birds such as the ostrich and emu have feathers that are primarily used for thermoregulation; the feathers on these birds do the same for the bird as the fur on an animal. Penguins have feathers for thermoregulation that act like the fur on a seal when it dives into frigid water.

You have probably seen birds take a bath in dust or water. This way they rid themselves of parasites and dirt. Then they begin the art of preening—putting each feather in place. After a bird takes a bath it will probably go to a safe limb and begin preening its feathers.

The main stem of the feather is called a quill. On either side of the quill are vanes that are made up of filaments or barbs. Each barb has many microscopic hooks called barbules, which have barbicels ending in hooks, and these work like miniature zippers. When the birds start their preening, feather by feather, they zipper all these barbules and barbicels into place, so the feathers fit tightly against the body. Most birds have a gland at the base of the tail that produces an oil that makes the feathers waterproof. As the bird preens the small gland is touched by the bill, and the feathers are zipped into place and waterproofed with the oil. This protects the body of the bird as it flies or as it swims or fishes.

God made the bird feathers to help protect and clothe the birds. The Scriptures say that if God has taken so much thought with the birds, He has taken even more thought with us. Thank God that He takes care of you and loves you.

SPERM WHALES

O righteous Father, the world hath not known thee: but I have known thee, and these have known that thou hast sent me. John 17:25.

Sperm whales are the largest of the toothed whales. They may grow in length to about 60 feet. These whales have a very blunt snout that looks like someone chopped it off. At the top of the nose is the "blow hole." About one third of the body is taken up by the enormous head. The sperm whale has a small, narrow, lower jaw loaded with teeth, which may be up to nine feet long.

There are three species of sperm whales, two of which are called pygmy sperm whales. Sperm whales are in all the oceans and have been the most hunted whales in history. The book *Moby Dick* concerns a sperm whale.

Early whalers have written about the sperm whale. In the early days they hunted and harpooned them from open boats. One man wrote that a whale slammed down on his boat with its head, then backed off and rammed it again, crushing the timbers and sinking the boat. Another report stated that a whale boosted its head out of the water, pitched its whole weight onto the boat, and ruined it, killing the midshipman.

When a sperm whale calf is born it is about 13 feet long. Its length doubles within about six months, which is the nursing period. The mother guards it, even if it is dead. The calf will usually stay with the mother for a period of about two years and mature at eight years. These whales generally take about 45 years to grow to the full length. They may live to be about 75 years old. Their diet consists mostly of squid and octopus.

Many in the world have known about the sperm whale, but few have known about the God of heaven. He has put us here not only to help the world learn about Him but He also wants us to know more about Him too. We have the opportunity to find out more about Him by reading from the Bible. Take time in your busy schedule to read and understand more about God. Ask Him to help you understand His Word today. It is a good "spiritual diet."

KEMP'S RIDLEY

*But be ye glad and rejoice for ever in that which I create.
Isaiah 65:18.*

Have you ever heard of Kemp's Ridley? Do you even have an inkling of what it is? If you do, you are ahead of me, as I had to read about it. The Kemp's Ridley is a species of turtle that lives on Rancho Nuevo beach along the Gulf of Mexico in southern Tamaulipos, Mexico.

The rarest of sea turtles, 99 percent of Kemp's Ridley has disappeared since 1947. Little is known about these turtles, since there are very few of them and they remain mostly at sea. As adults they weigh between 60 and 100 pounds. The females go ashore and lay their eggs in the sand. The males stay out at sea. The female turtles arrive at Rancho Nuevo generally between April and July. They nest only in the daytime. They dig a hole, lay from 50 to 135 eggs, then return to the sea. In 1947 a Mexican scientist filmed 40,000 females coming ashore and laying their eggs and returning to the sea. They did this in less than an hour. Today only about 500 to 600 females repeat this process every year. The large "arribada" (arrival), as the Mexicans call it, is a thing of the past.

Researchers are now trying to save the Kemp's Ridley from extinction. They have prepared artificial nests covered with wire. After the females have laid their eggs and returned to the sea, the researchers put the eggs in these nests. Eighty percent of the eggs are hatching now with this process. It takes the baby turtles 50 days to hatch and leave the egg. Researchers know that they can live for a minimum of 20 years, but they do not know the maximum. U.S. marine biologists, with special permission from the Mexican Government, are transplanting some of the Kemp's Ridley turtles to the southern coast of Texas, hoping they will remain there and have another nesting area.

Man does much to take care of certain creatures created by God. God does much to take care of His created children. Thank God that He cares for you today, and that He is interested in protecting you from extinction.

SMOOTH STONES

The waters wear the stones: thou washest away the things which grow out of the dust of the earth. Job 14:19.

Is there a boy who hasn't gone to the water's edge of a small stream, picked up a smooth stone, and tried to skip it across the water? For years as I have approached a body of water I have wanted to pick up smooth stones and skip them across the water. It is still fun to see how many times I can skip the stone on top of the water.

Have you ever wondered what made stones smooth? A rock hound, that is, a person who collects and polishes rocks, will pick up the ugliest rocks, put them in a tumbler and after some time take them out all smooth. What has happened? As the rocks roll in the tumbler, all of the sharp edges are worn off and the rock becomes smooth. A stream of water, or small river, or even the waves at the edge of the ocean, keep rolling the rocks, and over a period of time they become smooth. All of the sharp edges are worn off and the rocks become nice smooth stones. They are not made smooth in a day but over a long period of time. Nature's forces are often slow, but because they are steady they have been able to move mountains, carve new riverbeds, and create underground caverns.

We as sinners have rough edges caused by sin in our lives. The Lord wants to have all our roughness removed, so He allows us to go through trials that will help wear down the rough edges and make us a smooth and valuable "stone."

As we meet obstacles in our lives and conquer them, roughness is worn off; as we steadily meet trials and conquer them, our character is polished. God does not promise us a smooth life altogether, but He does promise to be with us and help us through the trials.

Ask God today to be with you as you go through the day. As the trials come, with His help you will be able to meet and overcome them.

EVERGLADES

Let not your heart be troubled: ye believe in God, believe also in me. In my Father's house are many mansions: if it were not so, I would have told you. I go to prepare a place for you. And if I go and prepare a place for you, I will come again, and receive you unto myself; that where I am, there ye may be also. John 14:1-3.

In the southern part of the State of Florida in the United States is a swampy marsh area called the Everglades. This area has been home to thousands of species of birds, mammals, reptiles, and amphibians, as well as to many species of plant families. More than five feet of rain falls here annually. The Everglades kept itself in balance until a few years ago, when developers came into southern Florida with the desire to build houses and inhabit the area. Their activity cut the Everglades wildlife habitat to about half what it was.

According to one national park biologist, the Everglades are now an area of extremes. There is either too much water or not enough. Engineers have routed the flooding from the large Lake Okeechobee so that the natural flow of water from this lake is no longer natural. A large canal has been built to handle the floodwaters. This has at times brought drought to the Everglades and at other times, flooding.

The fight has become a real one. The farmers want to raise their crops and they don't want any more water. The biologists and conservationists want to protect the wildlife, so the conflict goes on. Due to flooding, many alligator nests have been destroyed, and there have been no new little alligators hatched in three of the past five years. The nesting birds have not had a normal season in more than ten years. The wading bird population has dwindled to one tenth of what it was in 1930. Some say that the Florida panther is also endangered.

It will be great to get to heaven where there will be no more conflicts over the terrain and the wildlife. God has promised a place for each of us, and all of the wild and tame animals will be there to enjoy it too. Thank God this morning that He has prepared a place for you in heaven.

IRAS

And they that be wise shall shine as the brightness of the firmament; and they that turn many to righteousness as the stars for ever and ever. Daniel 12:3.

The Infra-Red Astronomy Satellite (IRAS) was launched the night of January 25, 1983, with the hope of finding out more about our universe. Dutch, English, and Americans had a part in this program.

The human eye cannot see infrared rays. These are what cause the sunburn on your skin; even the clouds don't cut them out. Through the use of the IRAS scientists have discovered that the atmosphere has truly a lot of dust particles (causing the varying hues of the sunsets), and that some areas are more concentrated than others. The dust particles may obscure infrared rays.

The IRAS carried a 22.4-inch telescope that was surrounded by liquid helium that lasted for a year. This helium was used to cool the telescope, so it could relay correctly the images in space that it saw. The IRAS passed around the earth twice daily; as it passed over Chilton, England, it sent more than 350 million bits of information down to the computers. It may be years before the scientists can complete their interpretation.

The whole universe has been opened up by the IRAS, although it lasted only a year. There are plans to have a better one in the 1990s. Astronomers now say that "a lot of astronomy books will have to be rewritten when all the results are in." IRAS has discovered five new live comets and one dead one. The Milky Way emits about half of its energy as infrared and Andromeda about 3 percent. Much will be discovered as knowledge increases until Jesus comes.

Thank God this morning for the knowledge that He has given us, and that you have the opportunity of participating in this knowledge explosion.

SPICE OF LIFE

Because thou hast forgotten the God of thy salvation, and hast not been mindful of the rock of thy strength, therefore shalt thou plant pleasant plants, and shalt set it with strange slips. Isaiah 17:10.

Early settlers experimented with all types of plants for spices to season their food, and many different spices were found. One person wrote that some of the plants tried may have poisoned their experimenters.

We generally think of most of the spices as coming from dried leaves that are crushed and put into bottles for serving. This is not necessarily so. There are seeds and dried fruits that are also used as spices. Caraway, anise, coriander, and dill are four spice seeds or fruits. Dill is used in the form of leaves as well as seed.

Many of the spices come from the tropical regions, and many of those from islands. Cloves and nutmegs came from the Moluccas in the East Indies; for many years they were called the Spice Islands. Cloves are made from the buds of a eucalyptus tree of the myrtle family. Nutmeg is produced from a hard nut, and mace is made from the powdered outer covering of the nutmeg nut. Cinnamon is made from the inner bark of the cinnamon tree. Ginger is made from the rhizome of a tropical herb.

Herbs have been used by witch doctors for years, in trying to dispel a sickness or a devil from a person. How the witch doctors decided on which herb, I do not know; each tribe, and in some tribes, each village, uses different herbs for the same purpose. Anise seed was believed by some to avert an evil eye. Coriander and fennel were used to summon the devils. Dill was an herb used in casting spells; it was also used to protect against a witch's spell. Sage is to give wisdom and life.

God is the greatest "Sage" this world will ever know. He planned everything and knows everything. We can go to Him for all of our answers. Thank Him this morning that He is the all-wise God and that He will listen to you.

WILD BURROS

Who makes the wild donkeys wild? I have placed them in the
wilderness and given them salt plains to live in. Job 39:5, T.L.B.

Back in the days when men used horses and donkeys for transportation in the United States, some of the animals got away or were turned loose. Today, as their descendants, there are several herds of wild mustang horses in the country, as well as many wild burros. The little burros are a very hardy breed. They have lived out on the deserts so long that they seem to be immune to disease.

In their struggle for survival on the deserts they eat just about anything they find and are overgrazing the area, not leaving anything for other animals. They are also leaving the desert soil in such a condition that it erodes easily. Farmers and ranchers, as well as national park rangers, are very concerned about this. There are groups of concerned citizens who want the wild herds left intact, while those who are not happy with them want to shoot them and reduce the herds. So the struggle continues.

Wild burros have an average life span of about 25 to 30 years and need very little water. In fact, they can go for about 24 hours without any water. They can smell water almost as far off as a camel can, and they will dig for it, which a horse will not do. Because of the hardiness of these creatures, a foal born to a jenny (female burro) usually survives.

There are about 350 burros living in the Grand Canyon. Others live in California, Arizona, Nevada, and New Mexico. They are not really "wild burrows" but domesticated burros gone native. To help out in the problem of these burros, the National Park Service has started an Adopt-A-Burro Program, and approximately 1,600 have been adopted out.

There are many of us who are running around this world just like these wild burros, tearing up things, especially our own bodies. Once the human body is damaged its repair is expensive, and many times it cannot be repaired. We can survive for a while, perhaps, but help is greatly needed. Ask God to send His angels to be with you today so that you might have a good day.

BIRCHES

Beware of false prophets, which come to you in sheep's clothing, but inwardly they are ravening wolves. Matthew 7:15.

Many birch trees have white bark—the bark that the Indians used in making their canoes. Birch bark is very beautiful, and these trees are sometimes called the "ghosts of autumn."

As the fall of the year comes around these white-bark trees with their colored leaves are a beautiful sight to behold. One photographer-writer said that as he walked through the woods of Vermont he could classify the different trees by a characteristic. The poplars are opportunists, because they are quick to take advantage of the situation—they grow fast. The maples are selfless providers, with their sugar and good firewood. The elms are autocratic and elegant, but a hard, tough wood to cut. The birches are elusive and standoffish, because they make you stand in awe as you look at them.

On a Pathfinder Camporee in the Southern New England Conference, two Pathfinder boys were helping me find a tree that would serve as a good flagpole. We found a lovely birch, and one of the boys volunteered to go up and string the rope. He was about 20 to 25 feet up when the tree broke. My heart sank, but the Pathfinder hung on to the tree, and it came down gently. We were able to catch the boy, and he was not hurt. I was then informed that these birches, which I believe are called the white birch, rot on the inside and one cannot tell from the outside that the inside is rotten.

I know that there are people who look good on the outside but are rotten on the inside. Their characters are not what people see, and they pretend to be something they are not. Look into your own life this morning and see if there is any rottenness in your life. If there is, ask Jesus to help you rid your life of sin and clean it up this morning. Only the clean life in Jesus will be in heaven throughout eternity.

LET YOUR LIGHT SHINE

Let your light so shine before men, that they may see your good works, and glorify your Father which is in heaven. Matthew 5:16.

In a little farming community in the State of Kansas where there were only a few stores, a variety store and a jewelry store stood side by side on the main street.

The window of the variety store displayed one sample of almost everything for sale in the store. The owner wanted to make sure people would see the items they were looking for and come into the store and buy. But there were so many items the store window was cluttered and did not look neat.

There was a marked contrast in the display window of the jewelry store. The owner of the jewelry store had thought through very carefully what he wanted to display in his window. He took some deep-purple velvet cloth and lined the walls and floor of the display area. Then he took eight pieces of wide white ribbon and from each of the eight corners, top and bottom, he ran the streamers to the center of the display. In the center, where all the streamers met, he put a small white box with purple velvet cloth in it. In the center of that purple velvet he put a beautiful diamond. He also installed a spotlight out of sight. The diamond sparkled as it reflected the light.

As people walked down the street and looked into these two windows they saw a great contrast. One was cluttered, the other was simple and beautiful.

Our lives can be like either of those two display windows. They can be cluttered with sin, or Jesus can be seen as we reflect Him shining forth from our lives. Can your friends see Jesus in you as evidenced by kindness, truthfulness, thoughtfulness? Or as your friends look at you do they see a life cluttered by selfishness, dishonesty, laziness, fretfulness, and rebellion? Ask Jesus to help you have a reflecting life today. Let your light shine for Jesus.

ANIMAL DEFENSES

*Thy word is a lamp unto my feet, and a light unto my path.
Psalm 119:105.*

God created the creatures of nature with many ways of
defending themselves. Because of the many varieties it is impossible, to consider at one time all of the interesting creatures
and how they defend themselves, but we will consider a few of
them.

There are some insects that blend into their surroundings.
You might see something like a twig move, but on touching it it
becomes a twig—when in actuality it is a walkingstick. You
might see a moth flying and land on the bark of a tree. As you
look for it, its coloring makes it look like the bark. Have you
ever been outdoors looking for different things in nature and
picked up what you thought was a pretty light-green leaf and
found you had a katydid in your hand?

The ptarmigan bird, arctic fox, short-tailed weasel, and snowshoe hare all turn white when winter come, camouflaging themselves. If the arctic fox or weasel chose to go after the ptarmigan,
it would be difficult for them to see the bird, and difficult for the
bird to notice them.

Skunks send off an odor to keep their enemies away, and not
many animals are interested in getting tangled up with them.
You've no doubt heard about the porcupine and its quills, and
the opossum and hognose snake, which as their defense, pretend to be dead. Some moths and butterflies have large eyelike
spots on their wings to protect them from the birds that want to
eat them. An owl will ruffle itself up so big with its wings and
feathers that its enemies will leave it alone, thinking that it is
bigger than it is.

God not only gave the creatures of the natural world defenses
from their enemies but He has given you and me a defense
against our enemy, Satan. He has given us His Word to read
and store up in our minds. When Satan tempts you, you can say
as Jesus did, "It is written," because you will know what the
Bible says. Also, the devil flees when you pray for help. Ask
God to help you in your study and prayer to get your defense up
against the enemy.

STRANGE PLAYMATES

But I say to you, Love your enemies and pray for those who persecute you." Matthew 5:44, R.S.V.

Have you ever heard of the word *mutualism?* This is a scientific word meaning "I'll scratch your back if you scratch mine." In other words, if you do something for me, I'll do something for you.

In Arabia there are several species of butterflies and ants that have an interesting relationship. The butterflies belong to what is called the "blues" family. When a butterfly egg hatches, a small caterpillar emerges. As the caterpillar grows it changes its skin five or six times. It can do little more than eat and grow.

The caterpillar is vulnerable to many enemies, especially ants, but there is one kind of ant that likes the presence of the blues caterpillars. The blues caterpillars have a special gland on the back that secretes a liquid similar to honey, and the ants eat this honey. They look for the blues caterpillars and eat the honey from the caterpillars' glands and protect them from parasitic wasps and assassin bugs.

These caterpillars actually need the ants to eat this honey because, if it is not eaten, a mildew develops on the caterpillar and kills it. Many times the ants drag or carry the blues caterpillar into their nest. There the caterpillar eats the immature ant eggs and the ant eats the caterpillar honey.

The caterpillar goes into a cocoon and comes out a beautiful butterfly. These butterflies are all colors of the rainbow, not just blue.

Jesus told us to love our enemies. We are to pray for them. Today, I urge you to ask Jesus in your prayer to help you love your enemies. Ask Him to help you treat and talk to them in a nice way. That will be sweet honey to them, and they will not be able to resist you. If you have unkind classmates, ask Jesus to help you love them today.

WALRUS

Which in his times he shall shew, who is the blessed and only Potentate, the King of kings, and Lord of lords. 1 Timothy 6:15.

The monarch of the arctic seas is the walrus. This is a large seallike animal that has two large tusks that hang down from the top jaw. Both the male and female have these ivory tusks.

Walruses weigh from 1,500 to 3,000 pounds and are about nine to 12 feet long. At birth, the baby walrus will be about four feet long and weigh 130 pounds. The female will have only one calf about every two or three years and may nurse each calf for two years. The mother walrus will do anything to defend her calf; she will even give her life to protect it.

These large creatures have stiff bristly hairs on the snout. The tusks are used to dig up the food. They eat mostly from the shallow bottoms of the ocean, which are usually less than 300 feet deep. When they are not eating they will lie around on ice floes. God created these creatures with very strong back teeth, strong enough to crack the shells of the mollusks that they eat.

Walruses enjoy one another's company; it is not uncommon to find hundreds of them living together. As many as two thousand have been counted in one herd. They are hunted by the Eskimos for their meat, ivory tusks, and skin. The ivory brings a very high price today. The skin makes good leather goods and boat hulls because it is almost hairless.

The walrus is not a great long-distance swimmer. It can swim quite rapidly for a short period of time, but it has to rest, either on land or ice, or it would drown through fatigue. Swimming in the cold arctic water would be enough to tire anyone out! Polar bears are the only real enemies that they have, and they will put up a good fight with them, usually to protect the calves.

As the walrus is recognized as the monarch of the Arctic, so we should recognize Jesus as monarch of the world and of our lives. He will be recognized as "King of kings and Lord of lords," so why don't you get a head start on the rest of the world and recognize Him as king today. Give your life over in service to Him today.

ICE

Wait on the Lord: be of good courage, and he shall strengthen thine heart: wait, I say, on the Lord. Psalm 27:14.

Ice is an interesting natural phenomenon. As the temperature of water gets below 32°F. or 0°C., it begins to freeze into ice. As ice is formed it expands and increases its volume by one eleventh. This is one of the reasons why ice is lighter than water and floats.

Ice is used for many things and is almost a necessity for life. Ice is used chiefly to preserve food. Many years ago in North America settlers used to cut the ice frozen on the lakes with large saws. They would store the blocks of ice in sheds insulated with sawdust. Ice is used for making drinks cold, for ice cream, sports, and many other things.

Ice can also be dangerous. When water pipes freeze the expansion of the ice can break the pipes. Ice floating down rivers has damaged ships and bridges. Icy roads are hazardous to automobiles and trucks. Icy sidewalks are dangerous for people to walk on.

As ice forms on the water from the top down, living things in the water can survive, as ice keeps some warmth in the deeper water. If ice were formed at the bottom of a lake and froze upward, most creatures in the water would die.

Ice was not part of God's original creation. Sin altered God's plan, but God has taken these alterations and made them work for the best. In life we make many decisions, some of which are not for our best good and would not have been made had we let God lead. However, He has taken these decisions and allowed the best to happen for us when we've asked Him.

If we ask Jesus to come into our lives He will warm us with His love. Invite Him to come into your heart, melt the iciness of sin, and bring the warmth of His love into your life, so that you may radiate that love in your associations with your friends today.

ICEBERGS

Put not your trust in princes, nor in the son of man, in whom there is no help. Psalm 146:3.

We talked about ice yesterday and how it can be good for some things and bad for others. This morning let's continue to talk about ice.

Icebergs are formed in the Arctic and Antarctic, regions where it is very cold. They are formed where the glaciers meet the sea. Large chunks of ice break off and drift away. Icebergs float on the water with only about one ninth of the iceberg above the surface. There have been icebergs that were 400 feet tall, and yet only one ninth was seen. Imagine the massive amount of ice that lay hidden under the water's surface. This is what makes them very dangerous to ships, especially at night, when they cannot be seen.

Radar picks up many things on the ships' receiving units, but icebergs are only frozen water. They have no metal or minerals so the radar cannot pick them up readily.

On the night of April 14, 1912, a ship named the *Titanic* was making her maiden (first) voyage. It had been advertized that the *Titanic* was unsinkable. It had a strong steel hull and was the safest ship afloat. On that fateful night, as everyone was drinking, dancing, and celebrating, the *Titanic* hit an iceberg. It ripped a long gash in the hull of the ship, which sank rapidly, taking 1,513 persons to a watery grave. An "indestructible" object met an iceberg, which unfortunately destroyed the indestructible.

We cannot put our hope, faith, trust, and confidence in men. All that man can make is destructible because only God can make something indestructible. We are not to put our trust in the things of this world. Put your trust in God this morning and ask Him to help you be indestructible today to Satan.

SNAIL KITE

Man shall not live by bread alone, but by every word that proceedeth out of the mouth of God. Matthew 4:4.

In the southern part of Florida, in the marshlands, lives a beautiful bird called the snail kite. The male is a dark gray in color, and the female is buff. These birds have been diminishing in number due to the development of southern Florida for houses and industry. The wetlands are being filled in and inhabited by humans.

The snail kite has only one item on its menu, and that is the apple snail. These snails live only in the wetlands of Florida and a few other places such as Cuba and Central and South America. Where the apple snails live, so do the snail kites. The kites eat about 50 snails a day to stay alive. They will go into the marsh, grab a snail with their long narrow talons, bring it up onto a limb, and with their pointed, curved beak, pry out the snail without breaking the shell.

The snail kites build their nest out among the cattails or on some smaller plant. Male and female work together and build the nest, and both parents will sit on the nest to incubate the three buff-colored, spotted eggs. When the eggs are about half incubated, one of the parents will leave and build another nest. They seem to be saying, "We'll have a spare nest, just in case something happens to this one." So, they will incubate two nests of eggs and, if no predator disturbs the nests, they will hatch two out of three eggs on the average.

To ensure the diet of the snail kite, the U.S. Fish and Wildlife Service has spent $2 million to build some water-filled impoundments in which to raise apple snails. An electric utility company was forced to spend $700,000 to reroute one of its high-tension power lines, so as not to molest the kites' nesting area.

Snail kites subsist on just one item in their diets, but God has told us that we are not to live on bread alone. Yes, we need to put much of God's Word into our lives; we need to be filled with it. If you want that, pray this morning, asking God to help you with your spiritual diet.

DRAGONS OF KOMODO

These also shall be unclean unto you among the creeping things that creep upon the earth; the weasel, and the mouse, and the tortoise after his kind, and the ferret, and the chameleon, and the lizard, and the snail, and the mole. Leviticus 11:29, 30.

You may wonder why God said that none of the creatures listed in this text are to be eaten. God gave specific orders concerning the right and wrong things to eat. I do not question God because He made me and knows what is best for me to eat.

Unfortunately, there are many people in the world who are not aware of what God said. There are others who, because of necessity, eat what they can find, and then there are some who eat what they want to and ignore what God said.

The world's largest lizards live on a few small Indonesian islands, one of which is called Komodo, from which they get their name. These lizards are members of the monitor family that we talked about some time ago. These lizards grow to about 12 feet in length, and weigh up to 300 pounds. They have very long tails and a short, stocky body. There is a lot of flesh on the body so the natives hunt them for meat.

The lizards were named dragon lizards because they look like the legendary "dragons." The bodies of the dragon lizards are covered with small dull-colored scales and rough skin, and they have large claws that they use to dig caves in which they hide during the night. They generally hunt during the day. They feed on eggs mostly and some small animals, usually locating them with their keen sight and sense of smell. The mouth is very large; as they open it, a large cavern with teeth that look like a saw is visible. The inside of its mouth is red.

God gave to us the things that are good to eat and forbade us to eat the things that are bad. Some people think that God was out of line in doing this. Was He? He made us, didn't He? And we belong to Him, don't we? Therefore He had a right to tell us what to eat and what not to. Thank God this morning that He took enough interest in you to tell you what to eat and what not to. If you are eating something you should not be, ask Him to forgive you and help you to replace it with something else.

LITTLE HAYMAKERS

Take therefore no thought for the morrow: for the morrow shall take thought for the things of itself. Matthew 6:34.

The pika is a small animal resembling a guinea pig. It has back legs that are slightly larger than its front legs. These little creatures have a series of bladelike enamel plates for teeth that are made for cutting vegetation. There are 12 species of pikas found only in Northern Asia; two other species live in the western parts of North America, from Alaska south to the High Sierras in California.

The pikas in North America live in rocky areas, but in Asia they live in burrows in the ground. The pika does not hibernate but lives throughout the winter down under the rocks or in the burrows under a lot of straw, eating the grass, herbs, and shrubs it has gathered and made into hay during the warmer months.

These little creatures are always planning for tomorrow and the future. As soon as the snow melts and the vegetation greens up the pika, or "little haymaker," begins to gather the green grasses and shrubs. It cuts the grass with its teeth, carries it back to the area of its "house," and lays it on the rocks or ground to dry. Then it stores it for the winter. Pikas may gather up to 30 different kinds of food for their winter supply. They need to gather up large amounts of food to eat since they have little fat on their bodies and their metabolic rate is high. Their main activity in life is to prepare for tomorrow and the winter.

Although we have a greater purpose in life than just preparing our meals for tomorrow, the pika gives us an example of preparing for the future. Jesus told us not to worry about the things of today but to prepare for eternity. He said, "Seek ye first the kingdom of God, and his righteousness; and all these things shall be added unto you" (Matt. 6:33). He'll take care of us if we prepare for heaven. I want to ask you this morning: Are you storing up in your mind Bible promises that will prepare you for the future? Ask Jesus this morning to help you prepare for eternity.

SPEWING VOLCANOES

But the day of the Lord will come as a thief in the night; in the which the heavens shall pass away with a great noise, and the elements shall melt with fervent heat, the earth also and the works that are therein shall be burned up. 2 Peter 3:10.

Although scientists are often aware, long before the "blowup," that a volcano is about to erupt, they do not know exactly when it will happen. They can only warn people that live nearby and hope for the best, because there is very little that anyone can do to stop the heavy lava flow or ash fall that usually comes out of a volcano.

In Sicily in 1983 an active volcano, Mount Etna, could not hold back the pressure any longer and blew up. The people in the surrounding towns were terrified and wanted something to be done. The hot molten lava started flowing from the volcano at the rate of 50 miles an hour, disgorging more than 2 million cubic yards a day. (A large dump truck can hold from 18 to 24 yards of dirt at a time.) The lava was engulfing buildings, houses, and many orchards and wooded areas, and turning them into an inferno. Naturally, the farther it flowed, the slower it moved.

Large bulldozers were brought in and men worked frantically to save three towns. A team of explosive specialists was brought in to see if they could use dynamite to divert the flow of the lava. They tried, but had many problems. Their explosives detonated from the heat of the lava before the workers were ready. They finally worked out a method, but it did not change very much the course of the lava flow. It seems that once lava begins to flow it takes its own course. They did save the towns, but it was a very difficult task.

We know that Jesus is coming, but we do not know the exact time. Men will not be able to stop His coming, and many will be weeping and saying all kinds of unkind things. Pray that you will be looking up to see Jesus and that you will be able to go with Him back to heaven.

SNOWFLAKES

All things were made by him; and without him was not any thing made that was made. John 1:3.

Some of you reading this have never seen snow, and others of you may be wishing that it would go away. But snow is an interesting phenomenon. Scientists are trying to figure out just what causes the snowflake to form. We do know that dust particles in the atmosphere come in contact with water molecules and then an ice crystal is formed. As more vapor freezes on the crystal the snowflake is formed. Each snowflake is different and has six points to it.

One scientist has tried to figure out by mathematical formulas just what happens, and he thinks that he has it all figured out. He has spent several years in trying to figure out how the snowflake is formed. By analyzing the physical laws that control the solidification of a fluid into a crystal, and then formulating the mathematical equations of growth for a hypothetical (make-believe) snowflake, this scientist has created a mathematical model that shows the beautiful hexagonal shapes of snowflakes. Can you imagine the time spent just to see how things in God's world are made? Yet this happens every day. One scientist wrote, "The structures of nature, animate or inanimate, complicated or simple, all seem to be controlled by the mysterious process of pattern formation."

To us as Christians it is not mysterious. God created this world. He spoke and it came into being. I don't read where God created snow in His Creation week, but when sin entered into the world, things changed. Yet we know that God still had His hand in all of this because without Him nothing was made. The tiny snowflakes that fall from the sky are all beautiful and different. Each one is unique.

God made each of us as individuals. We are different; we are all unique. There is no two of us alike. Scientists are still trying to figure out what makes the parts of the body function. They can't explain it, but God can. Thank God today that He made you a unique person. You are the only one of your kind.

JACKRABBITS

And the hand of our God was upon us, and he delivered us from the hand of the enemy, and of such as lay in wait by the way. Ezra 8:31.

There are several kinds of hares in the United States, but the jackrabbits are outstanding because of their very large ears. The black-tailed jack has black tips on the ears and the top of the tail is black. The white-tailed jack has, of course, a white tail, and is probably the fastest and largest of the jackrabbits. The antelope jackrabbit has the longest ears, which are about seven to eight inches long.

The original name of the jackrabbit was actually "jackass rabbit," named after the long ears of the jackass or donkey. The name was shortened to just "jack." Jackrabbits have very long back legs that allow them to jump with ease over a five-foot object as they run. They are able to dodge very easily, also.

These creatures live principally on the plains. Years ago, when the early settlers came, they killed off many of the predators of the jackrabbits, so the latter flourished. When the jackrabbits began eating gardens and crops, the settlers built large corrals and drove the rabbits in and killed them. On one such drive in southern California, more than twenty thousand were killed. At the large Los Angeles airport many jackrabbits are run over by airplanes. The carcasses attract buzzards and these buzzards are very dangerous to the airplanes.

In the State of Wyoming signs warn travelers to beware of the "jackelopes." The picture is of an extra large jackrabbit with large hind legs and huge ears, a cross between hares and antelopes. Of course there is no such animal, but with so many jackrabbits in Wyoming the people have to have a little fun.

In Arizona and northern Mexico is a real animal called the antelope jackrabbit. It can, at will, make its white underfur swing around to the side, and thus help it in its flight. One person described it as a "flapping pillowcase."

In our daily Christian walk God will help us avoid the enemy if we will ask Him to help us. Ask God to help you stay away from Satan today. He is the enemy to avoid.

MILKWEEDS

Not for that we have dominion over your faith, but are helpers of your joy: for by faith ye stand. 2 Corinthians 1:24.

The common milkweed plant is quite well known all over the United States because it is a native plant of America. The early settlers took some of these plants or their seeds to southern Europe where the great Swedish botanist Carl von Linné named it.

This very common plant has thick, broad leaves that are opposite to each other on stems that are covered with fine, misty hairs. These plants grow to a height of about two to six feet. There are about 25 other species of milkweed, but they have somewhat different characteristics.

The common milkweed gets its name from a white sap or milk that the plant secretes. This milk has entertained both children and adults alike for generations as a curiosity of nature. Thomas Edison and others experimented with this milk as a substitute for rubber, but the experiment failed.

North American Indians applied the milk directly on warts and used it in concoctions to control ringworm. It was used as a remedy for various intestinal disorders. It was believed that a mixture of milkweed root and marsh mallow leaves, steeped in a tea and drunk several times a day, would cure gallstones. This same tea was believed to help in cases of dropsy, asthma, and high fever. Most parts of the milkweed plant can be eaten if picked and prepared at the right time. Euell Gibbons in his book *Stalking the Wild Asparagus* tells how to prepare the milkweed plant parts.

I have used the silky seeds that come from the pod on the milkweed as a background in frames that I mounted butterflies in. I removed the seeds and just used the beautiful silk instead of cotton.

Imagine a common plant that can be so useful. God thought of everything, didn't He? God desires that each of us be as useful to humanity as the milkweed. We are to help our fellowmen and be as useful to them as we can. Ask God this morning to help you be a helper today to someone.

SCARAB BEETLES

And it shall come to pass, that from one new moon to another, and from one sabbath to another, shall all flesh come to worship before me, saith the Lord. Isaiah 66:23.

You have probably never heard of the scarab beetle unless you live in Egypt. For several thousand years the scarab beetle has been a symbol of the sun, of rebirth, and of life itself. Back in early Egyptian art, the artists used the symbol of the scarab beetle. It is legendary in Egyptian history.

The scarab beetle has legs that are well adapted for digging. These beetles will dig a burrow about 12 inches deep near an animal manure or dung pile. They will roll up some of the dung into a small ball and roll it to the hole—and down it goes. They will eat from it, then when it is gone they will fly over and begin another ball.

When the female is ready to lay her eggs, which are not many, she will make up a dung ball, push it into a hole, and lay one egg in it. Then she will move on, dig another hole, roll up another dung ball, and lay another egg. She makes sure that the dung is wet so that when the eggs hatch the larvae will eat the dung and eventually grow to adulthood. This whole process takes about thirty days.

As the early Egyptians observed these beetles pushing the ball of dung, then seeing the new beetles after a month, they related this process to the sun going down and the moon coming up, and within thirty days there was a new moon and new life. One Egyptian wrote in a papyrus more than 2,500 years ago, "On the twenty-eighth day, which the insect knows to be that of the conjunction of the sun and the moon and the birth of the world, it opens the ball and throws it into the water. From this ball issue animals that are scarabs." Scarab symbols were used as seals by religious and bureaucratic officials.

From one new moon to another one, we who are faithful will have the opportunity of worshiping the true God who created life—not a beetle that symbolizes life. Pray that God will help you in your worship of the true God.

SEQUOIAS

His branches shall spread, and his beauty shall be as the olive tree, and his smell as Lebanon. Hosea 14:6.

As God was willing to bless Israel, so He is blessing the giant sequoia redwoods in California. These trees are interesting. The largest of these trees is in the Sequoia National Park, in central California. It is called the General Sherman tree, 272 feet high and about 75 feet to the first limb.

Some sequoia trees are as much as 3,500 years old. They have some natural traits that keep them alive and growing. Their beautiful red bark is of a porous material, resistant to decay, disease, and insects, and it is fire-resistant. Many of the large trees have been scarred by fires that have gone through the area, but they still stand because the bark has saved the life of the tree. This bark may be up to 12 inches thick. It acts as an excellent insulation to protect the tree.

The trees also produce a natural fluid called tannin. Tannin is what provides the color of the bark, and also makes the tree insectproof. This is why redwood is so good for outdoor furniture. The redwoods also scatter millions of seeds, which fall to the ground. God gave the seeds power to germinate and grow, but most of these redwood seeds do not take root and grow.

Most of these tall redwoods have roots that extend for up to 200 feet, but they are only about six feet deep. Is it any wonder then, when high winds come, that some of these giants tumble to the ground? These giants also spread their limbs out over many feet in each direction.

God wants us to be "rooted and grounded" in His love, and He wants us to spread His love to everyone. He also wants us to be rooted deep in His Word, too. There are many who are spreading out and telling others about God's great love. Thank God this morning for the privilege you have of spreading His love to others. Ask Him to help you do that today.

THE GRUNION RUN

The Lord is good to all: and his tender mercies are over all his works. Psalms 145:9.

It is interesting to note that every species of animal life has its own individual ways of doing things. Take for instance the grunion fish. These little silvery fish, which grow about six inches long, live in the ocean not too far away from the shore. The females go up onto the beach, in what is called a grunion run, to lay their eggs. Several male grunion accompany the females. As a female wiggles her tail and digs into the sand to bury her eggs, a male will wiggle to the same spot and release from its body a liquid called milt, which goes down through the sand and fertilizes the eggs.

John Olguin, director of the Cabrillo Beach Museum in Los Angeles, says, "We know when the fish will come ashore, but we don't know how they know the correct time. It's possible that grunion have internal clocks—biological mechanisms that enable them to detect minute changes in ocean currents or other aspects of their environment." Year after year, from March to August, on certain beaches in southern California and along the Gulf of California, these fish swim up onto the selected beaches about every two weeks to lay their eggs. Some of the grunions will lay up to 3,000 eggs at a time.

These eggs must incubate in the sand before the tide can wash them away and break open their transparent membrane sacs. It is only during the nights of the new and full moons, when the tides are the highest, that the grunion run. Interesting, isn't it, to see how God has put His creation in such balance that they work together for each other?

At night, during a grunion run, thousands of people come onto the beach to watch these interesting fish completing and sustaining their life cycle of productivity. What a great Creator— God brought all forms of life into this world.

If God can take care of the little grunion, how much more He can take care of you. Pray just now that God will guide you today as He guides the little grunion. Ask Him to help you do what you need to do, just when you need to do it. He guides the grunion, and I know He will guide you, if you will ask Him.

WOODCOCK

Then many of the Jews which came to Mary, and had seen the things which Jesus did, believed on him. John 11:45.

The woodcock is a plump-looking bird, brownish in color, and generally lives where there is thick underbrush or thickets in wooded areas. A nickname for it is the "timberdoodler," because it spends so much time in the thickets.

Woodcocks are difficult to see. They are described as mysterious, sly, and recluse birds. In fact, some people don't even believe that they exist.

They have a very long bill for their size, about two and a half to three inches long, that is used to get earthworms, their principal source of food, out of the ground. They are about the size of a robin, and will sit and stare at a person with their bigger than usual eyes. You may not see them because of their colorings, which blend them right into the environment.

The male woodcock has a special aerial dance that he performs to encourage a female to accept him. He will fly out into the open and then straight up into the air. He will hover for an instant, make some musical sounds, then straight down to the ground. Once on the ground a "peent" noise is heard, which is a communication between the sexes. At times, two woodcocks may be doing it at the same time. At other times two males may fly at each other in the air; one dodges and continues on, and the other goes through the ritual aerial dance. This usually occurs at dusk, not during the bright daylight hours.

In their nests they will have a clutch of about four brown, spotted, buff-colored eggs. The eggs are difficult to be seen, so they have about a 60 percent chance of surviving, whereas other birds, such as quail, have only a 33 percent chance to survive. Although woodcocks migrate, they fly low and at night, so very few are seen by humans.

Although some of Jesus' creation is secretive and sly, Jesus did all of His work out in the open, never hidden, so that all might see and understand. He wants us to believe in Him. One way is for us to be able to see what He can do. Ask Him to help you in a special way in your life.

SALAMANDERS

But Jonathan Saul's son delighted much in David: and Jonathan told David, saying, Saul my father seeketh to kill thee: now therefore, I pray thee, take heed to thyself until the morning, and abide in a secret place, and hide thyself. 1 Samuel 19:2.

Salamanders are little lizardlike creatures that have short legs and a long tail. They walk or run like a lizard but they are not lizards. They belong to the frog and toad class. Most of these little creatures are quite small, three to four inches in length. They are more abundant in the United States than any other country in the world. But the largest salamander is found in Japan and is about five feet long. The most well-known salamander is the spotted salamander in the United States, which grows to about six inches long.

Being cold-blooded amphibians, salamanders adapt to the climate around them. They cannot live in a climate that is too severely cold. They spend most of their daylight hours under moist logs, rocks, bark, and leaves. Most salamanders are land creatures; however, there are a few varieties that are water creatures. Some of the water ones are waterbound—they never leave the water. One variety lives on the bottom of streams and ponds. There are also some salamanders that never leave the egg until they are mature; then they venture out. Others hatch and grow to maturity.

The salamanders have been created by God in such a way that if they lose a tail or a foot, they can grow another one. I wish that this were possible in humans, don't you? I wish that some of my friends who have lost an arm, hand, leg, or foot could grow another one, but God never put that ability in humans. I believe that the creatures that I saw most in summer camps during the time I was a camp director, were salamanders. Boys and girls seemed to enjoy bringing the little creatures back in their hands. They had found them as they rolled over rocks and rotten trees and lifted up leaves and other debris.

God is in a secret place; one of these days He will come back and take us home with Him to His "secret place." Ask Him this morning to help you be ready to go with home with Him.

FROST-FREE

And ye shall know the truth, and the truth shall make you free. John 8:32.

For many years scientists have been going into the Antarctic's icy waters, trying to discover what really makes things "tick" in the very cold water. They have discovered a fish called the ice fish. This fish puzzled marine biologists for many years, who wondered how it could survive in the frigid water under the ice. Doing much research on these fish, scientists came to the conclusion that ice fish have a protein in their blood that is a type of antifreeze, similar to that used in the radiators of automobiles. They believe this protein is what keeps the fish's blood from freezing.

Scientists are not sure why some of the other antarctic creatures do not freeze to death. One scientist captured a sea spider, small shrimplike creatures called krill, and a giant isopod. In the laboratory he discovered that these creatures do not have a protein like the ice fish to prevent freezing, but they have an extra amount of salt in the blood. He believes that this extra amount of salt is what keeps the animals from freezing.

Scientists are still trying to unlock the mysteries of the Antarctic. As one scientist put it, "We could study for a lifetime and never unlock all of the secrets of this ice world."

Since there was no ice or real coldness in the original Creation, God must have made some adaptations in the creatures that would live in this world changed by sin. It was when sin entered that God placed into action the plan of salvation, which was a change in His original plan for man.

Jesus died that we might be free from sin; with that would come a new life throughout all eternity. As Jesus changed His plan and gave life to the creatures in the Antarctic, so He changed His plan and gave to us the plan of salvation that we might live. Thank God in your prayer this morning for that wonderful plan that brings to you a new life in Christ Jesus, free of sin.

127

PRECIOUS STONES

And the merchants of the earth shall weep and mourn over her [Babylon]. . . . The merchants . . . shall stand afar off for the fear of her torment, weeping and wailing, and saying, Alas, alas that great city, that was clothed in fine linen, and purple, and scarlet, and decked with gold, and precious stones, and pearls! Revelation 18:11–16.

Precious stones or gems come in all colors, some more valuable than others. We have already talked about pearls, which come from mollusks, and coral from sea creatures. Amber comes from the resin of fossil trees, and jet from fossil coal. This morning we want to talk about real gems. They are minerals that look like pretty stones, which are lodged generally in other rocky substances.

Color determines not only the beauty of the gem but it helps in the value of it too. There are two types of color: (1) essential, and (2) nonessential. The true color of the gem is "essential"; the "nonessential" is that which is the result of some impurity.

The degree of hardness determines whether it is classified as a gem or not. Minerals are classified by hardness on a scale of one to ten, with ten being the hardest. Diamonds are classed at ten; that is why they are used in cutting tools. In order to be classified as a gem, the rock must be a hardness of seven to ten. This hardness means that it cannot be cut with a knife or scratched by glass.

Opal and turquoise are found in areas where there is very little moisture. The prominent sources for turquoise are in the Southwestern United States and Tibet. Emeralds, topaz, and tourmaline are found in areas where erosion has exposed the old, once-molten rocks at the surface. Topaz comes from Germany and Russia, but the best are found in Brazil. The best rubies come from Burma, the best sapphires from Kashmir, the best diamonds from Africa, and the best opals from Australia. Value of the gems is determined by color, rareness, demand, hardness, and brilliance.

Since precious stones were used to build that beautiful city of Babylon, which was destroyed, God has said He will build a more beautiful city with even more beautiful and precious stones. Thank Him for the beauty in the rocks and minerals today.

THE PRAYING INSECT

Keep watching and praying, that you may not enter into temptation. Matthew 26:41, N.A.S.B.

I remember that when I was a boy, my uncle, who was living with us, went out into the field beside our house and found some egg cases. He put them on his windowsill.

He said he didn't know what kind they were but maybe we would soon find out. One day he arrived home from work and entered his room. Soon he called me. I went running to his room and saw little green creatures all over his window screen, window, desk, bed — well, all over the room — hundreds of them.

"What are they?" I asked.

He replied, "These are baby praying mantises."

"What is that?" I asked.

"The praying mantis is an insect about four inches long. It has funny stilted legs for walking and two spiny jointed front legs that are used to catch other insects for food. They have a triangular-shaped head with large eyes," he said.

"Why are they called praying mantises?" I asked. My uncle told me that these mantids raise the front feet up in a posture of praying. The mantis will sit up and be quiet for long periods of time. It is not praying but waiting for food. Mantises are so still that when an insect passes by they reach out quickly with their two front legs and capture it, then eat it. Although the praying mantis is an enemy and only fooling the other insects, it is friendly to gardeners, because it eats many pest insects. These insects are caught off guard and lose their lives because they did not recognize the enemy.

In our spiritual life we have an enemy whose name is Satan. As our text for today says, we need to be on guard that he will not attack us without our knowing it. We need to watch for his false ways. He will bring many things into our lives to trick us into his arms of sin. We need to stay close to the Lord so that we can identify Satan when we see him.

Ask the Lord today, as you pray, to help you recognize Satan and his ways so you will not be caught as his prey. God will help you identify him if you will only ask Him.

VINES, VINES, AND MORE VINES

Stand fast therefore in the liberty wherewith Christ hath made us free, and be not entangled again with the yoke of bondage. Galatians 5:1.

It seems that the only place that you can avoid vines is in the middle of a desert. Vines are all around us, some of them are useful and some of them are poisonous. Others are simply pests. I have a cartoon of a little boy who was at camp. He came to the nature director with a handful of vines and said, "Look at these new vines that I found." The picture shows the nature director backing away, because the vines were poison ivy.

There are always some who find interesting vines that they haven't seen before, and that is probably because there are so many of them. Vines vary in size from that of a thread to as large as a person's body.

Vines usually grow up on some other natural object. They rely very much on chance on finding something to grow up on. If there is no rock, tree, or other climbable object, they will grow horizontally on the ground. For many vines, the upward climb to light is what keeps them alive. Some vines will just spiral around their object, while others will use barbs, prickles, hooks, thorns, and aerial roots to hang onto the captive object.

The large vines of tropical rain forests that have a woody texture, the kind that children like to swing on, are called lianas. Grapevines also belong to this group. Monkeys and other animals in the jungles and rain forests use the vines that extend from tree to tree to walk, crawl, and jump on. Some of you have rattan furniture in your house. The rattan is a good-sized vine that climbs part way up the tree, attaches itself with spines, then goes from tree to tree. Rattan palms grow up to 650 feet long and store drinkable water in them.

Christ came and died in this world that you and I as sinners might be freed from the bondage of sin. As the vines wrap themselves around their victims, so sin wraps itself around its victims; only the blood of Jesus can set you free. Thank Him for that freedom today.

SCULPTURES OF TIME

Great peace have they which love thy law: and nothing shall offend them. Psalm 119:165.

Many stand in awe as they look at the beautiful rock formations in caves and caverns. Time does not stand still in a cave; there are usually on-going changes.

Many formations grow through interaction between water and rock surfaces. How the specific forms come about may depend on the amount of water in the cave and the type of minerals in the water. In standing water within a cave, minerals in the water precipitate out to form clusters of crystals. These clusters of crystals take on various shapes and forms and are called cave coral.

We have all heard of stalagmites and stalactites. Stalactites grow from the ceiling down and stalagmites grow from the floor of the cave upward. Both of these types of formations are formed by constant dripping of water. The water evaporates and the calcium carbonate, or calcite, forms deposits. What is fascinating is that in each cave or cavern there are many types of formations. One of the prettiest types of stalactites is the "soda straw." As the stalactite is formed the carbon dioxide released from the water "fizzes" away and leaves beautiful crystals on the stalactite.

Gypsum crystals finer than human hair have been photographed. These crystals grow parallel to each other; they look like a lovely "angel hair" decoration, like the kind some people use on their Christmas tree.

There are formations called mothballs, twisted currents, aragonite crystals, calcite chunks, gypsum flowers, cave pearls, gypsum needles, and crystal bunches. Almost all of these formations are made from calcium carbonate, gypsum, and calcite.

There are many people who live what is called a "hard life." They have left God out of their life and their hearts have turned to stone. Ask Jesus to help you live a happy, peaceful, and satisfied life.

SUNSPOTS

And the city had no need of the sun, neither of the moon, to shine in it: for the glory of God did lighten it, and the Lamb is the light thereof. Revelation 21:23.

Sunspots. Are there such things? Yes, according to the scientists, there are. When I was using radio for communication, there were times that I could reach some places that at other times I could not reach, and I was told that it was due to sunspots. A policeman in West Virginia was calling on his radio for a helicopter to come and take an injured person to the hospital. This message was picked up in Santa Monica, California, some three thousand miles away, by a police radio operator. Normally these radio messages go out only a few miles. What made the difference? Sunspots.

Sunspots are solar activity that are magnetically enhanced regions of the sun. There are not always the same number of sunspots each day, and there may not be the same each week or month. At times they are more intense than at other times. They run in cycles that last about 11 years. Solar flare explosions and other disturbances of the sun are related to distortions of the solar magnetic field.

Some years ago, pilots in a Concorde passenger plane, flying at an extremely high altitude, noticed that their radio system was going wrong. They lowered their altitude and found that it started working correctly again. Sunspots can do interesting things.

The Bible says that in God's New Jerusalem there will be no need of the sun. The brightness of the glory of God will light up everything. We now depend on the sun for much light and heat, but in the New Jerusalem that will not be necessary. It might be well for us to start to depend on God today and every day from now on, so that when Jesus does come our dependence will have been such that we will continue to depend on Him. In your prayer this morning, talk to God about your dependence on Him and ask Him to help you be more dependent on Him.

HURRICANE OR TYPHOON

The Lord is slow to anger, and great in power, and will not at all acquit the wicked: the Lord hath his way in the whirlwind and in the storm, and the clouds are the dust of his feet. Nahum 1:3.

Do you know the difference between a hurricane and a typhoon? It depends on where you live as to what name you give to the tremendously powerful storms that develop over the oceans. The hurricane develops over the Atlantic Ocean and the typhoon over the Pacific and Indian oceans. During the summer months the warming of the oceans' water causes a patch of warming air to begin to rise producing an area of low pressure. As the wake trails upward, it sucks in more air, and as the air is warmed, it in turn joins the updraft. This phenomenon is called a "tropical depression." The rising column of warm, moist air is cooled at higher altitudes and condenses into huge clouds that spread outward. The "chimney" in the center becomes the center of the storm, and as the air rushes inward and upward it begins to whirl, in a counterclockwise direction in the Northern Hemisphere and clockwise in the Southern Hemisphere. As the whirlwind accelerates, this tropical depression becomes a driving storm. As the storm moves across the water, the winds may get up to more than 300 miles per hour, but the storm as a whole may be traveling only about 30 miles per hour.

Theophrastus, who was a student of Aristotle, wrote a book that gave 50 ways to forecast a storm. Mariners have coined the phrase, "Red sky at night, sailors delight. Red sky in the morning, sailors take warning."

God is the Creator of the universe, and therefore He understands what is happening even though scientists do not. God is waiting for you and me to make our decision to follow Jesus. It is not His desire that any of us should perish; that is why He holds back the storms of total destruction. But the day is coming, and I believe soon, when God is going to destroy this earth.

While there is time, while He continues to warn us—through His Word, events, and storms—I invite you to make your decision to be with Him throughout all eternity. Ask Him to help you today. You can trust Him, because He is a God who acts.

DESTROY THE WEEDS?

The field is the world; the good seed are the children of the kingdom; but the tares are the children of the wicked one. Matthew 13:38.

Destroy the weeds? Are all weeds bad? It certainly seems that way, doesn't it? But there is good in everything; let's try to find out the good about weeds. Someone has said that a weed is only a plant that is in the wrong place; even a tomato plant in a row of beets may be considered a weed because it doesn't belong there.

Granted, there are good weeds and bad weeds. However, even the bad weeds can do good. Bad weeds will hold the soil, keeping it from blowing or washing away. Their tough root systems break up the hard soil. Some of them have such deep roots that they bring some minerals up toward the surface of the ground; other plants can use these for nutrients to live on. Other weeds are used for medicines, dyes, and other useful purposes.

Think with me about the beauty that can be found in many weeds. Look at the beautiful purple flower of the thistle, the lovely yellow flower of the dandelion, the blue flower of the chicory, the yellow flower of the mullein, the pink flower of the motherwort, the white flower of Queen Anne's lace, and so on. Many weeds have a very deep root; they can be cut with a hoe but they will continue to come back. Weeds also seem to have a tolerance for a lack of water and care that most cultivated plants do not have. Weeds are just a pest to most of us; they seem to survive for a purpose, yet they are still weeds.

Have you ever noticed that shortly after a piece of ground is abandoned, weeds begin to grow? It is evident that weeds need no care to grow. They can spring up and grow most anyplace. Cultivated plants need tender loving care to survive. Those who follow the leadings of the devil are allowed by him to just grow on their own, but those who follow Jesus are given that tender loving care needed for survival and for eternity. While all have value in God's eyes, the day will come when He will have to separate the weeds from the true plants. Ask God to help you be a "true" plant in His love, and not a weed of the devil.

SOME YELLOW JACKETS
STEAL AND KILL

Our inheritance has been turned over to strangers, our homes to aliens. Lamentations 5:2, R.S.V.

Yellow jackets are small wasps. They are very aggressive little creatures; sometimes the little wasps come to share your picnic lunch.

Yellow jackets usually build their nests in underground caverns. They attach the nest to the top of the cavern. The nest, made of a soft paperlike material, is chewed-up wood, mixed with saliva of the yellow jacket, spit out, and formed into the desired shape.

Yellow jackets live in a "colony," which is made up of one queen and many workers. The new queens mate in the fall of the year, then hibernate throughout the winter. As spring approaches, the new queens fly around seeking new homes for themselves.

Studying the habits of yellow jackets, scientists discovered that there are really two kinds, the *Vespula squamosa* and the *Vespula maculifrons*. For simplicity, let's refer to these as yellow jackets A and B, respectively. In the nests of the yellow jacket A, scientists discovered some yellow jacket B eggs. However, they found no yellow jacket A eggs in yellow jacket B nests. As these researchers continued their study they found that the yellow jacket B queens were allowed to enter the yellow jacket A nest by the queen. The yellow jacket B queen would take advantage of her welcome and lay a few of her eggs there. Then the daughters of the yellow jacket A queen take over and nurture the yellow jacket B queen's young along with their own.

As we live a Christian life, doing things the way God would have us do, the old devil, Satan, tries to sneak in and take us away from God. He tries to lead us into the paths of sin and entice us into places we ought not to go, trying to kill our spiritual experience. He does not want us to have that heavenly home Jesus has prepared for us. Pray today, asking Jesus to help you keep Satan out of your life so he will not be able to destroy your inheritance. Jesus is waiting for your invitation today. Invite Him into your life now.

QUIET HUNTERS

Now then, do not let my blood fall to the ground away from the presence of the Lord; for the king of Israel has come out to search for a single flea, just as one hunts a partridge in the mountains. 1 Samuel 26:20, N.A.S.B.

The cat family has many varieties, representing many different sizes and colors. For the next few mornings we will look at these different "silent hunters," largely from the Asian area, where many of them are concentrated. They roam over the southern part of Russia and the northern part of India; throughout the countries of Nepal, Pakistan, eastern China, Java, Sumatra, Borneo, Tibet, Burma, and Thailand; and the island of Iriomote, which is the southernmost of the Japanese Ryukyu Islands.

There are twenty different kinds of cats in this area of Southern Asia. We are, of course, familiar with the tiger, probably the most famous and receiving the most attention. Many other cats live in tiger territory, quietly going about their business. We will look at them from the largest to the smallest.

The Asian lion, known as the "king of beasts," is not as populous as it once was. There are only about 200 now in the Gir Forest in Gujarat, India. There are three species of leopards, the spotted, the clouded, and the snow. The spotted leopard is the most noticeable in Sri Lanka, with the black being more prevalent in the tropical rain forests. The snow leopard lives in the Himalaya, Pamirs, Altai, Kush, and Tien Shan mountains. The snow leopard must eat about 2,000 pounds of food a year to stay alive. It has not been known to attack people, like the spotted leopard has.

When David was being hunted by King Saul, he asked the Lord to watch over him. The devil is silently going around hunting his victims. Ask God to help you to not be one of the devil's victims today.

ASIA'S FASTEST
AND DIFFERENT CATS

Wilt thou hunt the prey for the lion? or fill the appetite of the young lions, when they couch in their dens, and abide in the covert to lie in wait? Job 38:39, 40.

The cheetah is the fastest animal; it runs at speeds of more than 70 miles an hour for short distances, enough to catch its meal. The cheetah is nearly extinct now in Asia, but in the olden days the Mogul emperors of India had it trained to hunt game animals for the emperor's table. It is a spotted, sleek, and slender animal, with long legs.

The clouded leopard of Nepal and Borneo lives in the rain forests. This creature has a lovely clouded coat that resembles the mint leaf; thus the natives have given it the name "mint leopard." These small leopards hunt their prey and slap them off their feet with a forepaw before they move in for the kill. The lynx, about the size of the clouded leopard, has a short bobbed tail, weighs about 40 pounds, is brown, and has long distinctive ear tufts. It generally dwells in the forests.

The caracal is a smaller version of the cheetah. It is the size of the lynx but with a longer tail and slimmer body. In the past caracals were trained to hunt like the cheetah; they are the fastest and best-jumping cats of their size. They have a light tan-colored fur and are quickly approaching extinction.

The Asiatic golden cat ranges from Tibet to India and Sumatra. These cats are rarely seen because they do not adapt well where there are humans. They are smaller than the caracal and about the same color. In Burma and Thailand, the fur of this cat is burned to keep away the tigers, so there it has been named the "fire cat."

The fishing cat, which lives in much of Asia, weighs from about 17 to 25 pounds; it is gray in color, with beautiful patterns on the fur. It goes to the streams and lies down and waits for the fish. When it sees a fish, as quick as lightning it can throw the fish out with its slightly webbed paw. Considered a timid cat, it can be fierce.

God was challenging Job in the text today, because Job was feeling sorry for himself. God took care of Job; although He didn't let Job have everything, still He watched over him. We may not get all we want, but God still watches over us.

ASIA'S PRETTY CATS

They hunt our steps, that we cannot go in our streets: our end is near, our days are fulfilled; for our end is come. Lamentations 4:18.

As we read the text for this morning we see an interesting situation that we wouldn't want to get into. Yet that is what happens with the prey of various Asian cats. The jungle cat ranges from the Volga River south to Egypt and east to Vietnam. Although the name doesn't so indicate, it dwells in high grass, shrubby plains, and thick brush. It is not particularly shy of humans, and lives near villages. It has a beautiful grayish-brown fur and is active in the daytime.

A very beautiful cat is the marbled cat, which looks something like the clouded leopard. The fur is yellowish with black markings that merge together like marble. It is confined to the evergreen forests of Nepal, Sumatra, and Borneo. It is scarce and afraid of people.

The leopard cat is a miniversion of the leopard, found in the Amur Valley of the Soviet Union and western India to Indonesia. It is the only cat in the Philippines and is called the "money cat" in China, because the spots in the fur resemble Chinese coins. It is one of the few cats that seemingly mate for life, and is probably the most common cat in Southeast Asia.

In 1967 the Iriomote cat was discovered on Iriomote Island. It is the newest cat in the cat family, and very little is known about it. The authorities say there are only about 40 of them on the island, making it the rarest of all cats. The native islanders have discovered that the flesh of the Iriomote cat is very good to eat, so that may cut the number further, if the islanders can find them.

Someday soon, and maybe sooner than we think, we as Seventh-day Adventists may be hunted for our belief in God and the practice of our beliefs. Ask God to help you today to be strong for your faith and for Him; this will help you be strong when the time comes to stand strong for God.

ASIA'S SMALLER CATS

Thou huntest me as a fierce lion: and again thou shewest thyself marvellous upon me. Job 10:16.

The desert cat is reported to be a relative of the common house cat. The former are scarcely seen by humans; they live in the drier areas of Northern Africa to the Central Asian steppes and central India. They can adapt to drier climates and droughts by eating insects instead of rodents. They have a brownish-yellow fur and look like a house cat. The Chinese desert cat is generally found on the deserts, scrublands, and dry grasslands of Mongolia, eastern Tibet, Kansu, and Szechwan, where tigers have not been seen for many years. This creature is so scarce that little is known about it. It does have a light-brown fur, with spots on the rump. A very striking cat.

Confined to the northern part of the island of Borneo is the Bornean bay cat. It was first discovered in 1856 and has not been seen much since. It has black tips on the ears and is mahogany in color, or it may be a blackish gray. A beautiful little cat. Pallas' cat, in Central Asia, is unique in that it has a large rounded head with both eyes facing forward, and small rounded ears. It has long fur underneath to protect it from the cold ground, as well as short stocky legs and a fat little body. It hunts mostly in rocky areas.

Flat-headed cats are one of the smallest and weigh from four to six pounds. These are found in southern Thailand and Borneo. Their ears are low to the head, thus giving the flat-head look. They live along streams and are excellent swimmers. The smallest of all the cats is the rusty-spotted cat. It is about half the size of the house cat, has a soft, fawn gray color with brown spots and bars on the fur. It lives in the dry forests of India and humid forests of Sri Lanka. Very little is known about this animal.

Job was feeling sorry for himself and feeling that he was being hunted by God. God hunts us only to show to us His love. He does not hunt us to cause us harm, like the devil does. Thank God this morning that He is interested enough in you to want to be with you.

BARNACLES

The Lord shall reign for ever, even thy God, O Zion, unto all generations. Praise ye the Lord. Psalm 146:10.

Scientists want to know how to make it; dentists want to use it in the repair of teeth; and others want to use it too, but no one can figure out how to make it. What am I talking about? I'm talking about the glue that holds the barnacles to any object that they decide to attach themselves to. Scientists have analyzed what the substances are that are contained in the barnacle glue, but they have not been able to get the right proportions so that they can duplicate it.

Barnacles may attach themselves to a rock where the waves constantly dash against them. It is estimated that they withstand forces that would be equal to a human being trying to stand up in a 300- to 400-mile-an-hour wind. Yet these creatures hang on, day after day, year after year, sometimes as much as forty years or more.

Different sea creatures such as turtles and whales have barnacles attached to them. Sometimes these barnacles are attached to the same whale for its entire lifetime; many outlast the whale. According to sea-life specialists, barnacles are choosy as to which surfaces they adhere to. Of the more than 1,500 species in the world, each has a preferred surface. Many times they stay permanently, although they can move if they want to.

In Florida, coastal engineers have noticed that barnacles attach themselves to dock posts and seawalls at the surface of the water. The engineers claim that during the last few years the ocean water has risen several feet, thus boosting the theory that our earth temperature is warmer and the ice fields are melting and raising the ocean level.

As barnacles hang on seemingly forever, so God will reign forever; there will be no letting up in His reign. It will be forever and ever; there is no end. Pray that God will help you stick to His gospel, and remain "stuck" to Him for eternity.

THE RAVEN

The eye that mocketh at his father, and despiseth to obey his mother, the ravens of the valley shall pick it out, and the young eagles shall eat it. Proverbs 30:17.

There are three kinds of ravens in North America, but they all have similar characteristics. They build their nests with sticks in a very crude manner and line them with animal hair, shredded bark, moss, seaweed, or grass. These nests are usually quite large and located on the top of a cliff or at the top of a large tree. There are usually from three to eight eggs laid which are greenish-gray with brown spots. The raven has a wingspan of up to three feet; it is a very strong and hardy bird.

The raven is an impressive bird because it has a shiny black luster to its feathers. Boys and girls with black hair are often called "raven haired."

Ravens have good eyesight and are constantly on the lookout for food. They eat a lot of insects, grain, small rodents, and bird's eggs; they also eat on dead animals. When ravens come to a fallen animal the first thing they do is peck at the eye. God has given them the instinct to know that if the animal tries to cover the eye, it is not dead. If the animal does nothing then the raven knows that the animal is dead and it begins to eat the animal. Other birds such as the eagle come and eat on the dead animal, also.

Sometimes when a young person starts to show a rejection of his mother and father and others in authority, he may be showing by the patterns in his life that he is dying spiritually. There may be reasons why a young person is rejecting others, but that young person is leaving himself or herself open to Satan's temptations. Satan will look into the eyes, as it were, and if he sees a spiritual dying, he will work hard to cause a spiritual death. Today you may not appreciate being told what to do by your parents or teachers, but if you respect them and do as they ask, when you are older you'll see you did the right thing. Don't give Satan a chance to pluck that Christian gleam from your eye. Be the kind of person that you know God wants you to be—kind, loving, and obedient.

THE TOAD WORLD

And of every living thing of all flesh, two of every sort shalt thou bring into the ark, to keep them alive with thee; they shall be male and female. Genesis 6:19.

Of those creatures that came from the ark when Noah landed safely, some were toads. Today there are many varieties of toads. They exist in almost every country of the world except Australia, New Guinea, New Zealand, and Madagascar. After the Flood subsided there weren't many places these toads didn't hop to.

In Mexico and Trinidad there is the giant toad that is about nine inches long. South Africa has the smallest toad, called the rose toad; it is only about one inch long. England has a popular toad called the natterjack toad. It has short legs, runs instead of hops and butts with its head. There is an African toad that gives live birth to its babies, into a stagnant pool of water.

Toads adapt very well to the temperatures and climates where they are found. The boreal toad of Alaska and British Columbia does very well in colder climates, and the green toad of the Himalayan Mountains lives up to 15,000 feet elevation. The Colorado River toad is at home in the southern deserts of the United States and the northern deserts of Mexico. Its skin is so baggy when born that it looks like a man who lost a lot of weight but still wears his old suit. It has to grow into its skin!

Found in the waters of Trinidad is a toad called the granular toad. It is covered with warts, but fortunately it doesn't give warts to people any more than any other toad does. This toad can even sing under water. Toads singing in the tropical rain forests provide a real musical treat. I used to lay in bed at night and listen to the toads singing in the Amazon jungle. One night we recorded a program in our house for broadcast over the radio. When it was broadcast the next night, we heard the toads, providing their "background musical chorus."

I'm thankful that God spared the lives of toads, as well as many other species of His creation, at the time of the Flood, so we can enjoy them. Thank God this morning for His thoughtfulness; ask Him to help you enjoy His creation more.

NEW JERUSALEM FOUNDATIONS

And the foundations of the wall of the city were garnished with all manner of precious stones. The first foundation was jasper; the second, sapphire; the third, a chalcedony; the fourth, an emerald; the fifth, sardonyx; the sixth, sardius. Revelation 21:19, 20.

Today and tomorrow we will talk about the twelve foundation stones that God will use in the walls of the New Jerusalem. Some of these precious stones are more common than others.

Jasper is a mixture of quartz and iron oxide. It comes in many colors, such as green, yellow, brown, black, and red. Sapphires come from corundum and are usually blue in color. The deeper the blue, the more expensive the sapphires are. There are other sapphires that are called the pink sapphire, the "oriental emerald," the "oriental topaz," and the "oriental amethyst."

Named after the town of Chalcedon in Turkey, where these gems were found, chalcedony has been referred to as "thunder eggs." There are many varieties of this gem, which has also been called the "white agate" because it is semitransparent to translucent with spots and circles. Petrified wood has deposits of chalcedony in it.

In larger sizes, emeralds are almost as expensive as diamonds, because they are very rare. They are usually from a pale to a rich green in color and have a six-sided form. They are a type of beryl, which is usually found in a rocky substance with many layers of pegmatites. A variety of agate, which is a form of quartz or chalcedony, is sardonyx, usually cut flat from layers of banded masses of agate. This is the cheapest of the gems and used widely in jewelry.

Sardius, orange-red in color, comes from the iron compounds of chalcedony that permeate the colloidal silica, today known as carnelian. It is used extensively in jewelry. Mohammad is said to have used it in a ring to seal his important papers.

Why will God use these precious stones in foundations, you ask? Why not? He made them, and He wants the best for His children. The streets will be pure gold, so why not foundations of precious stones? God is a lover of beauty, and these gems are beautiful. Seek Him this morning, asking Him to help you enjoy that beauty forever.

MORE FOUNDATION STONES

The foundations of the city walls were decorated with every kind of precious stone. . . . The seventh chrysolite, the eighth beryl, the ninth topaz, the tenth chrysoprase, the eleventh jacinth, and the twelfth amethyst. Revelation 21:19, 20, N.I.V.

This morning we take a look at the other six foundation stones. Chrysolite is a type of peridot or olivine, which is a magnesium-iron silicate. The colors are yellow, brown, and green, the best colors being yellowish-green to green. The chrysolite that is yellowish-green, is the most expensive of all of the peridots.

Beryl are popular crystals because they are among the largest, some of them weighing up to several tons. Within their gem materials are smaller and more valuable crystals, which are slightly harder than quartz. They vary in color from bright grass green to a dull bluish green, yellow, pink, or white.

In early days the name topaz was used to designate the colors from yellow to orange. Some of the topaz colors vary from brown to pinkish-red. Topaz is a mixture of aluminum silicate and fluorine, and one of the hardest of the gems. Some of the crystals are colorless; the largest of the colorless crystals weighed nearly 600 pounds.

Chrysoprase also a chalcedony, is a combination of nickel and colloidal silica. It is easy to get a high luster from polishing this transparent apple-green gem, thereby making it one of the most beautiful of gems. Jacinth is an orange colored gem that is probably a sapphire, which is also a corundum. It is a very hard mineral and almost transparent.

The last of the foundation gems mentioned by John is amethyst. It is a quartz and gives a show of "zones" in its purple color. The large crystals are beautiful as they radiate the zoned look. Interestingly, the best of most of these precious foundation gems come from Brazil. It is a country rich in natural resources.

What a privilege it will be to see all of these precious gems in the new earth and have them all around us. We cannot imagine how bright and brilliant they will be as they reflect the light shining from God. Ask God to help you be faithful so you can live where precious stones are the foundations.

PALM TREES

The righteous shall flourish like the palm tree: he shall grow like a cedar in Lebanon. Psalm 92:12.

There are many types of palm trees around the world, and many of these are quite useful. In the country of Israel I saw beautiful date palms with very large dates on the trees. Date palms are also cultivated in the State of California; that is where the majority of the dates are grown that are eaten in the United States.

In the country of Peru, in South America, there are palm trees that have other types of fruit. The aguaje (a-GUAW-he) palm produces a fruit that is barrel-shaped, about three inches long, with scales for skin. The Peruvians peel the skin off with their teeth and eat the meat of the fruit, which is only about one fourth of an inch thick. They also make a drink and ice cream out of this fruit.

The country of Brazil, also in South America, has probably the largest variety of useful palm trees. There is the carnauba palm with a very large, fan-shaped leaf that produces wax. From these trees companies harvest the wax that is used on automobiles and wooden floors, as well as in some furniture polishes. There is also a very famous tree called the chonta or palmito palm. People cut these trees down and harvest the heart of the tree. This is cut up into pieces or strips like ribbon and cooked, or served raw in a salad; it is very good.

From a certain type of palm tree in Brazil, people gather the fruit, squeeze the juice, and make a drink called assai (as-SIGH-ee). It is a very nutritious drink. Still another palm tree produces nuts; the Brazilians make cooking oil from them.

In His creation, God created all types of trees for man's use, and man has made use of most of them. Interestingly enough, most of the palm trees grow rapidly and straight and usually flourish well in hot desert areas. As Christians, we are to grow, with God's nurture, like the palm trees and bear fruits of righteousness to our friends and neighbors. Ask God to help you bear fruit to someone today as you associate with your friends.

145

SHAMANS AND PLANTS

And by the river upon the bank thereof, on this side and on that side, shall grow all trees for meat, whose leaf shall not fade, neither shall the fruit thereof be consumed: it shall bring forth new fruit according to his months, because their waters they issued out of the sanctuary: and the fruit thereof shall be for meat, and the leaf thereof for medicine. Ezekiel 47:12.

Shamans, which we call witch doctors or medicine men, are a vital link in the indigenous traditions and rituals among most of the South American and many African tribes. The shaman is the central figure; as such, he is able to tell the people what he wants them to do. Because of fear or loyalty, the tribes people will listen.

For years shamans have been using various plants to "drive out the devil" or treat some types of diseases. Scientists have decided that maybe the shamans knew something valuable about using plants for medicinal purposes, and many of these researchers have spent time living with South American Indians. After gaining their confidence, they have been able to find the "secret" plants that are used to treat different diseases and physical disorders.

While we were living in Iquitos, Peru, some years ago, we met Nicole Maxwell. She had come to the Amazon to learn about the medicinal plants that the Indians used. Through her friendships with the Indians, she was able to obtain many of their medicinal secrets. Nicole fell on her machete (large knife), cutting her arm. An Indian chief made a brew from a common bark. She drank this and the bleeding stopped within three minutes. About 1,370 different plants are used for ailments, most of them successfully.

Indian shamans have helped discover, through trial and error, plants that are today used in the treatment of heart failure and leukemia. Some of the poisons they use on arrows are used by modern doctors as anesthetics because they do not kill, but temporarily paralyze.

We cause much of our own illnesses by how we eat. In heaven there will be no sickness, and we will eat those delightful foods that God has prepared for us. Ask God today to help you live a healthful life.

ENERGY PRODUCTION

By what paths is the heat spread abroad or the east wind carried far and wide over the earth? Job 38:24, N.E.B.

During the past few years in the United States people have been trying to come up with energy alternatives, and some have come up with some real winners.

Did you ever hear of the rabbit-heated greenhouse? Bill Schultz of Grants Pass, Oregon, had a greenhouse that was expensive to heat. He knew that rabbits had warm bodies, with a temperature of about 102.6°F. He bought 400 rabbits; with the heat radiating from their bodies—about 180,000 BTU's, which was equivalent to the output of one commercial greenhouse heater—he heated his greenhouse. When the temperature was 32°F. outside, his rabbit-heated greenhouse was 56°F. inside. He not only got the heat from the rabbits but he also had so many baby rabbits that he sold them for fryers to the local markets.

In Chicago and many other cities in the United States, commercial firms are burning garbage to produce heat and electricity. With the heat from only 22 percent of the garbage in Chicago, they are able to heat a large candy factory, a large car garage, and the garbage-burning facility itself. Other areas are using cow manure to produce methane, which powers generators that produce electricity. In Henniker, New Hampshire, a factory is producing digesters that enable a farmer to use the manure from his cows for heating purposes.

The large Prudential Insurance Company contracted with a man who brought in a large snowmaking machine and built a 60-foot-high mound of snow. He covered it with an insulated blanket and all through the summer the company used the melting water to cool the large building. The company said they saved $12,000 in one year on air-conditioning.

I am glad that my God made so many things that are useful to us. Thank Him today for being such a great God.

SCREAMING DEMONS

Behold, the Lord hath a mighty and strong one, which as a tempest of hail and a destroying storm, as a flood of mighty waters overflowing, shall cast down to the earth with the hand. Isaiah 28:2.

Forces of nature such as wind, fire, and water can be very destructive. This was not in God's original plan but, as we have said before, sin changed things in God's world.

The Lord didn't create His world to be destroyed, but that is the result of sin. As storms come, especially thunderstorms, which bring lots of rain, hail, and wind, there is the possibility of a tornado. Scientists are not sure exactly what does happen, but they think that it has something to do with the meeting of layers of cold and warm air.

You may have seen a tornado funnel in real life or in a picture. This is a part of the cloud that extends down and may even touch the ground. The speed of the air as it whirls inside this funnel may get up to the speed of a jet plane, and the funnel itself as it travels along the ground may have the speed of an automobile. It has such force that it destroys much of what is in its path.

A tornado acts like a giant vacuum sweeper. It inhales the air as it goes along so that when it hits a house or building, the air is sucked out and the house falls in on itself with the force of an explosion. That is why it does so much damage. It is no fun to be in a tornado. There is an area in the Midwestern United States called "tornado alley"; many of you reading this today know what we are discussing. It is a frightening experience.

God will be sending Jesus back to this earth, and when He comes, this earth will be destroyed. No human will live on this earth after that experience, until Jesus remakes it. I want to be in the group that will escape the destruction of this earth, don't you? Ask God this morning to help you be in Jesus' group that will live forever.

FIRE IN THE SKY

His lips are full of indignation, and his tongue as a devouring fire: and his breath, as an overflowing stream. Isaiah 30:27, 28.

Most of you have probably seen a volcano, either in a picture or the real thing. As a child, I had the opportunity of traveling with my parents, and, in our travels, we saw several extinct volcanoes. Also, I had seen many pictures of volcanoes, and they fascinated me.

While living in South America it was my privilege to travel over the Andes by air, and through the Andes by car, train, and horseback. We even went across Lake Titicaca by boat at night. During those seven years in Peru, I always wanted to see an active volcano, but did not have such luck.

Several years ago our family went to the Hawaiian Islands. We saw results of active volcanoes. We saw how the lava had boiled out over the top of the mountain and run downhill, covering everything as it flowed. We saw where trees had once stood but were destroyed as the flowing hot lava hit them. We saw a bubbling volcano and smelled the sulfurous gas coming up out of the cracks in the ground and from the bubbling mud. One evening as we looked from our hotel balcony, we saw fire shooting up into the sky. Now I had seen an active volcano. I was happy that the eruption was not a large fireworks that would destroy property and animal and plant life, and possibly human life. However, later it did.

As the gases under the ground get hot and expand, there has to be a way of releasing pressure, and so there are volcanic eruptions.

In life, there seem to be many times when we develop emotional pressure inside. Our friends, parents, and teachers aggravate us until we cannot take it any longer and we erupt just like the volcano—spewing words out all over the place. God is a God of love, and He will help us not to explode if we want His help. In your prayer this morning, tell God you want your life to be changed. If you have been an eruptive type of person, ask Him to help you change your life to do good.

FLOWERS OVERHEAD

Verily, verily, I say unto you, He that believeth on me hath everlasting life. John 6:47.

We naturally enjoy the beautiful flowers that we see around us on the ground and bushes, but have you taken time to see the beautiful flowers that are over your head on many of the trees? Springtime is a beautiful time to see many of these beautiful flowers.

We may be familiar with the blossoms of the cherry, apple, peach, apricot, and pear trees, but what about all the other trees that have flowers or flowerlike cones. Some of the trees that have flowers on the branches are the maples, oaks, and birches; flowerlike cones are found on the pine, cedar, fir, and tamarack trees. In order to produce seeds, they must have a flower. Some of the flowers are not large; that is why you have to look for them. According to the information I have, there are about 100 different types of conifers (evergreens) in the United States and more than 650 broad-leaved trees. With this many trees, a variety of flowers are produced. Some are small and dainty and others are broad and large.

As one walks underneath the broad-leaved trees there is a buzzing world overhead. These trees depend largely on bees and insects to pollinate them. The pollinators work busily, collecting nectar and spreading pollen. Conifers don't need the insects to spread the pollen but depend on the breeze and the wind.

These flowers add to the beauty of God's world for a short time. I can imagine when God spoke at Creation and all the vegetation came forth, it must have been like spring all at once. The Garden of Eden was a beautiful place. All the plants were new.

Thank God this morning for life. Every morning thank Him for the new life that He gives to you daily. As He takes care of the flowers, so He will take care of you and give you everlasting life.

DWARF MONGOOSES

For this cause I bow my knees unto the Father of our Lord Jesus Christ, of whom the whole family in heaven and earth is named. Ephesians 3:14, 15.

Mongooses live principally in the Serengeti area of Kenya and Tanzania, although some live in Asia. There are 31 species of mongooses, and this morning we want to talk about the smallest of the bunch—the dwarf mongoose. I heard a story about a man who wanted a mongoose for a pet. Then he decided he wanted two of them in order to raise mongooses. He didn't know if the plural for mongoose is "mongooses" or "mongeese". He didn't want to show his ignorance so he sent a letter to a friend in Africa and asked his friend to send him a mongoose, and "while you are at it send me another one."

Dwarf mongooses are very small, not much larger than a rat. They weigh less than a pound. They live together in colonies or communes and have a dominant male and female as the leaders; their selection is usually determined by age. The dwarf mongooses, which live largely on termites and other small insects, will go into the ventilation channel of an unused termite nest and have their young. Each female will have two to three litters with a total of up to six young during the months from November to May. The young will stay in the nest with the mother for several weeks, then go out foraging with "mama."

At times, a mother mongoose may fall prey to another animal, so other females take over and nurse the young. There may be in the commune a mother that has lost her litter and is lactating (dripping milk). She may help feed the young of another female in the nest. It takes from 12 to 24 months for a mongoose to mature. At that time it may have to leave its commune or pack and go to another one, or try to form a new one.

Like the mongooses, we are to help take care of one another. When one is sick, handicapped, or aged, we should visit and help out where needed. When one is discouraged, we should cheer him or her up. We are to help one another, as members of God's family. Thank God this morning that you belong to His family, the largest family on earth.

CORK

And when he had gone a little farther thence, he saw James the son of Zebedee, and John his brother, who also were in the ship mending their nets. Mark 1:19.

For centuries men have been fishing with nets. One of the things that they have depended upon in using the nets, was cork floats to hold up the edge of the net. History tells us that men used cork floats as early as 400 B.C. The Romans wore cork sandals to keep their feet warm. Cork bottle stoppers have been around since the 1600s.

Cork is a lightweight, soft, spongy substance that comes from the bark of the cork oak tree. This tree is a live oak, which means it is green year-round and doesn't lose its leaves. These trees grow to about 50 feet high and live from 300 to 400 years. They grow mostly in Portugal and Spain. The third largest producer is Algeria.

The outer layer of the cork oak bark is composed of dead cells, whose thin walls have become thickened and waxy. Trees must be about 20 years old before cork can be harvested. The workers strip the cork or outer bark off only once every ten years. Long-handled hatchets are used to cut the cork into long oblong sections, from the top of the lowest branch to the bottom of the tree. The cork is then stripped off very carefully, so as not to disturb the inner layer of bark, because the inner layer will not grow any more cork if it is damaged.

Next the cork is boiled to soften it and remove the rough, gritty, outer layer. Boiling also dissolves the tannic acid in the cork. It is cut to whatever size needed and shipped. Cork has been used for many years as insulation in freezers. Linoleum is made by mixing cork powder with linseed oil and spread as a paste over burlap or canvas, and left to dry.

Jesus wants to take the rough skin of sin out of our lives and allow us to grow new fresh Christian skin. Ask Jesus to help you get rid of the old skin of sin and grow a new Christian skin, soft with kindness and buoyant with love.

FLY IN THE FRUIT

I will send swarms of flies upon thee, and upon thy servants, and upon thy people, and into thy houses: and the houses of the Egyptians shall be full of swarms of flies, and also the ground whereon they are. Exodus 8:21.

Flies have been a plague since before the days of the children of Israel and Pharaoh in Egypt. There have been many species of flies that have made life miserable for the human family as well as for the rest of the animal kingdom. They do remind us of sin.

There is a species of fly that likes fruit, called the Mediterranean fruit fly, better known recently in the United States as the "medfly." This fly has become a real pest in the world, and has made things miserable for fruit growers as well as for fruit eaters. These fruit flies destroy the insides of many varieties of fruit and vegetables, including apples, apricots, most citrus fruits, nectarines, peaches, plums, mangoes, and tomatoes.

These pests were discovered in the early 1800s in Africa. They spread to Australia, South America, Hawaii, Europe, and other areas. They were discovered in Florida in 1929. There have been attempts to exterminate them but with little success, so most countries have just learned to live with them. These little flies plant their eggs in the ripe fruit.

Although the females' reproductive period is only about a month, one female in hot areas can lay up to 500 eggs and have about 12 to 13 broods of offspring in a season. These eggs hatch into larvae in a day, then they begin to eat the fruit, which causes it to drop to the ground prematurely. When the larva is about seven days old, it leaves the fruit, bores a hole in the ground, and after nine days comes out a mature fruit fly, ready to begin the process again. Think of the millions of fruit flies that are reproduced this way.

Could it be that God is trying to tell us, like He did Pharaoh, that His people are going to remain and be victorious over sin? He'll take care of the flies eventually. He'll rid this world of all sin. Thank God for that promise this morning.

GREAT WHITE SHARKS

So then because thou art lukewarm, and neither cold nor hot, I will spew thee out of my mouth. Revelation 3:16.

There is much that ichthyologists (fish scientists) don't know about the great white shark. The reason is that they have not been able to keep any of these sharks in captivity for a length of time, and they have not been able to study them in the ocean. These sharks go places where they cannot be followed, and they will attack anyone who bothers them. In fact, they attack for no reason at all. They are usually found along the California coast and around the country of Australia.

Only 33 divers have been bitten by these sharks in the past 53 years. Of these, only four have died, and their death was caused by bleeding. In almost every case, after biting a human, the white shark has spit him or her out. We just don't taste good to the white shark.

Scientists can only speculate how large the babies are at birth. They have never seen one born, but they know that these little calves are born live.

When attacking, white sharks will zoom toward their prey. About seven or eight feet before reaching the target they will open the mouth, on the bottom side of the head, roll their eyes to the back of the head, and let their electrical sensing device zero in on the prey. Many times they miss, but the white shark is quite agile for its size. They seem to have a built-in heater that keeps their body six to 18 degrees warmer than the water they are in. With this added heat they are able to move faster, as the muscles respond more rapidly with a higher temperature.

As scientists desire to know more about the white shark, so we should desire to know more about God. He does not want us to be lukewarm, but hot in our Christian experience. Pray that He will help you be a "hot" Christian and that you will not be "spit out" of His mouth, which means to be left out of heaven.

YOU VULTURE

There is a path which no fowl knoweth, and which the vulture's eye hath not seen. Job 28:7.

When I was a small boy I heard a friend of mine call another boy a vulture. I really didn't understand why he said it, but it wasn't nice.

Vultures fly very high and look for food on the ground. They are known for their ability to spot the carcass of an animal at a great distance. Vultures do not kill for food but eat the carcasses of dead animals.

When we lived in Brazil and Peru it was against the law to kill these birds, and they were everywhere. There were many animals killed by trucks and cars, and the vultures would come in by the dozens and clean up the carcasses. There wasn't much left when they finished. According to scientists, these birds seem to be immune to poisons that may have killed the creatures they eat.

There are many species of vultures all over the world. In North America there are the black and turkey vultures and the California condor. Vultures have about a four- to six-foot wingspan; it is a beautiful sight just watching them soar in the sky for they seldom move a wing. They have been given a special ability by God that allows them to stay aloft by catching the rising warm air columns produced by uneven solar heating of the landscape.

Have you ever noticed the head of a vulture? It has no feathers. Do you think God in His plan thought about the "clean-up" crew that would be needed after sin entered this world? If these birds were going to be cleaning meat off the bones of animals and reaching into the carcass with their heads, feathers would get in the way and not be very hygienic. They may look ugly, but this featherless head is very practical for their way of life.

As the miner digs under the ground for precious minerals and the vulture searches for food, you can dig for and find God's wonderful promises in His Word. Ask God to help you as you search for these precious truths.

COUCH'S SPADEFOOT TOAD

But God hath revealed them unto us by his Spirit: for the Spirit searcheth all things, yea, the deep things of God. 1 Corinthians 2:10.

About three feet underground in the Sonoran Desert in Arizona live the Couch's spadefoot toads. These are not just any ordinary amphibian. These toads stay under the hot desert sands during the day and come out to feed only at night.

These toads have little spurlike projections on the back feet, which they use to dig their way down into the sand. They await the torrential rains to breed, but these come sporadically only during the months of April to August. God has given these creatures a built-in alarm clock to tell them when the time is right. They await the vibration of the rain on the desert floor, then they come out at night to the water holes that have been made by the rains.

They come out at night to lay and fertilize eggs and to eat. The females will lay their eggs and the males fertilize them. A female may lay as many as 1,000 eggs a night. By morning they are back in the ground to escape the heat. These toads have to eat enough to last them for the extended dry periods that they aestivate underground.

The eggs hatch in record time for any amphibian, about 24 to 36 hours. The tadpoles develop and grow in the 100°F. pools of water. In 15 to 40 days they are fully developed. They are too young to dig but spend a day or two in cracks. Then they begin to dig into the sand. Those that cannot find cracks die of the terrific heat. Those that survive eat like there is no tomorrow and prepare for the long stay underground.

There are many things on the surface and in the depths of this earth that man does not fully understand. In God's Word also there are some tremendous challenges that we do not fully understand. But God is willing for us to understand, and if we will ask Him for the wisdom necessary, the Holy Spirit will provide it. Ask Him this morning for the power of the Holy Spirit to bring you that wisdom to understand the depths of God's Word.

OOMINGMAK

So Christ was once offered to bear the sins of many; and unto them that look for him shall he appear the second time without sin unto salvation. Hebrews 9:28.

Our title sounds strange, I know, but that is what the Eskimos call the musk-oxen. Oomingmak (o-MING-mack) means the "bearded ones." Musk-oxen are making a comeback in the State of Alaska. The last of the wild musk-oxen on this continent were seen 120 years ago. Desiring them back in this area, the United States acquired 34 in Greenland and transported them to Norway, then on to New York, Seattle, and finally Alaska. They were put into a herd at the research quarters of the University of Alaska.

Much research has been done on these creatures since they landed in Alaska. In 1969, the first animals were taken out to the wilds to live. One researcher was watching the musk-oxen when he saw one making a dash for him. He thought what he might do to escape the charge; then he decided to just stand still and sidestep the charging animal if necessary. As the musk-ox came to within fifty feet of the scientist it stopped, got down on its front knees, and began to back up. It was later realized that all this "pet" wanted was his head scratched.

Musk-oxen are small in stature, probably not more than five feet high. They have a long shaggy fur that at times reaches to the ground. Underneath this fur is a silklike hair that scientists say is eight times warmer than wool.

For their defense against attackers such as wolves or wild cats, the muskoxen, usually in herds of 20 to 30, will stand in a circle, facing out, with the young calves on the inside of the circle. This way they can fend off the predator. Predators generally work on one animal at a time to conquer it. The muskoxen's method of defense does not permit this, therefore they are rather safe from predators.

As the musk-oxen have returned to their native home of Alaska, so Jesus will return to His home after He has taken His family with Him from this earth. I am happy for the promise that Jesus is coming again, and that He will take the faithful home. Ask God this morning in your prayer to help you be faithful, so you can return "home."

UNITED THEY STAND

Behold, how good and how pleasant it is for brethren to dwell together in unity! Psalm 133:1.

The "playful penguins," as they are often called, are very intelligent, family- and society-oriented, and they mate for life. Year after year they will come back to the same breeding grounds. The males will find their nesting place and as the arriving females begin to arrive at the icy nesting area, the males will make a sound like "gug-gug-gug-gug-gaaaaaa." The arriving females seem to know the sound of their respective male partner; and they will slide on the snowy ice toward them.

As the arriving female gets to her companion, the two will put their beaks high in the air and shout over and over again. They seem to be saying, "We belong to each other." Two weeks after they mate, the female will lay one or two light-green eggs on the stone nest that her mate has prepared for her. As soon as she lays the one or two eggs, she, along with all of the other females, will go out into the water to eat their favorite food — fish, squid, and krill (shrimplike creatures). If all goes well, the females return to the nesting area in about two weeks. During this time the males have been sitting on the nests, or incubating the single egg by holding it on their feet. A blizzard sometimes comes upon them, but the males will endure it to preserve their families. The male will lose about one third of his body weight while incubating the egg and awaiting the arrival of his mate.

When the female returns to the nest, they say their goodbyes, and he is off into the water to eat his fill, along with all of the other males. After their two-week stay in the ocean, eating, the males come back, do their welcome and goodbye dance with their mate, and the hungry females go back into the ocean again looking for more food. They do not stay too long the second time because when they return they will probably find the egg already hatched. Then the mother and dad penguins take turns going into the ocean, eating and bringing back food for the youngster.

I thank God that He loved me so much that He called me out of this world and put me into His body, the church. Thank God today that He has called you.

MANGROVES

For he shall be as a tree planted by the waters, and that spreadeth out her roots by the river, and shall not see when heat cometh, but her leaf shall be green; and shall not be careful in the year of drought, neither shall cease from yielding fruit. Jeremiah 17:8.

Mangroves are an important part of the ecosystem, necessary to preserve the lives of many creatures. Mangroves are found all over the world. They are not the nicest-looking things, but very important. A mangrove thicket consists of hundreds, yes, thousands of trees that grow by the edge of water or in the water. Their prop (aerial) roots project into the water and get tangled up with other roots. They look like a tangled mess. They are anything but pretty but have a land-forming function from the deposited silt and debris that collects around them.

A mangrove swamp can be a forbidding place. It generally has a spongy mud base; many thousands of creatures live in and around these mangroves. In some areas such as in the tropics, there may be up to 50 varieties of trees in a mangrove thicket. The leaf coverage is dense, and it is difficult for the sunlight to penetrate. Mosquitoes buzz all around the place. Because of their unbeautiful appearance, and the "bother" they are, some people have begun clearing them out to make room for housing developments. But scientists are now finding that this destroys not only the trees but the breeding and living areas for many thousands of wildlife creatures.

How does a mangrove swamp provide life for so many creatures? Let's look. The droppings from the trees, such as leaves and buds, hit the water and are eaten by tiny organisms such as plankton, worms, crustaceans, and mollusks. These then are eaten by larger creatures such as shrimp, mollusks, crabs, and small fish, which in turn are food for larger water creatures such as larger fish, birds, and other water inhabiters.

When we have a personal relationship with Jesus, the Good Book tells us that we will be as a tree planted by the river. We will really be in need of nothing and will bear fruit. That is the way the mangroves are. This morning talk to Jesus and ask Him to help you through this day to have a good relationship with Him.

WHICH END IS UP?

A land which the Lord thy God careth for: the eyes of the Lord thy God are always upon it, from the beginning of the year even unto the end of the year. Deuteronomy 11:12.

Have you ever wondered how plants know which end is up? I have often wondered as a boy growing up, why, when I planted seeds, the seeds opened and the shoot went up and the roots went down. How does the seed know which way to send the shoots and roots?

Biologists have been stumped for many years as to why the shoots go up and the roots go down. They related this to gravity and called this plant reaction "geotropism." Biologists still do not know how the plants get their directions straight. Darwin found that on the roots there is a small cap that acts like a helmet that offers protection as the plant sends the roots digging through the dirt. When the caps were removed the roots became confused. He asked, "Is there a brain inside the little cap that somehow directs the roots?"

In the 1920s a hormone called auxin was discovered, that causes the shoots to grow but does not do anything for the roots. Calcium seems to play an important part in strengthening the plant cell walls of the roots, making them stiff and rigid, which enables them to grow downward into the earth.

Scientists now are looking at how auxin reacts to gravity within the plants' cells. As the auxin is pooled in a specific area by gravity, the hormone enhances shoot-cell growth and inhibits root-cell growth, which causes the shoots to bend up and the roots to bend down. Scientists speculate this is a polarity that comes from electrical charges, which are different between upward and downward growth. As one scientist put it, "It's all speculation, but it's tempting to think that, because of this polarity, a plant *always* knows which end is up."

Isn't it great to know we have a God who knows, who has designed the seeds with the "know-how" to shoot the shoots up and the roots down? I'm thankful for such a great Creator. Tell God this morning how thankful you are to Him for His wonderful creativeness and how He cares for you.

GOD-GIVEN STRENGTHS

The Lord is my light and my salvation; whom shall I fear?
the Lord is the strength of my life; of whom shall I be afraid?
Psalm 27:1.

It is not possible to talk about all of the "strengths" that God has placed in the natural world that He created, but it is fun to look at a few creatures and see just how God created them.

Some of the strongest creatures in God's world are very small. A beetle was observed pulling an item about 90 times its own weight. That would be equal to a human dragging about a seven-ton load. Just an ordinary flea has the strength to jump more than 130 times its height. For you to equal that you would have to jump into the air almost one quarter of a mile. The flea can also jump 13 inches in distance, or about 700 feet for a human. A grasshopper can jump over obstacles 200 times its size. An American salmon can jump up to 12 feet in the air, and the killer whale, weighing more than nine tons, can propel itself out of the water more than a body's length.

A four-inch abalone can hook itself onto a rock with more than 400 pounds of force. A bolt of lightning can strike the earth with a force of more than 15 million volts of electricity. A small electric eel can send out a charge of electricity of more than 600 volts, or more than five times that which you would feel when you get a shock from a light socket. A tidal wave has the force of nearly 500 miles per hour of speed as it rolls through the ocean.

Then there are the jaws of the crocodile, which come together with a force of about 1,540 pounds, while the jaws of a human can exert about 40 to 80 pounds of pressure. Quite a difference, isn't it? The little ant has the strength to lift a bundle 50 times its weight. The ruby-throated hummingbird can beat its wings at the rate of 90 times a second, and the common mosquito can best that with about 1,000 times a second. The strength of the skunk's scent is so strong that it can be smelled a mile away.

Jesus has told us that we cannot do anything by ourselves (see John 15:5). Our only hope to conquer the devil is through Jesus Christ, as only He can give us the strength to do it. Ask Him this morning for the strength that you will need today to overcome the devil's temptations, and He will give it to you.

BEARING ANOTHER'S BURDENS

Bear ye one another's burdens, and so fulfil the law of Christ. Galatians 6:2.

Today I want to call your attention to some camels that have no humps. They are called the "camels of the Andes," and are divided into two species, the llama (YA-ma) and the alpaca (al-PAK-a). These animals belong to the camel family and work like camels. The larger of the two species is the llama. It has long, stringy fur that keeps it warm in the high altitudes of the Andes. Llamas weigh from 250 to 400 pounds each and are about three to four feet tall at their shoulders. They are able to carry about from sixty to one hundred pounds of baggage for distances of 15 to 20 miles a day. The llama has a head shaped much like a deer's head. It has a long neck and as it walks along it reminds one of a very proud person walking with his head held high. Many baby llamas and alpaca die shortly after birth because of the coldness of the high altitude in the Andes. After death their fur is tanned, and this very soft "baby" fur is used to make slippers, rugs, and coats.

The alpaca is somewhat smaller than the llama and has a heavier, softer fur. Alpacas are used also for carrying baggage, and their fur is used more widely for coats, sweaters, slippers, and rugs than the llama's.

The camels of the Middle East and South American countries are used to carry burdens for people. As these creatures walk through the deserts and over the mountains, they do their work very faithfully.

As animals carry another's burdens so we are to bear one another's burdens, and do it willingly and faithfully. In other words, we are to help one another. Maybe you have a friend or relative who is sad or needs help with his or her work. Go to that person and offer to help him. In this way you help to carry his burden.

As you pray this morning, ask God to help you find someone with a burden today that you can help carry. He will show you that person who needs your help.

BRAZILIAN FIRE ANTS

Ants are creatures of little strength, yet they store up their food in the summer. Proverbs 30:25, N.I.V.

A feisty little creature from Brazil that is uncontrollable and hated by people is the fire ant. These little red ants are tough on those that they land on. People who live in Brazil and in the southern part of the United States have learned that you don't stand very long in one spot if there are fire ants around.

These little creatures have a sting that is very toxic. When stung, a person will begin to scratch the itchy sensation. As the spot is scratched a welt develops, and it may take up to a week to get rid of it. One scientist was desirous of seeing what could be done to combat the sting. He took a large number of these fire ants and whizzed them up in a regular kitchen blender. He then took the liquid and used it as an antitoxin against the fire ant bite. It worked, just like snakebite antitoxin.

Sometime in the year 1918, the Brazilian fire ant was brought to the southern part of the United States. It is thought that the fire ants came aboard a ship. Now the little creatures infest more than 230 million acres in many of the Southern States. They are moving northward, but very slowly.

In the South, soybean fields have been infested by the fire ants. These little ants build their nest so that it extends from about three feet underground to about a foot above ground. The ants have a hardening liquid in their saliva so that when they build their nests they harden like rock and damage the combines used to harvest the beans.

Fire ants spend much time in gathering their food for the winter months. Even though these ants are hated, and people try to exterminate them, they still carry right on with their business. God expects us to carry on with our business and prepare for eternity. Ask Him this morning to help you prepare for eternity, just as the fire ant prepares for the future.

NESSIE, THE LOCH NESS MONSTER

Behold, he cometh with clouds; and every eye shall see him, and they also which pierced him; and all kindreds of the earth shall wail because of him. Revelation 1:7.

Since the year A.D. 565, there have been reports of a monster inhabiting the now-famous Loch Ness. Loch means lake in Scottish. People have claimed to have seen this monster; they say it is about 30 feet long and occasionally parts of it rise up out of the water of Loch Ness. I have seen purported pictures of the monster, but they were not clear. This monster has been named Nessie.

Nessie is supposed to be living in this lake, which is about 24 miles long and one mile wide. The lake is reported to be about 950 feet deep at the deepest point, which is directly offshore from the ruins of the Urquhart castle. For many years, divers have gone down into the depths of this lake, trying to find Nessie, but no one has seen it up close.

This is the largest lake, in terms of water volume, in Scotland. The waters are not only cold and deep but dark. Below 50 feet it is impossible to see more than a couple of feet in any direction. Divers have taken very large and powerful lights into the depths of Loch Ness, only to come back without locating Nessie.

There is a great amount of vegetation growing in Loch Ness, and some biologists believe that gases released by decaying vegetation have brought some of it up to the surface, and people imagined it to be the Loch Ness Monster. No one has seen even this phenomenon for many years.

We all know that Jesus is coming back to this earth, one of these days. We don't know when He will return, only that He will. As people are keeping their eyes open for Nessie we should keep our eyes open, watching for Jesus' return. The apostle writes that everyone will see Him. I thank God that we shall all be able to see Him come, no matter where we live. Thank God this morning that you will be able to see Jesus come back to this earth. It will be no mystery.

THE WOODPECKER

Give unto the Lord the glory due unto his name. Psalm 96:8.

On many occasions as I have walked through woods, I've heard a familiar sound—that of a woodpecker drilling a hole in a tree with its beak. I've wondered how these creatures can do this and not splatter their brains. I continue to marvel at how God thought of every little detail for everything.

There are about 23 species of woodpeckers in North America, ranging from the six-inch downy to the 20-inch ivory-billed. Part of the reason the male woodpecker pecks is to build a nest, but another part is to tell any female woodpecker around that he is an available mate.

God created the woodpecker with very strong neck muscles; these act like the "motor" that drives the head and bill. There is a sturdy protractor muscle inside the head that controls the upper part of the beak. This muscle braces the bill and acts like a shock absorber as the woodpecker drills the hole.

A study found that an acorn woodpecker's beak goes about 15 miles per hour as it strikes the tree. This means about a peck every one-thousandth of a second. The researchers believe that the way the beak hits the tree—straight on—is probably what keeps the brain from being splattered.

A pileated woodpecker, about the size of a crow, pecks out a nesting place about eight inches wide and 24 inches deep. That's a lot of pecking, isn't it? Red-bellied woodpeckers communicate by pecking, about two to three seconds, with 20 to 40 taps in a series. Other woodpeckers communicate by taps or pecks and find the tree they will build their nest in. Interestingly, woodpeckers don't return the next year to the same nest, after all that work.

When David turned his life over to God, he glorified God and acknowledged what a great God He is. Give God the glory due Him in your prayers this morning. We cannot understand His greatness. We can only give Him the praise and glory for what He has done.

OUR RATTLING CONSCIENCE

Having a good conscience; that, whereas they speak evil of you, as of evildoers, they may be ashamed that falsely accuse your good conversation in Christ. 1 Peter 3:16.

Today I want us to look at the rattlesnake. The rattlesnake is a much-feared snake. There are many varieties — 34, to be exact. Only eight species are not found in some part of the United States. Rattlesnakes are not altogether bad. They will bite humans only in self-defense. They are helpful to humans by eating mice, rats, and other small rodents and pests.

When a baby rattler is born it has what is called a little "prebutton," just a round tip on its tail. After about two weeks, when it sheds its skin the first time, the first little button of the rattle forms. Each succeeding time that the snake sheds its skin it adds another segment to the rattle. The rattle is made up of a number of segments that interlock loosely with one another to form a jointed string. It is longer than it is wide and it vibrates sideways. The rattling noise is made by vibrating the segments rapidly (about 48 times a second). The segments strike each other, and because of the rapid vibration, a buzzing sound is produced. The rattling noise is the snake's warning to "stay away." The rattle is one of the most remarkable structures in nature. There is nothing remotely resembling the rattle in any other group of snakes.

God did not make us with a rattle, but we do have a conscience. If we desire to go someplace or do something questionable, the conscience says, "You know you shouldn't go there or do that."

In your prayer this morning, ask God to help you listen to the warnings of your conscience. You would not go near the rattlesnake if you heard its warning, would you? Our conscience, guided by the Holy Spirit, should be our guide in our life today. God will send the Holy Spirit to help us, if we ask Him. Ask Him now!

BEWARE: POISON

He hath made every thing beautiful in his time: also he hath set the world in their heart, so that no man can find out the work that God maketh from the beginning to the end. Ecclesiastes 3:11.

There are many beautiful flowers and plants on the face of our earth. God certainly didn't create poisonous plants at Creation; the Bible says everything He made was good. Why there are poisonous plants can be blamed only on sin. Let's look at a few of these poisonous plants this morning.

Take rhubarb as an example. The stalk is good for food, but the leaf is poisonous. The potato tuber that we eat is good, but the rest of the plant is poisonous. Many mushrooms are poisonous, and other plants and weeds cause traumatic body disorders. Some plants are harmful to man but not to some of the creatures in the wild.

These poisonous plants do not necessarily kill a person, but they can make one very ill. In each of these plants is some chemical substance that harms or kills an organism. This is why it is very important to learn which of the wild plants and berries can be eaten safely.

Not all plants produce the same reaction. Some produce a weakness or paralysis; some interfere with the circulatory system; some disrupt the chemistry of the blood; some affect the mouth and the digestive tract; others irritate the skin or cause burns. Scientists say that a person must eat a substantial amount of most poisonous plants before a real serious illness or death occurs, but let's not take any chances. OK?

Poison hemlock looks like parsley leaves. This was the plant that was used to poison Socrates. Some people have been poisoned by using oleander branches to grill their meat on. White snakeroot is said to cure snakebites, but this carrotlike plant, eaten by cows, can poison the milk. It is reported that Abraham Lincoln's mother died from this type of milk poisoning.

Thank God today that He has given us as humans the power of the mind. Ask Him to help you use it to the best of your ability to keep you safe from eating unknown plants.

WOLVERINE

I know all the fowls of the mountains: and the wild beasts of the field are mine. Psalm 50:11.

For many years the youth leaders at Camp Au Sable in northern Michigan wanted to have a stuffed wolverine for their beautiful nature center, but they could not find anyone who owned one. The wolverine is Michigan's State animal, but there are almost none in the State, unless in the far north near Canada. Finally the youth leaders located someone in Montana that had one; now it is in the nature center, representing the State of Michigan.

Wolverines are the largest member of the weasel family. They may grow three to four feet long and weigh about 40 pounds. They have very rugged-looking teeth and could frighten anyone. Like so many other animals, they have been misunderstood. They have been accused of killing everything in sight, even bears, coyotes, and large game animals such as deer, moose, and elk.

During a five-year study of wolverines in Montana, where there seems to be a sizable group of them, scientists found where the wolverines had killed and eaten smaller animals, but never in the five years of their study did they find any evidence that they had killed large game animals for food.

Wolverines are very shy and do not come out in the open very often. They generally will stay in the wilderness where it is uninhabited. In the study mentioned above, it was found that they travel up to 100 miles at times, just looking for food. But although they travel a lot, they usually try to stay away from human civilization.

I am happy that God made many animals so that life here on this earth is exciting. As we study His creation we marvel at what He created. Thank God this morning for creating interesting animals for your enjoyment.

ACID RAIN

These men are those who are hidden reefs in your love feasts when they feast with you without fear, caring for themselves; clouds without water, carried along by winds; autumn trees without fruit, doubly dead, uprooted. Jude 12, N.A.S.B.

Cries are being heard all over the United States and Canada that lakes are being polluted and forests are being destroyed. Something needs to be done about it. It is estimated that more than 20,000 lakes in Sweden have been affected. The beautiful Black Forest of West Germany may be beyond hope.

What is happening? you ask. The smoke that comes out of the smokestacks from coal-burning power and industrial plants is carrying large amounts of sulfur dioxide and nitric oxides. As it lands on the water or land it kills many living things. In and around the lakes that once flourished with beautiful fish and wildlife, the fish have been killed off and the chirping tree frogs, loons, and kingfishers have disappeared.

Can something be done to stop this? Scientists are hoping that by cutting back on the emissions of sulfur that pour out of the smokestacks, the damage done by acid rain can be curtailed. Workers are spreading lime on some lakes in the Northeastern United States to counteract and neutralize the acid so that the aquatic creatures will not be killed off.

To think that the world in which we live is being destroyed by us because of our selfishness and greediness is frightening.

In our Christian experience also there are pollutants that harm our bodies and our relationship with Jesus. With God's help we can overcome the destroyer, Satan. Jesus will take care of the pollutants in your life if you turn it over to Him.

I invite you to turn your life over to Jesus, today. Allow Him to purify it, taking out all of the sinful pollutants. You'll have a nice clean life.

MUSKRATS

Deliver me, O my God, out of the hand of the wicked, out of the hand of the unrighteous and cruel man. Psalm 71:4.

If there is any animal that would echo the words of David if it could, it would be the muskrat. This animal is trapped for its fur; trappers are always on the lookout for it.

When I was a young boy two little irrigation streams went through our farm. They abounded with muskrats. My father and the other farmers were not happy with so many muskrats because they made many holes in the banks of the streams, and this caused the banks to cave in. My father bought me some traps. I would set a trap by each hole, for one den might have two or three holes. Every morning before dawn I would put on my rubber boots, get a flashlight and a gunnysack, and go to the streams. I always found several muskrats in the traps.

I would take them back to the house and skin them. Their fur sold for 25 cents each. That was good money in those days. Today the muskrats are still being trapped, as the fur is quite valuable.

Muskrats have from two to four families a summer; each litter will have from five to seven young. The young are born blind and hairless, but within a month they are gathering food on their own, even though they may stay with their parents for a month or more.

Muskrats are not altogether bad. As they eat mostly plants, they will thin out some vegetation so that it will produce better and the other wildlife and waterfowl can survive. In the winter when ice is formed on the bodies of water, the muskrats eat aquatic vegetation and various aquatic animals.

David wanted to be delivered out of the hand of the devil. This should also be our desire. As the muskrat is trapped for his hide, so Satan tries to trap us. Ask God this morning to deliver you from Satan's traps today. He'll be glad to warn you before you get into the trap, if you will listen.

AN APPLE A DAY

And I went unto the angel, and said unto him, Give me the little book. And he said unto me, Take it, and eat it up; and it shall make thy belly bitter, but it shall be in thy mouth sweet as honey. Revelation 10:9.

You've no doubt heard the saying "An apple a day keeps the doctor away." Apples provide pectins and an acid that help in digestion, as well as bulk and water that help in the body functions. The natural fiber in apples helps in controlling cholesterol levels in the human body. Maybe that is why this expression came into existence.

Wildlife have also discovered that wild apples and apple trees are especially good to eat. Deer and grouse have an appetite for apple leaves. Scientists report that the leaves have more calcium and vitamin A in the carbohydrate-type food than the apple fruit itself. Mice, porcupines, deer, and rabbits like the inner bark of the apple tree. The bark contains more carbohydrate than the leaves. The seeds are enjoyed by birds and squirrels as well as by other animals that eat the whole apple. The seeds contain the most concentrated dose of nutrition.

Ruffed grouse, ring-necked pheasants, and bobwhites like the apple buds as well as the fruit and seeds. In New England, ruffed grouse ate so many of the apple blossoms that the crops of apples were endangered, since the blossoms are what turn into the apples. For some years, in some Massachusetts townships, there was a bounty of 25 cents for each grouse shot or killed. In New Hampshire, a law in 1915 required the State to pay to apple growers a sum of money for crops damaged as the result of wildlife that were on the protected list. Since 1972, no money has been paid to apple growers.

Apple trees provide a benefit for humans and wildlife. Jesus has suggested to us that His Word should be very attractive to us because in it we can find all the elements necessary to live our spiritual life. Ask Jesus this morning to give you an appetite for God's Word today and in the future, so that you may be nourished by it.

DEADLY OR
DELICIOUS NIGHTSHADES

And it shall come to pass, that the man's rod, whom I shall choose, shall blossom: and I will make to cease from me the murmurings of the children of Israel, whereby they murmur against you. Numbers 17:5.

There are more than 2,000 species of plants that belong to the nightshade family. These range in size from a small wildflower to some very large bushes and small trees. Diverse as these plants are, they all have five-petaled flowers that are shaped like funnels or wheels.

Many of the plants belonging to the nightshade family are poisonous, but not all. Probably the most toxic is the jimsonweed, which got its name from Jamestown, Virginia, where a group of English soldiers were poisoned from eating it, back in 1676. It has also been called the "thorn-apple." American Indians have used the seeds from this plant in their religious ceremonies, because of its narcotic effect.

A second deadly nightshade is the Italian-named belladonna, meaning "beautiful lady." Italian women used this plant to dilate the pupils of their eyes, because large pupils were considered attractive. Today eye doctors use belladonna or a derivative to enlarge the pupils of their patients' eyes, so they can be examined.

Edible plants of the nightshade family include potatoes, tomatoes, chili peppers, and eggplant. Tomatoes were discovered in Mexico when the Spaniards overran the Indians of Mexico. The Spaniards sent the seeds back to Europe, and they were called the "love apple." Later, in the 1550s, the Italians experimented with eating them and later developed the tomato-sauce base for their cooking. Potatoes came from the highlands of Peru and Bolivia and found their way to Europe, also. Chili peppers were discovered by the Aztec Indians in Mexico, and the eggplant was discovered in India.

Because He is the Creator, God can make bloom what He wants to bloom. If you want to bloom for God and look beautiful for Him as a Christian, ask Him to help you do that now. He will be glad to help you be a "blooming Christian" today. A Christian always looks nice for the Lord.

THE ANT LION

Be sober, be vigilant; because your adversary the devil, as a roaring lion, walketh about, seeking whom he may devour. 1 Peter 5:8.

The ant lion is not like the African lion. It is much smaller. In fact, the ant lion is not a lion at all, but an insect similar to the damselfly.

The ant lions have four narrow transparent wings like the damsel-fly, and they fold their wings over their backs. When the ant lion is alarmed by an intruder of some kind it will raise all four of its wings together over its back. The head has two large eyes and two antennae that resemble those of the butterfly. Ant lions are of different sizes, from the size of a damsel-fly to less than an inch across the wingspan.

Larval ant lions feed basically on ants. In their larva stage they are very ferocious for their size. They have short legs and tough bodies and heads and live in soft sand. Even at this young age, the larvae know how to work. With a quick twist of the head, these larvae also called "doodlebugs," throw grains of sand or small stones. They dig a funnel-shaped hole that has steep sides consisting of fine, loose grains of sand. As ants walk around looking for food they may approach an ant lion hole. The sides are so loose that an ant cannot hold on and it slips to the bottom of the hole, where the ant lion larva is waiting, hidden under the sand. The ant lion larva grabs the ant with its powerful fangs and sucks out the body fluids until the ant's body is just a dry hull. Then it is discarded.

I thought about another creature that lies in wait for us. Satan goes around as a roaring lion looking for his prey—you and me. Satan will try to tempt you, maybe several times today, to do or say something you know you should not. Before you pray for God's help today, let's read Psalm 34:7: "The angel of the Lord encampeth round about them that fear him, and delivereth them."

Now pray that God will deliver you from the temptations of Satan today.

ELEPHANT SEALS

At that day shall a man look to his Maker, and his eyes shall have respect to the Holy One of Israel. Isaiah 17:7.

Elephant seals are the largest of the seals. They get their name from the fact that the male of the species has a trunklike snout that extends down like that of an elephant, except not quite as large. Male elephant seals grow to about 15 to 18 feet long and weigh more than 5,000 pounds. They have been hunted almost to extinction for their blubber containing a valuable oil. Females are about one half the size of the males, and they do not have a trunk.

The northern species lives in the waters off the coast of southern California and Mexico. There are several islands that they inhabit where they breed and raise their families. A newborn calf will weigh about 40 pounds. The mother nurses it for about six weeks. By that time it will have grown from about 250 to 300 pounds. I'd say that mama elephant seal milk is very nutritious if it can put that many pounds on a calf that fast. When the calves are born they are black but as they grow their color turns to a silver-gray.

Adults come to the islands to raise their families from December to March, and remain there through most of the summer months. During this time they molt (lose their hair). During the day they cover themselves as much as possible with sand to protect their tender skin from the sun. They do their hunting for food at night. During August the adults leave and will be gone until December for the males, and January for the females.

When the males return to the islands they will not eat until the females arrive. They are not afraid of humans; if they are sleeping, you could quietly slip up and sit on one. However, he might attack you if he awakes. They don't like humans to come too close.

The big bull seals have respect for each other. More importantly, we should respect the Creator of the universe. Tell God how much you love and respect Him this morning, then show Him by your actions today.

RED-WINGED DIVE BOMBER

But take good care to keep the commands and the law which Moses the servant of the Lord gave you: to love the Lord your God; to conform to his ways; to observe his commandments; to hold fast to him; to serve him with your whole heart and soul. Joshua 22:5, N.E.B.

One of the more common birds to be seen after the winter months is the red-winged blackbird. The male is black with a reddish-orange epaulet at the bend of the wings; the female is a brownish color with dark-brown to black stripes or splotches of color.

I have often wondered why the male species of most birds have such pretty coloring and the females so drab a color. I think I know why. In most instances, the female sits on the nest to incubate the eggs laid. Her coloration fades into the nest and brush or foliage, so that enemies have difficulty in seeing her. God camouflaged these female birds for a purpose.

The female red-winged blackbird takes about six days to build her nest. She will build it of cattail, sledge, and swamp milkweed leaves. She will intertwine them closely so that they are very tight and supportive. When the nest is finished the female will lay three to five eggs in it. Only after the third egg is laid will she begin to incubate them.

During the nest-building and egg-incubation period the male red-winged blackbird will continually guard the area of the nest. You may have been out on a walk sometime and had a male red-winged blackbird sound the alarm several times and fly out and "dive bomb" you. This is his way of saying, "Stay clear, this is my domain."

God's holy angels are by our side. Should any of the devil's angels come into our territory and get near us, God's angels fly to the evil angels to protect us and say, "This person is mine." There is a constant battle of the angels over us, and who wins out is our decision. Pray that God will help you decide and stay on His side.

OPEN MOUTHS

The Lord shall preserve thee from all evil: he shall preserve thy soul. Psalm 121:7.

When animals open their mouths they may just be yawning, but even the yawns take on important meanings in some animal species. Take for example the lion family. When a lion opens its mouth, it may just be yawning from boredom or sleepiness, but it may also be a courting procedure or a territorial signal. If the teeth are showing, it may signify that the lion is ready for action.

A yawn seems to gear an animal up again for activity. If the respiration is slow, the yawn gets the body working at a greater speed again. The sudden intake of air rushes fresh oxygen into the bloodstream. The heart reacts immediately, with more blood to the sluggish muscles. When the animal stretches, it squeezes the blood veins and the lymph system, speeding up the blood and reducing the amount of carbon dioxide buildup.

A hippo will open its mouth against another hippo for territorial possession. As these large animals come "mouth to mouth" and "lip to lip," they are saying, "I'm the boss here." This is also demonstrated by the javelinas that live on the deserts in Arizona and by some species of baboons and monkeys. Crocodiles will open their mouths and allow birds to go in and pick the food from around their teeth, because they cannot clean them with their tongue. This helps both the bird and the crocodile.

The zebra says different messages by the wideness of the open mouth. The wider open the mouth, the stronger the message. If the ears are straight up then the message is a greeting, but if the ears are layed back and the mouth very wide open, look out, the zebra is angry.

So the open mouth can mean danger. David said, "Save me from the lion's mouth" (Ps. 22:21), meaning from the devil. Our text says God preserves us from evil. Only God and His angels can do that. Pray that today you will be kept from the open mouth of danger of the evil devil.

CURSED BY GOD

And the Lord God said unto the serpent, Because thou hast done this . . . upon thy belly shalt thou go, and dust shalt thou eat all the days of thy life. Genesis 3:14.

One of the most beautiful creatures in the Garden of Eden was the serpent. It had wings and could fly. It was the serpent that Satan used, as it sat in the Tree of Knowledge of Good and Evil, to tempt Eve. After man's fall into sin, the serpent was cursed by God to crawl on its belly on the ground.

My family and I had been in Brazil only a short time when into our backyard slithered a big red and black snake. Our little maid cried, "Cobra." I left my Portuguese-language lesson to go kill the cobra. When I arrived I saw that it wasn't a cobra, but I proceeded to kill the snake anyway. As I picked up the dead snake I said to Domingas, "This is not a cobra!" "Oh, yes, it is," she said. My wife settled the argument. It was a "cobra," because that is the Portuguese word for snake. All the time I had thought Domingas was talking about the Old World poisonous snake.

God used snakes back in Moses' day. You remember that when Aaron and Moses were before King Pharaoh, Aaron's rod became a serpent and ate up the other rods that only looked like serpents (see Ex. 7:12). Also, the children of Israel were pitching camp and were afraid of the snakes and God told Moses to make a serpent of brass and put it on a pole. Moses made a brass serpent and put it up on a pole. If the people were bitten by a serpent they looked at the brass serpent on the pole and lived (see Num. 21:6-9). God used the serpents in these and other cases to teach lessons.

Satan disguised himself in the form of a serpent in order to talk to Eve in the Garden of Eden, and he was successful in getting her to doubt God's word and sin. He is disguising himself in many forms today and enticing many to sin. He makes sin look attractive and fun. Pray today that God will help you not to be attracted to the deceptive beauties of sin like Eve was attracted to the beautiful serpent.

177

FOODS OF THE WORLD

Nevertheless he left not himself without witness, in that he did good, and gave us rain from heaven, and fruitful seasons, filling our hearts with food and gladness. Acts 14:17.

When my wife, Millie, and I went to Brazil in South America, my father-in-law told me that I would find some delightful and delicious fruits and other kinds of food there. He said that I might not like them on the first try, but that God has placed in all parts of the world food for people to eat. Some would be different from what I was used to, but they were still good.

As we arrived in Brazil, we were served mangoes. Millie loved them, but I had never tried one. I liked them right away. However, when they gave me a papaya, I wasn't so sure I liked that. Now I could eat it every day of the week. There was also the custard apple, passion fruit, breadfruit, acerola fruit, aguaje fruit, and some other fruits. Then there was the yuca, mandioca, farinha (far-IN-ya), plantains, inguere (in-GEER-ee), and other roots and vegetables. A person has to learn to like these things or in some instances go hungry, except one can almost always get beans and rice.

In other parts of the world there are taro roots, coconuts, bamboo shoots, water chestnuts, Chinese peas, sweet potatoes, and oh, so many other good things to eat. Yes, God has given to each place, food that the people of the region can eat. I didn't mention many other foods we found in South America, because in North America they are known well; bananas, grapefruit, oranges, lemons, limes, and so on.

The native people in each country have ways of fixing their own foods. Sometimes they will mix them; other times they will use the simple, common food. I believe that the reason the people in many of the countries are so healthy and live so long is that they eat good food, prepared in a simple way.

God wants to fill our lives with food and gladness, and the only way He can do that is if we let Him. God will fill your life with health and gladness if you ask Him to and follow His simple diet. Try it; you'll like it, and you'll feel good.

THE ICY PLANET

He was in the world, and the world was made by him, and the world knew him not. John 1:10.

It was not until 1930 that a 22-year-old Kansas farm boy named Clyde Tombaugh, using his homemade telescope, discovered the planet Pluto. He sent his drawings of his sightings to a professional observatory in Arizona. They had just acquired a 13-inch telescope but had no money to hire anyone full-time. When they received Clyde's drawings they contacted him and hired him part-time to study the heavens.

As Clyde continued to study the stars, planets, and constellations, he started taking photographs and discovered more about Pluto. It was the ninth planet to be discovered in our solar system, and the fartherest away from Earth. Others started looking through telescopes to learn more about Pluto. They used the 150-inch telescope atop Mauna Kea in Hawaii, the 200-inch telescope on Mount Palomar in California, and an 80-inch telescope on a mountain in Arizona. They noticed that Pluto rotated on its axis every 6.4 days.

As James Christy was studying Pluto with the telescope in Arizona, he noticed that there was a smaller celestial body next to it. Further investigation revealed a small moon. Christy named this moon Charon, pronounced "sharon," for his wife, Charlene. He also noticed that this moon revolves around Pluto every 6.4 days, the same as the planet's rotation on its axis. There was much speculation as to the size of Pluto and what type of material it was made of. This investigation went on for twenty-six years, from 1953 to 1980, when there was brought to light the fact that Pluto has a large mass of ice on it. The moon, Charon, puts out enough heat to melt some of the ice. This releases methane gas that is in the frozen state, and this causes a wispy atmosphere around Pluto.

As scientists have tried to understand the universe, and especially the little-known Pluto, Jesus smiles from heaven, understanding all about it because He created it. The world did not know Him but He knew the world. He knows and understands you, and He will help you in your spiritual life if you will ask for His help. Thank God He knows and understands you.

"AIR SCENTING"

And he gave some, apostles; and some, prophets; and some, evangelists; and some, pastors and teachers. Ephesians 4:11.

God not only gave different talents to different ones of us to be able to do different things, He also created many of His animal creatures with different instincts and capabilities. A special training that has been given to German shepherd dogs in recent years is that of "air scenting." According to researchers, our bodies are made up of more than 60 trillion cells. They claim that more than 50 million cells are shed and regenerated each day. This exchange causes an odor (not BO) that we as humans cannot detect but dogs can smell. Trainers work with these dogs for about a year to really make them effective. With training, a German shepherd can smell a person, not only because of clothing or other odors but also because of this cell-changing odor.

On March 31, 1982, a 22-year-old ski-lift operator was buried under an avalanche of snow. She was in the employees' locker-room area. She was pinned down by the lockers and remained in this situation for five days. Rescue workers didn't know that anyone was there, but a German shepherd named Bridget was brought in by her trainer, Roberta Huber. Because of her training in "air scenting," Bridget smelled Anna under 12 feet of snow. She was the first avalanche victim saved by a dog in North America. Bridget detected Anna's scent through air spaces in the collapsed building.

I am happy that God not only gave each of us talents to be able to do things but that He also gave His creatures special features. These features have helped save many lives. Anna lost a foot by frostbite, but she could have lost her life. Bridget had been trained, and her God-given instinct saved Anna's life.

God has given you at least one special talent, and probably more. Use those talents for God. Pray in your own quiet way this morning, thanking God for your talents and ask Him to help you to develop and use them.

EXPLORING PONDS

Charge them that are rich in this world, that they be not highminded, nor trust in uncertain riches, but in the living God, who giveth us richly all things to enjoy. 1 Timothy 6:17.

Think for a minute about all of the creatures that are around or in a pond. There is a whole tiny world in every pond. Students in outdoor-education classes are finding some very interesting things about ponds. They get right down into the pond and explore all of the life that is there. A pond is full of life.

You've probably noticed those little skaters on top of the water. No doubt you have wished you could skate on the water like these water striders. There is another skater, called the whirligig, which is actually a beetle. It has a water-repellent body like the water strider. These beetles usually spin around in circles. Then there are the back swimmers and water boatmen, which are "true" bugs. They move along in kind of a rowing fashion. The back swimmer swims upside down.

Looking down into the pond, you will see crayfish, turtles, snails, and other creatures as they rummage around for food. If you put some pond water on a glass slide and put it under a microscope, you could probably be able to see some one-celled protozoans.

Around the pond fly all kinds of birds and insects. This is a place of busy activity. Many creatures will build their nests in the broad-leafed trees; others will use the tall grass nearby. Water lilies will float on the water, giving some support to frogs and small birds that want to rest and sun themselves. In the cool dirt around the edge of the pond you might see some salamanders, lizards, and worms.

God has given to us everything to enjoy. He especially wants us to enjoy His creation. One way to do that is to sit and watch all of the activity around a pond, or get in it and examine the creatures. Thank God today that He created everything for your enjoyment, and go out and enjoy it.

BEAVERS

I have therefore delivered him into the hand of the mighty one of the heathen; he shall surely deal with him: I have driven him out for his wickedness. Ezekiel 31:11.

This text fits well our subject this morning, as we will be talking about the beaver. We all know that beavers have a big flat tail that is used as a rudder when it swims, and that it can signal other beavers when danger is near by slapping its tail on the water. But beavers can also do much damage.

Beavers like to cut down trees by chewing them close to the ground with their very large front teeth. They will then cut off and pull the branches into a stream. By using many small trees, branches, and mud, they can dam up a stream and make a nice lake, which they can use to swim around in as well as build a nice lodge, or beaver house. While it may seem nice to have a beaver pond nearby, where we can watch the beaver in action, these beaver ponds can be destructive to farmers' crops as well as other wildlife and vegetation.

Many smaller animals have their homes in the same areas as the beavers. At times, when the beaver gets his dam built, the homes of these other creatures are destroyed by the rising water. Also, trees and other vegetations can be drowned by the water that backs up from the beaver dam. In fact, in many areas the beavers have been so destructive that the dams have been broken to let the water flow. Sometimes the beavers will rebuild the dam, so the only way to get the stream flowing freely again is to take the beavers away or kill them. Most wildlife people would rather take them away and not kill them, even though they have been destructive.

Pharaoh was a wicked man, and God said that He would deal with him. God drove him out for his wickedness as men have driven out the beaver. God does not want to drive us away from Him for our sinfulness; He wants to forgive us and have us close to Him. This morning ask God to forgive you of your sins and draw you close to Him.

BULLDOG ANTS

Be glad in the Lord and rejoice you righteous ones, and shout for joy all you who are upright in heart. Psalm 32:11, N.A.S.B.

Bulldog ants are an inch long. Their sting feels like a hot needle has been plunged into the skin, and the pain from the sting can last for ten days or longer. One scientist said that 30 bulldog ant stings can kill a person. The ants are very feisty and aggressive creatures; they are not afraid to tangle with another creature larger than they are. There are 65 species of the bulldog ant in the world. The species that I've chosen to talk about today is from Australia.

The hub of a colony of bulldog ants is, like many other ant species, a queen. She is a matriarch of absolute power and may live up to ten years. Without her tremendous egg output—one egg per hour—the colony would die out.

The devoted workers, which are females, are considered midwives. With their antennae they stroke the abdomen of the queen, which stimulates her to lay eggs. As the eggs are laid other workers carry them to a pile where they are constantly licked with a saliva that prevents fungus growth. Worker bulldog ants are also capable of laying eggs. These are used for food that is fed to the larvae.

When danger approaches the workers rally to protect the queen. She is put into the safest part, deep down in the nest. Immediately next to her are the "teen" ants, and then the infants. The worker ants are willing to fight and give up their lives, if necessary, to protect their queen and her colony.

God has placed a value on each person's life; that value is the same for everyone, because we are all equal in God's sight. We are not like the ants that have different values. God's "colony" will be forever!

I hope that you will give your life to God this morning, and ask Him to guide you, so that you will be among the righteous who will shout for joy at Christ's second coming and live in God's "colony" forever.

FALLING LEAVES

The one who listens to you listens to Me, and the one who rejects you rejects Me; and he who rejects Me rejects the One who sent Me. Luke 10:16, N.A.S.B.

Let me share a parable with you. One day a leaf saw other leaves floating from place to place and decided that would be fun. So the leaf said to the tree it grew on, "I don't need your sap anymore. See how pretty I am? I can take care of myself and I want to be free like the other leaves." The leaf detached itself from the tree and floated in the breeze to the ground. It made many friends with the other leaves as it went from place to place. Life seemed to be very exciting!

One day the leaf noticed that its beautiful color was beginning to disappear and brown spots were developing. A few days later, all its surface had turned brown and life wasn't exciting anymore. Some of its friends had already died, and it was beginning to feel sick. It didn't float from place to place anymore. It had been put into a pile with the other leaves, and it wasn't long until it was dead and burned up by fire. It had completely rejected the life-giving sap offered to it by the tree, and now it was too late!

The pleasures of sin are fun for a while, but they are not things that make us truly happy for any length of time. They bring only temporary satisfaction. The leaf in our parable thought it would be great to be free and do what it wanted, but it found out that it was fun only for a while and ended in destruction by fire.

There are occasions when some young people reject help from their parents, teachers, and others. They feel that they are big enough now and can succeed on their own. But later they have found that this was not the wise course to follow, and they have returned home, like the prodigal son, for the help and love they needed.

We cannot reject Jesus and expect to live forever because He says, "Without me ye can do nothing" (John 15:5). We don't need to worry about that fire if we keep a close relationship with Jesus every day. Ask Him to help you be a beautiful Christian today.

ARTICHOKES ON LEGS

His scales are his pride, shut up together as with a close seal.
Job 41:15.

One of the ugliest creatures that I have ever seen in pictures is the pangolin, called by some "an artichoke on legs." These animals have scales that act as their skin, covering their upper body and tail. They are the only animal in their group that has scales. They have no teeth, so they do not chew their food.

Pangolins are nocturnal animals, living in Africa and Asia. With their scales, they rather look like pinecones come to life. These scales grow continuously. They are sharp-edged and can be opened out at will. A pangolin can curl up in a ball for protection; stories have it that it takes several strong men to unroll one. This curling procedure is part of the pangolin's defense mechanism.

Pangolins have a long snout, with a small mouth way back up underneath. They live mainly on ants and termites. They also have a clear protecting cover over their eyes in case they get into a stinging-ants nest or termite nest. They have a tongue that is about a foot long and rolls up in their mouth. This tongue contains a sticky substance on it that acts like flypaper to small insects. One dead pangolin was found to have more than 200,000 insects in its stomach, which was a one-day supply. That would mean that it would eat more than 70 million insects a year. Quite a large diet, right?

There are seven species of these pangolins, three living in Asia and four in Africa. Some live in trees, others in burrows in the ground. After birth young pangolins will nurse for about a month, then they begin to eat insects. Shortly they are on their own.

I am thankful that we have a God who looks after us. I am glad also that He has given us earthly parents to love and protect us, as well as provide for us. Thank God today that you have parents, and that you have a mother who will take care of you for a long time.

TREE-CLIMBING LIZARDS

He shall pray unto God, and he will be favourable unto him.
Job 33:26.

The tree-climbing lizard of the Old World is also called a chameleon. Chameleons are intriguing reptiles. They live mostly in trees and shrubs and even have tails that help them climb. A few do spend most of their time on the ground, but even these can and do climb.

These tree-climbing lizards are rather odd to look at. They have two large eyes, one on each side of the head. Scientists have discovered that each eye works independently of the other, so they can be looking forward with one eye and backward with the other, if the head is held right. They can see two complete pictures at the same time. Our eyes normally focus on the same object and we see a whole panorama in living color, but not these chameleon lizards. Their eyes work independently and are protected by fused eyelids forming a cone-shaped shield open only at the tip. No doubt, God created these tree-climbing lizards with this special optical system because of their unique way of hunting food. Chameleons have tongues that may be shot forth at prey over a distance often greater than the length of their bodies. When they see a small or medium-sized insect, the tongue is quickly ejected. In less than a third of a second the tongue, which has a thick mucous secretion on its surface, is attached to the insect and it is taken into the mouth for food.

This chameleon has a built-in defense mechanism—yellow, black, and white pigments in special skin cells called chromatophores, which are located near the skin surface and, when activated by the nervous system, allow the chameleon to change colors so as to look nearly the same color as the object it is on or near.

God has given us adaptability, too. We can go from hot to cold climates, from sea level to high elevations. We can adapt to good friends or questionable friends; to good habits or bad habits; to good motives or bad motives; to good attitudes or bad attitudes. This is the adaptability that God has given to us.

Today ask God to give you the ability to adapt to good friends, good habits, good motives, and good attitudes. You know which are the good ones.

THE CAMEL BIRD

Casting all your care upon him; for he careth for you. 1 Peter 5:7.

Many years ago some Chinese people saw an ostrich and called it the "camel bird" because it was so large, had a long neck, and its feet were similar to those of a camel. The ostrich has been written about in history for several thousands of years. Early Egyptians used the ostrich feathers as a symbol of justice because the vanes on either side of the shaft are exactly equal in width.

Ostriches are the largest birds on earth and are found in several places—the Middle East, Africa, and Australia. They stand seven to eight feet tall and weigh about 300 pounds each. They can run up to about 40 miles an hour, but 30 miles an hour is their usual pace. They can run that pace for about an hour without getting too tired.

The female ostrich will lay as many as 15 eggs. The ostriches are good parents. The female will sit on the nest during the day, and the male will sit on it at night. After the chicks hatch the mother finds lice, fleas, and worms and feeds these to her young until the chicks start to graze.

In 1960 in the Nairobi National Park, workers recorded a situation in which the male ostrich was sitting on a clutch (nest) of 40 eggs. He was driven off by a pride (group) of lions. The lion cubs played with the eggs as though they were balls, batting them all over the area. When the lions left, the male ostrich gathered the eggs back into the nest and sat on them. Amazingly, they hatched. Ostrich eggs are so large—with a capacity of two pints—that in the olden days the shells were used to carry water.

As the ostrich parents guard and provide for their young, so God guards and provides for His children. This morning as you pray, ask God to take control of your life today and keep you from all harm. He will do it, because "He careth for you."

187

COUGAR

Where is the dwelling of the lions, and the feedingplace of the young lions, where the lion, even the old lion, walked, and the lion's whelp, and none made them afraid? Nahum 2:11.

The cougar, catamount, mountain lion, puma, or panther, as it is called in different regions, can live in just about any terrain. For many years the cougar has had the reputation of being a killer, that it would lie in wait and kill anything that came along. Probably Hollywood films have done more to discredit the cougar than anything else. In the movie films, the cougar crouches and at the right moment it lets out a roar and pounces on a person or animal.

Fortunately, that is not the true story of the cougar. According to wildlife researchers in Idaho, many cougars live in the same area where sheep are pastured, yet there are only two or three instances reported each year where a cougar has killed a sheep.

Cougars are carnivorous (meat-eating), and therefore do kill to eat. Deer and antelope are their main diet. But they are not on the prowl all of the time. A cougar will stalk an animal when hungry, but usually the ones they catch are the older or sickly animals. This way the cycle of life is kept in balance. An adult cougar may kill a deer or antelope only every two weeks or so, depending on the climate and the scarcity of food.

Many of those people who for years hunted the cougar to kill it have now become their protectors. They see that cougars are not bad creatures. They also realize that cougars are not really dangerous. In fact, many of these people would be delighted if they could only see a cougar out in the wilds.

God doesn't desire us to go around in a sneaky way and get the best of people. He wants us to share with them what He has done for us. God wants us to show how His power can work through us. Ask God today to give you "lion" power to overcome the devil when he tempts you.

DRINKS AROUND THE WORLD

Let us eat and drink; for to morrow we die. 1 Corinthians 15:32.

I have always enjoyed different fruit juices. When I went to South America I found many drinks that I didn't know existed. People who travel to the United States find drinks such as root beer that they hadn't known before.

Around the world, God has given many different things to drink, and man has made others that God didn't plan for him to make. When sin entered, man decided to do some things his way; he has paid for it through poor health and death.

People in Brazil make a drink from the guarana (gwar-ANN-na) fruit. This is kind of a national drink and is usually carbonated. They also mix avocado, sugar, and milk to make a drink called *abacatada* (a-BAA-ka-ta-da). They also make ice cream out of it. Brazilians make a drink from a palm fruit called assai (ah-SIGH-ee). It is usually very thick and a deep purple. Juice is also squeezed from sugarcane. People like to suck the *cana* (CON-ya) right from the stalk.

Coconut milk is a common drink, not only in South America but in other tropical places. Pineapple, guava, orange, grape, grapefruit, passion fruit, and other tropical fruits make nice *refrescos*, as the Peruvians call their drinks. Many people will take grains such as wheat, rice, barley, corn, oats, and rye and make "cereal coffee" from them. They toast them first, then boil them to make the "coffee." They will also take many leaves from shrubs and trees and make "teas" out of them. My favorite from Peru is a sweet grass that *yerba louisa* is made from. Oh, is it good. Apple leaves, lime or lemon leaves, garlic, and many grasses are used to make teas.

I have had many people offer me drinks that were fermented, but these destroy the brain and I have said No. Why numb the brain when there are so many good things to drink that are pure and sweet? God doesn't want us to just eat and drink because we are going to die. He has better plans for us—a good life for eternity. Thank Him for that plan, and enjoy the "good" drinks.

BUFFY

Behold, I stand at the door, and knock: if any man hear my voice, and open the door, I will come in to him, and will sup with him, and he with me. Revelation 3:20.

There were an estimated 60 to 70 million buffalo, or bison, in the early 1800s in the United States, Canada, and Mexico. It was not unusual to find herds of up to 4 million in one location, and they would roam in an area of about one thousand square miles. The early settlers began to kill the buffalo for food.

In 1889, conservationists began a movement to save the buffalo because only 541 buffalo were left. Today there are an estimated sixty thousand in the United States, Canada, and Mexico in private, state, and Federal herds. The State of Kansas has several herds; each year they must thin them out, so some calves and older buffalo are made available for sale to the public.

At the church camp in Kansas, Broken Arrow Ranch, we decided we'd like to have a buffalo for the campers to observe, so we put in our order to the Kansas State Fish and Game Commission. They honored our request, and on a set day we went to pick up our buffalo. We found it to be a 6-month-old female calf. She was wild, right off the range. The game commission workers vaccinated her and sent her down the ramp into our pickup truck, which had iron cattle railings. She didn't like that at all.

When we arrived at the camp we turned the buffalo, which we named Buffy, loose in the large corral with our Appaloosa stallion, Arapaho. Buffy and Arapaho became good friends. When we took Arapaho out of his pen to ride, Buffy would cry and whine. We could even let her out when we took Arapaho for a ride, and she would follow right along like a colt.

Jesus wants to be our friend. Jesus wants you to trust Him as Buffy did the stallion. He wants you to open up your heart and tell Him your joys and sorrows, and let Him know what you need. Take the time and open up your heart to Him right now. Tell Him how much you love Him, and that you want Him as your best Friend. "Prayer is the opening of the heart to God as to a friend"—*Steps to Christ*, p. 93.

BLUEBIRDS

And Jesus saith unto him, The foxes have holes, and the birds of the air have nests; but the Son of man hath not where to lay his head. Matthew 8:20.

At one time some birds were abundant but today they are scarce. Many people are trying to help the bluebird make a comeback. They are building bluebird houses by the hundreds and thousands, hoping to bring them back to the numbers they once were.

Where I grew up bluebirds were plentiful. We used to feed them and observe them. We enjoyed watching these birds with their pretty blue feathers. Today the three species of bluebirds are not very plentiful in the United States. It is hoped they will be again. The eastern bluebird is probably the one that has been affected the most, because the old wooden fenceposts that they nested in have rotted and have been replaced with steel fenceposts. The males of this species have a bright-blue back, blue tail feathers, and rust breast feathers. Their habitat is from the Rocky Mountains to the East Coast.

The mountain bluebird, which has more open space, has fared quite well. It lives in the areas of the northwestern part of the United States, through western Canada and as far north as Alaska. The males are all blue except for a whitish belly. The western bluebird ranges from the Pacific Coast to the Rockies. The males are blue except for brownish feathers on their backs. All three species have suffered, because the hollow trees that the bluebirds have been using for nesting and raising their young have been cut down for new shopping centers and housing developments.

It has been difficult for these birds to survive because of the lack of nesting places. In Jesus' day there was not the building developments of today and the birds did have places to nest. But today it is very difficult. Although Jesus had no place here to call home, He now has a beautiful home in heaven, and He wants to come and take His children back to share His home. Ask God this morning to help you be a faithful Christian so you can enjoy His home with Him forever.

OCEANS

The sea is his, and he made it: and his hands formed the dry land. Psalm 95:5.

As you look at a map or a globe of the world you will notice that about 70 percent of our world's surface is covered with water. Each of the bodies of water has a name, although they are connected. The Pacific Ocean is the largest expanse of water; the Atlantic Ocean, second largest. The others are the Indian, Arctic, and Antarctic oceans. The Pacific Ocean covers about 64,000,000 square miles, or about one third of the earth's surface.

Challenger Deep, in the Marianas Trench close to Guam, is the deepest spot in all the oceans. Its bottom is 37,782 feet below the surface. If we could put Mount Everest, at 29,028 feet the tallest mountain in the world, into the Challenger Deep, more than a mile of water would cover its top.

The ocean is never still, it is always moving. This movement is caused by wind and earthquakes and by the gravitational pull of the sun and the moon. The moon's pull is so strong that it causes the tides.

Many of the islands in the oceans are nothing more than the tops of mountains that project out of the deep water. Around most continents there is a plateaulike formation called the continental shelf. It gradually slopes down from the shoreline until it is under about 650 feet of water. There the shelf ends abruptly and the bottom drops away to what is called the abyss.

I am thankful there is a God who created this earth and all that is in it. Although sin has changed many things, I know that God is in control, and that strengthens my faith. God said it, and I believe it, and that is good enough for me!

As you think about these thoughts this morning, thank God that He is in control.

A PRICKLY WORLD

And lest I should be exalted above measure through the abundance of the revelations, there was given me a thorn in the flesh, the messenger of Satan to buffet me, lest I should be exalted above measure. 2 Corinthians 12:7.

Cacti are considered to be all-American plants because all but one of the more than 1,500 species are confined to the Americas, from Canada to the tip of South America. The hub of most of the cacti is the near-desert lands of northern Mexico and the Southwestern United States.

When we think of the cactus we immediately think of the spines, or stickers, that most cactus plants have. Those spines are the reason why different ones of the cactus plants have been named pincushion, hedgehog, porcupine, eagle claw, prickly pear, and fishhook. Not only do the spines of the cactus plant keep away animals that would eat it, but they also play a very important part in the life of the plant.

Spines have the important function of helping the plant live in the hot desert temperatures. Have you ever wondered how cactus plants live where it is so hot? Here is how. The spines screen the sun's rays and help keep the plant cool by trapping an insulating layer of air close to the plant. They reduce evaporation by breaking up the drying winds and air currents, and they collect raindrops and dew, gently dropping this water to the ground beneath the plant, where it can soak up the moisture.

Spines come in different sizes and shapes. They always are in clusters, in rows, or in spirals, and grow from spots on the plant called areoles. Some spines are short and stout, while others are long and straight. Some are curved, others are barbed, hooked, feathered, or hairlike.

The apostle Paul talked about a thorn, a problem, in his life. Some people, like the cactus, just naturally live a thorny life. However, with Jesus in the life it will be less thorny. Not all of the thorns will be removed because they help us develop a patient character. I thank God for the thorny growing experiences; what about you?

DESERTS

[The desert] shall blossom abundantly, and rejoice even with joy and singing. Isaiah 35:2.

Deserts are interesting places. Much can be learned from observing nature on the deserts. Ellen White, describing the results of the Flood in the book *Patriarchs and Prophets,* wrote, "Where once had been earth's richest treasures of gold, silver, and precious stones, were seen the heaviest marks of the curse."— Page 108. Could she be talking about the vast desert wastes on our Planet Earth? I believe that she is.

In the sands of the deserts are millions of little seeds that are doing nothing. Some wait in the soil for several years until they have the right conditions to grow.

Although we know that some animals burrow under the sandy soil to escape the heat, it is also true that some plants in a way do the same thing. Take, for example, the "living stone" plant, which is a native of Southwestern Africa. It grows in the sand with only a part of the leaves above the ground. These portions are called the windows, because they take in the sunlight. The plant must lose as little water as possible, and living almost totally submerged in the sand, helps it do that. In fact, reducing water loss in one way or another is a trait of most of the desert vegetation.

The plants that survive on the desert have become so adapted to their situation that water loss is at a minimum. Some plants have a waxy surface that helps keep the water in; others have dense mats of silvery hairs that reflect the sun, thus reducing evaporation. As water becomes scarce some plants shed their leaves, so as not to need so much water; when the rain comes they grow their leaves again. With moisture and rain, the desert blossoms out in a magnificent way.

God is waiting for the time when He can see His world in full bloom again. He also wants to see us blossom for Him in a spiritual way. Ask God to help you blossom as a Christian today, and ask Him to come soon so you can see the earth made new, in full bloom and living color.

THE AMERICAN SYMBOL

They are passed away as the swift ships: as the eagle that hasteth to the prey. Job 9:26.

Various nations on Planet Earth have a mammal, bird, or leaf as a national symbol. On June 20, 1782, the U.S. Congress adopted the bald eagle as the national symbol of the United States. There was some resistance because the eagle has characteristics that are not honorable. Ben Franklin wrote, "He is a bird of bad moral character. He does not get his living honestly." Richard B. Morris, a historian, wrote that the bald eagle is a "gangster bird, a hijacker . . . a symbol of espionage . . . an image of frightfulness."

Because the eagle will many times take a fish from an osprey that has caught it, or take food from other birds or animals that have killed it, the eagle is not looked upon very favorably. It is reported, believe it or not, that the eagle is a real coward.

Bald eagles are very good caretakers of their young. As far as research can tell, they also mate for life. The bald eagle does not get its white feathers on its head until it is 5 years old.

In past years the eagle was used as a symbol of imperial might, swiftness, and brute power. The Persians and Romans carried standards with the eagle symbol into battle. Emperors of Rome bore ivory sceptors topped by an eagle, and the American Indians worshiped the eagle because of its beauty.

Bald eagles were put on the endangered species list, owing to their fast disappearance. Today it is estimated that there are only about 5,000 with about 1,400 nesting pairs. Research effort on eagles is limited because they are very complicated creatures.

One of the lessons we can learn from the eagles is that they take care of their families. God is interested in His family and wants to take care of us. The eaglets will allow their parents to take care of them. Do we allow God to take care of us? Or do we want to do things our way, by ourselves? God will take care of us if we allow Him to. Invite God into your life this morning and ask Him to take care of you. Turn your life over to Him today.

FLIERS WITHOUT FEATHERS

Who are these that fly as a cloud, and as the doves to their windows? Isaiah 60:8.

We generally think of birds and insects when we think of creatures that fly. But a number of other creatures, while they do not actually fly, have membranes they use for gliding.

Probably the greatest gliders of all the animals are the colugos of Southeast Asia. The colugo, which looks something like a lemur, is about the size of a house cat. It has also been called the cobego and flying lemur. Colugos can jump from high in a tree and sail up to 100 yards. A baby colugo will cling to its mother tightly as she glides.

In Australia there is a gliding opossum; it is the smallest gliding mammal. It is only about six inches long, and half of that may be tail. In the jungles of Southeast Asia there is the flying dragon, which has folds of skin on its sides. As it leaps from limb to limb it stretches out these folds of skin and can glide up to about 50 feet. It can twist its body while flying and go to the right or left. The flying gecko lizard has webbed feet and skin flaps on its sides that it spreads to glide from tree to tree. Some Asian frogs have tremendous folds of skin between the extremely long toes on their feet that act like a parachute when they jump.

Flying fish are a beautiful sight as they soar through the air. Actually the fish are not flying, but gliding. These fish will build up speed, then shoot out of the water and, with extended paired fins, glide for a short distance. At times the wind may help them glide farther, and at times as they begin to come back down they will vibrate their tail fin in the water to keep the body above the water and glide a greater distance.

There will come a day when you too can fly. God will give you the ability to travel and explore through His universe to your heart's desire, throughout all eternity. Pray that you will have that opportunity.

FAITHFULNESS AND MODESTY

That their hearts might be comforted, being knit together in love, and unto all riches of the full assurance of understanding, to the acknowledgment of the mystery of God, and of the Father, and of Christ. Colossians 2:2.

In the language of flowers, violets stand for faithfulness and modesty. They have been gathered for their beauty, too. Violets come not only in violet but in shades of yellow, white, and blue. They have been used as food, medicine, cosmetics, and as omens. Children have enjoyed running into the fields and woods and picking handfuls of violets. The United States has more than 60 different violet species. There may be others in other countries.

According to Greek myth, the god Zeus created violets for his lover Io. Hera, Zeus's wife, found out about it, and Zeus hid Io by transforming her into a heifer. When she complained about the coarse grass she was having to eat, he created the white violet for her to eat. The purple violets are said to have come from the Roman goddess Venus, as a symbol of love, since she was the goddess of love. I'm certainly glad I don't have to believe all of that, aren't you?

In the Middle Ages violets were used to make violet syrup, violet sugar, violet jam, and violet greens. Modern-day wild-food enthusiasts proclaim that violet leaves are high in vitamin A content and that the leaves and flowers have more vitamin C than oranges. They are also a good laxative.

Violets reproduce in three ways, by self-fertilization, vegetative runners, and open pollination. Usually at least one of these methods will work. The activity of insects and birds around the flowers causes mature seed capsules to erupt. When they do, the seeds shoot up to five feet away. The smooth yellow violets sometimes eject the seeds up to 15 feet away.

Many things that God has done are a mystery to humans, but we can trust Him, knowing that He did all for our good. Thank God that one day we shall understand much more. Ask Him for wisdom in your studies today.

NURSERIES OF LIFE

And God said, Let the waters bring forth abundantly the moving creature that hath life. . . . And God blessed them, saying, Be fruitful, and multiply, and fill the waters in the seas. Genesis 1:20–22.

When God created this earth He told everything that He had created to multiply and produce more of the same. God gave each species the power to procreate its own kind. He gave this command to the creatures of the sea, and they go about fulfilling God's command in different ways.

Along the coastal areas of many of the countries in the world there are swampy areas called wetlands. Most people feel that these wetlands, which are also found in other parts of the continents, are a waste of space, that they need to be filled in with dirt and made usable. Because of the value of the locations, many real-estate developers want to use the nice coastal areas for cabins and houses.

To protect these very important areas for the benefit of sea creatures and other wildlife, the U.S. Government passed the Wetlands Act, which protects many of the areas but not all of them. The Wetlands Act is very important to natural creatures as well as to naturalists. Not only can the creatures multiply, but scientists can study their life cycles and habits.

Many creatures that cannot multiply in the open seas are able to come into these marsh wetlands and have their families. As the tide goes out to sea, many small creatures are caught in small ponds. Most of the time this is beneficial to them.

When man develops the wetlands into living space for humans, he endangers many species of sea life, birds, and other wildlife. Many times one type of creature will depend upon other creatures in the wetlands for its food and life.

As Christians we should be good conservationists, doing all we can to preserve these areas. God told all of the creatures to multiply, and these are the only areas where some of them can do so.

In this world filled with sin, thank God that you can look into these areas and see and enjoy His creatures. They can teach us many lessons if we will take the time to observe them.

NO DRINK

For the Lord is great, and greatly to be praised: he is to be feared above all gods. Psalm 96:4.

The koalas of Australia rarely drink water. In fact, in a primitive Australian tribe the word *koala* means "no drink."

Although koalas are often called bears, they are in fact marsupials, or pouched animals. They carry their young in these pouches for a period of three to six months. After leaving the pouch, the babies ride around on the mother's back until they are about a year old.

The koala spends most of its life in trees. It is especially fond of eucalyptus trees; it eats the leaves and young shoots. Although there are about 350 species of eucalyptus trees in Australia, koalas eat the leaves from only about 20. Interestingly, koalas in different parts of the country eat different kinds of eucalyptus leaves. These leaves contain substances that affect body temperature. Those koalas in the cooler climates eat leaves that contain phellandrene, which increases body temperature. On the other hand, the koalas in warmer climates eat leaves that contain cineole, which decreases body temperature. Koalas eat so many eucalyptus leaves, about two and a half pounds a day, that they smell like eucalyptus. They get most of the water they need from eating the leaves.

Generally, koalas will come down from a tree only to walk over and climb another one. While on the ground they lick soil and gravel to aid them in digestion. These little "teddy bears" may live to be 20 years old.

Many children love their toy teddy bears that are imitations of the koalas. The koalas have a nice soft fur and look like lovable little creatures. We have a God who loves us. He has done so many wonderful things for us. He wants us to accept His love that He gives to us. Thank Him for His love this morning and ask Him to help you be a lovable Christian today.

THE LADY WITH SPOTS

For thou art great, and doest wondrous things: thou art God alone. Psalm 86:10.

"Ladybug, ladybug, fly away home; your house is on fire and your children will burn." This is a little saying that I learned when I was a small boy. I don't know where the saying came from and I don't know the meaning of it, but maybe I said it just so the small ladybug would fly away.

Ladybugs are beetles that are beneficial to the human family. There are about 150 species of ladybugs in North America, and they are found all over the world. These little creatures range in size from that of the head of a straight pin to that of a large thumbnail. They may have no spots or up to 22 of them on their back.

Like many other insects, ladybugs go through a four-stage life cycle. Theirs lasts about 27 days. They will pass from the egg to the larva, then pupa, and finally to the adult. The female will lay her eggs in clusters on the bottom side of a leaf or in the crotch of a tree. A female ladybug may lay as many as 1,500 eggs in a two-month period. When an egg hatches and the larva comes out, it looks like a small alligator with hair. Ladybug larvae will eat all types of small insects, but aphids are their favorite. During the larval stage they will shed their skin four times. They also vary in color, most of them quite bright.

The ladybugs are so beneficial that gardeners and farmers buy them by the gallon to put on their plants to save them from many small pesty insects. There are about 135,000 ladybugs in a gallon. Their fame as pest killers was established in 1888, when the vedalia beetle, a species of ladybug, was imported from Australia. This beetle saved the California citrus crops from the cottony cushion scale insect, which also came from Australia and feeds on the sap from leaves and twigs.

Yes, God does wondrous things, and one of them is to save you from the enemy. He can make life more pleasant for you. Thank Him for His care today.

HIDDEN IN THE CORAL REEF

Deliver me, O Lord, from mine enemies: I flee unto thee to hide me. Psalm 143:9.

Among the most interesting and yet misunderstood works of God is the coral reef. Coral reefs are made by colonies of the coral polyp, a tiny sea animal. Reefs grow in shallow seas from the bottom of the ocean upward, and each type of coral polyp depends on some sunlight. Coral grows in warm water areas that have very little change in temperature.

Some oceanographers claim that coral reefs are the mightiest structures ever built by any form of life on this planet. The largest reef known is the Great Barrier Reef off Western Australia. It is 1,250 miles long and said to contain more than 5,000 cubic miles of limestone. The little flowerlike coral polyps deposit a molecule of lime, or calcium, at a time, and thus the limestone coral reef is made.

Each type of coral has its own growth pattern that produces a characteristically shaped structure. The brain coral resembles the human brain, and the branch coral looks like small trees and plants. Other types are not so smooth and branchy.

The coral polyps are the architects and landlords of the reef. Coral reefs provide food, housing, and protection for many ocean creatures. Around some coral reefs in the Pacific Ocean, more than 3,000 different varieties of sea life have been counted. They include shellfish, fish, snails, eels, lobsters, sponges, starfish, and sea fans.

We have a Protector, God, who will hide us from our enemy (Satan) if we are willing to stay close to Him and be sheltered by all His love and protection. Ask Jesus this morning to help you stay close to Him today and to put His loving arms of protection around you. He will!

THE SOLITARY STALKER

All our enemies have opened their mouths against us. Lamentations 3:46.

One of the most stately and beautiful birds is the great blue heron. These birds stand up to four feet tall, have a wingspan of more than six feet, yet weigh only five to eight pounds. They have a bill that can strike with accuracy and force and is usually deadly to the prey.

These birds are found from Canada to Mexico; they can adapt well to the area where they are. They like to fish in shallow rivers or lakes and delight themselves with the crayfish and other small creatures that are found in the water.

As an extremely skillful stalker, the great blue heron can hold still for a long time, waiting for the instant when it can strike. One day I watched one in a lake in northern Michigan. It stood still for about a half hour, then bingo, it had the fish in its mouth.

Great blues make their nests high up in the trees. These nests look quite flimsy yet hold the eggs and the parents as they incubate them. The female will lay from three to five eggs in a nest, and the parents will take turns incubating the eggs. After about 28 days the little chicks will peck a hole in the shell and appear saying in bird language, "Hi, I'm here and I'm hungry." At first it is necessary for the parents to regurgitate food, a little at a time, into the baby's mouth. Later, as the chicks grow, the parents will bring in small snakes, mammals, softshell crabs, and fish. It is a real trick for the parents to find and bring all the food necessary for their offspring because they eat about one fourth of their weight daily.

Just as the great blue heron is an enemy to many creatures, there are many evil angels flying around that are enemies to God's children. They want to feed us things that will corrupt our minds and that will be harmful to our spiritual well-being. Pray this morning, asking God to take control of your mind today so the evil angels have no room to feed you any trash.

ALLIGATOR OR CROCODILE?

And Peter opened his mouth and said: "Truly I perceive that God shows no partiality." Acts 10:34, R.S.V.

As you look at the long slender rough body with lots of tail, a big snout, four short legs, and a mouth full of teeth, what do you call it? Some people might call it an alligator and others a crocodile. The two are not the same, but people get them confused. One of the easiest ways to tell these two creatures apart is by the teeth. In the crocodile's lower jaw the fourth tooth from the front on either side fits into a notch in the upper jaw. These two teeth protrude out farther than the other teeth when the mouth is shut. Also, the crocodile's snout usually is longer, more pointed, and narrower than the alligator's.

Crocodiles range in length from 7½ to 12 feet. The record length in the United States is 15 feet, and in South America it is 23 feet. There are about a dozen species living in Asia, Africa, Australia, Madagascar, and North and South America. They enjoy the shallow water, rivers, swamps, and marshes. With their long, powerful, flexible tails, they are excellent swimmers. As they float along on top of the water, the eyes, which are up on top of the head, look forward out of the water.

I have had the opportunity of going up and down the Ucayali River in the jungles of Peru and seeing very large crocodiles crawl from the bank or sand bar into the water right underneath our canoe. It gives a person an uncomfortable feeling as he wonders where the crocodile went and what it is doing. We've seen many of them and they didn't seem to be looking for a "missionary" dinner. They were trying to get away from us, for they were just as wary of us as we were of them.

To most people all crocodiles and alligators look alike, but an expert knows them apart. Jesus can tell who we are, too, and calls us by name. I am thankful I know a God who is great yet He knows me by my name. I hope you are glad also.

Jesus shows no partiality. We are all equal in His eyes. Thank God today that He is a personal God, that He knows your name, and that you have just as much status in His sight as anyone else.

THE CAPYBARAS

Who gave himself for us, that he might redeem us from all iniquity, and purify unto himself a peculiar people, zealous of good works. Titus 2:14.

Venezuela is the home for the capybaras. These are the largest rodents in the world. Their front legs are shorter than their hind legs, and they live where the environment is somewhat swampy. The capybaras may weigh up to 120 pounds each. They are not fast or enduring runners. These creatures are non-aggressive; they grow fast and require very little care. Social animals, they live in small family groups, usually dominated by one adult male.

Young capybaras mature quickly; females are able to reproduce in about 15 months. The females produce three litters of babies every two years. They normally live from eight to ten years, and a female could produce 36 young in a lifetime.

Capybaras are excellent swimmers, because of partially webbed feet. They can dive and stay submerged for a long time. More than 300 years ago, because of the close association of the capybaras with water, the Roman Catholics classified capybaras as fish and could eat them on "meatless" days. This has since changed, but the capybaras are used today for meat. In fact, the salvation of these creatures came when it was discovered that these rodents could be eaten. Large farms in Venezuela raise them like cattle for their meat, which is said to taste like a combination of pork and beef. These creatures are in abundance now.

As the capybaras are different from all other rodents, so God has chosen to have a people who are different from other people. Different does not mean to be funny or odd, but different in lifestyle and beliefs. God wanted a special people, a chosen people.

As the capybaras are valuable to the Venezuelan cowboys, so we are valuable to God. Thank Him in your prayer this morning that you have been chosen by Him.

THE FLYING ARTIST

And he garnished the house with precious stones for beauty:
and the gold was gold of Parvaim. 2 Chronicles 3:6.

In New Guinea and Australia there is a kind of bird called
the bowerbird. There are 18 species of these birds, which are
about the size of the robin. The males of each of the species are
artists, some better than others. They express themselves like
human artists do, with different designs and colors.

All but two of the 19 species build what is called a "bower,"
or a display area of sticks and grass. Each species builds a little
differently. The birds take weeks to build a bower. After the
birds have built these bowers to suit them, they will go out and
look for decorations to adorn the entrance to the bower, which is
usually about a foot high.

The decorations used by the male birds are different from
bower to bower. They generally use different-colored mosses,
fungi, fruits, leaves, flowers, pebbles, shells, feathers, and anything else of beauty they can find. Sometimes they will use all
one color, depending on the species and likes of the males. The
adornments will be spread out at the entrance. The purpose is
to attract the females.

The males of different species have different coloring. Eleven
of the 17 bower-building males have a colorful crest on top of
their head, like a rooster. Some of them have beautiful colored
feathers while others have plain brown feathers. The males do
not help the females build their nests or incubate the eggs. They
only build their bower, and then they are through.

Solomon built his Temple with the most beautiful materials
and colors to glorify the Lord. He was an artist, I would say, in
the use of beautiful materials. Jesus has gone to prepare mansions for us in heaven. We have no idea what they will look like,
only that they will be beautiful. Thank God today for Jesus, and
that He has gone to prepare a beautiful home for you in heaven.

DEPENDENTS

And if any man ask you, Why do ye loose him? thus shall ye say unto him, Because the Lord hath need of him. Luke 19:31.

In the context of our text today, Jesus needed an animal to ride into the city of Jerusalem, so He told His disciples to go and get a donkey colt.

There are plants that God created that need each other too. It is interesting to see how many plants need each other. We have talked about pollination, how some plants need pollen from other plants, like themselves, to bear fruit. There are also plants that depend for their life on other plants. These we call parasites.

Parasites can grow in several ways. The true parasite will grow on the plant, attaching itself to the plant, and taking its nourishment from the host plant. Some dependent plants grow from the ground and use the host plants to support themselves but do not take anything from the host plant; these are not parasites.

Some common parasites, though you may not have realized that they are such, are mistletoe and dodder. Mistletoe is a parasite that attaches itself to the limb of a tree and lives by boring its rootlike tentacles into the tree and sucking out the water and dissolved minerals necessary for life. Interestingly, one mistletoe may attach itself to another mistletoe, living off of its own kind. Few other parasites do this.

There is a tropical parasite that lives inside the host plant; it is called the rafflesia. This plant bores into the host plant and spreads thin filaments through the internal tissues. It literally grows inside of the host, and it is difficult to tell the parasite from the host. Rarely does it come into the open, but when it does it produces the largest flower in the world, about three feet across. The flower is brown and purple, and stinks.

Ask Jesus to help you in your need today. He gives life, and it is free.

BEI-SHUNG

Happy is he that hath the God of Jacob for his help, whose hope is in the Lord his God: which made heaven, and earth, the sea, and all that therein is: which keepeth truth for ever. Psalm 146:5, 6.

What is it that is black and white, fuzzy, and lovable? If you guessed a giant panda, you guessed correctly. The giant panda, a native of China, has been imitated by stuffed-animal creators. Thousands of these pandas are sold each year and cuddled by small children and older girls.

Bei-shung is the Chinese name for this animal, which is related to the raccoon. The panda is mostly white with black ears, shoulders, legs, and feet, and black trim around the eyes. Pandas are great lovers of sweet bamboo shoots. They will eat forty pounds or more of bamboo shoots a day. They also like fruits and berries. It is estimated that pandas spend about two thirds of their time eating. Young pandas climb trees, but the adults live mostly on the ground.

Pandas weigh more than 200 pounds and are about five or six feet long. When a baby panda is born it will not weigh more than three pounds.

It was not until 1869 that a French missionary reported to the Western world about the giant pandas. Before that time, only the Chinese knew they existed.

The Creator created things that we could enjoy, and the lovable pandas are just one such creature. All creatures were lovable in the beginning, and will be again in the new earth. This morning let us turn our thoughts to the great Creator and thank Him for creating such wonderful creatures for our enjoyment. Ask Him to help you be kind and loving toward others today.

WATERSPOUTS

Deep calleth unto deep at the noise of thy waterspouts: all thy waves and thy billows are gone over me. Psalm 42:7.

I am curious to know how David knew about waterspouts. Do you suppose there were geysers back in his time? If not, how did he know about them? I'm puzzled; how about you?

There is some water under the earth's surface, just as there is oil and other substances. The water that many people drink comes from wells. On some islands, such as Bermuda, rainwater is caught on roofs or in large tanks. Most of us use well water, or purified river or lake water, or seawater that has been desalted.

In most areas where there is underground water, the rocks and sand that hold it are cool. In some areas the water table (the depth underground at which water is found) is shallow, and in other places it is deep. We used to have a six-foot well in our backyard in Colorado. Also along the Platte River in Nebraska the water table is just a few feet deep. In other places people have to drill hundreds of feet to find water.

There are areas underground where the rocks are hot and the water is under pressure. As the water runs into these reservoir areas, it heats to a superhot boiling point. Under this pressure, water and steam spout out from cracks or fissures into the air. This is how a geyser works. You may have seen those in Yellowstone National Park. A famous one is Old Faithful, which spouts off at regular intervals. The repeat performance of the geyser is caused by more water running into the heated area; when it becomes superhot it spouts off again.

As David recalled his love for the Lord and his desire to serve the Lord, he realized that his life needed some help. That help could come only from the Lord. Pray as David did, that God will come in and take over in your life. Thank Him this morning for His ever-abiding presence in your life.

FLAME FLOWER

And he shall be like a tree planted by the rivers of water, that bringeth forth his fruit in his season; his leaf also shall not wither; and whatsoever he doeth shall prosper. Psalm 1:3.

One of the largest multimillion-dollar plant businesses in the world is the raising and selling of poinsettia plants. It all started back in the mid-1820s when a man named Joel R. Poinsett of Charleston, South Carolina, was sent as the first United States ambassador to Mexico. As Mr. Poinsett walked through the hills and valleys around Mexico City he came across some crimson shrubs that were from six to 16 feet high. The Mexicans called them "flame flower." In English they have taken the name "poinsettia."

What especially interested Mr. Poinsett was the bright crimson color. Botanists tell us that the crimson parts are not really petals but bracts. The bracts surround the real flowers, which are clusters of little yellowish-green buttons.

The "flame flower" has become a symbol of Christmas. In California there is a ranch that grows nothing but poinsettias, under 20 acres of fiberglass roofing. If the temperature is not just right, or the soil is too soggy, the plant will lose its leaves. Then, of course, the color is gone. This ranch has produced a plant that will hold its leaves longer than most varieties.

The Bible writer likens the righteous person to a plant or tree that will not lose its leaves. That person will continue to be a beautiful tree, and others will be introduced to Christ through his or her life. Jesus wants us to show our true color as a Christian and let others know about Him.

It does take a lot of care to make a poinsettia pretty and keep it that way. Jesus is willing to spend time in helping us to remain pretty, if we will let Him. Ask Him today to help you be a true Christian and allow others to see your true color—a life that radiates Jesus.

MY BLACK WALNUT TREE

That ye, being rooted and grounded in love, may be able . . . to know the love of Christ. Ephesians 3:17–19.

There are several species of black walnuts in the United States, and a smaller variety in Japan. The eastern black walnut is the largest of all. It can grow to a height of nearly 150 feet and may have a trunk with a diameter of six feet. It is reported that one walnut tree in western New York had a trunk diameter of 36 feet. It was 80 feet to the first limb and the trunk was five feet thick at that point.

The black walnut tree is known principally for its beautiful hardwood, which is almost a purplish brown in color. Cabinet-makers and other wood craftsmen especially like the black walnut wood because it can be sanded and polished to a very high luster. Black walnut wood is quite expensive.

The black walnut tree also bears fruit. The nuts are embedded in pulplike husks. The aroma of black walnuts can be smelled some distance away.

In Kansas we had a large black walnut tree by our master bedroom window. Kansas has many lightning storms. During the storms in our area it seemed like the lightning wanted to climb through our bedroom window. One day as I was talking to a farmer I told him that I enjoyed having that large black walnut tree by my house but that every time we had an electrical storm the lightning seemed to want to climb in my window. He said, "Don't you know why you have that sensation?" I said, "No, why?" He continued, "The black walnut tree has a very large taproot [a central root that goes straight down into the ground], and it acts as a ground for electricity. When lightning flashes, it is conducted through the root of the black walnut tree in the ground."

Now I understand our text of today. As a Christian, I am to be a conductor of the radiant love of Jesus to those I meet. In order to be that kind of person, I must have my faith grounded deep in Jesus. That comes by a study of His Word and by talking with Him. If you have your taproot down deep in His love, Satan cannot move you with all His forces. Ask Jesus to help you to be rooted deep in His love, your only safety.

THE LESSER LIGHT

And God made two great lights; . . . the lesser light to rule the night. Genesis 1:16.

The moon has been one of the most fascinating objects of man's attention. For many years man had the desire to go to the moon. People were almost certain there was no life up there, yet there were many unknown things about the moon that had intrigued them, so they continued to search for a way to get there. We know that the United States finally put men on the moon on July 20, 1969. Did this great feat take away the curiosity man had concerning the moon? Some, but not all. Scientists still do not know all about the moon. From God's Word we know why the moon shines. The moon reflects the light of the sun. God made it to rule the night.

As we study the moon and God's Word, we see that the moon has a specific purpose. It was created by God to light up the night. The moon also controls the tides in the ocean. It has a very important part to play in our world.

The moon reflects the sun's light, so we as Christians should reflect the light from Jesus to others, that they might see Him in our lives. But is that all? No, it isn't!

The moon plays a secondary role to the sun, in giving light. Though the moon is number two, it still keeps reflecting and doing its job. In fact, it keeps working even when it cannot be seen. This tells me that I don't always have to be the "big shot" and get all the attention. I should do my assigned job willingly, even if it isn't a task that will give me attention or prominence.

What about you today? Will you follow the moon's example? By beginning the day with God—by reading the Bible, thinking about what we have read, and asking that the Holy Spirit control our thoughts and actions—we are placing ourselves where light from the Sun of Righteousness will shine on us. Ask God to help you reflect Jesus in your life today.

FISHERS

Behold, I will send for many fishers, saith the Lord, and they shall fish them; and after will I send for many hunters, and they shall hunt them from every mountain, and from every hill, and out of the holes of the rocks. Jeremiah 16:16.

In the northern part of the United States there is a fur-bearing animal called the fisher. These animals are one of the larger members of the weasel family and are known by several other names—fisher marten, pekan, black cat, and black fox. The fisher has a beautiful fur that is soft and silky. Around the neck and shoulders the tips of the fur are an attractive silver, which gives the fisher a grizzled appearance. Most fishers also have some small irregular white spots on the throat and underparts.

The males are 30 to 40 inches long, which includes a 13- to 15-inch tail, and weigh seven to twelve pounds. The females are about one third smaller and half the weight of the male. Fishers are opportunistic feeders and eat whatever is close by—plants and animals. Baby fishers are called kits, and in each litter there will be an average of three.

Wildlife experts are happy to have the fishers around. The State of Wisconsin imports them from other States because they help control the rabbit and porcupine population. While fishers like rabbit and porcupine meat, they also like squirrels, mice, some fish, and various berries, leaves, and buds. When they are hungry, they have been seen jumping from tree to tree like a squirrel, chasing a squirrel. They are quite agile in the trees but do not spend much time there. They prefer the ground and like living in hardwood forested areas. They are great hunters and roam over about a ten-square-mile area.

Jesus likened His kingdom to a large net. He wanted His followers to be fishers and hunters of men, going anywhere to find them and teach them of His great love for them. Thank Jesus that He has found you this morning. Ask Him to help you be a "hunter" for Him, and share His love today with a friend.

MOTH RADAR

If ye shall ask any thing in my name, I will do it. John 14:14.

Unlike butterflies, which flit from flower to flower and shrub to shrub during the daylight hours, moths are generally nocturnal creatures. Moths and butterflies belong to the same order of insects, but they are different. One of the main differences is the antennae. Those of the butterfly are bare and have a knob at the end, but the moth antennae are like graceful tapering filaments; on some species it looks like a feather.

The largest and most showy of all moths is the giant silk moth. Industrialists thought to use these to spin silk threads, but that idea caught on only in the Orient, not in the United States. These moths have a five- to six-inch wingspan. The life span of an adult is very short.

Like butterflies, moths go through a metamorphosis process, from an egg to a larva or caterpillar, to a pupa, and finally to an adult. The female will lay its eggs on the leaves or twigs of a specific species of plant, according to the species, because only these plants will provide food for the offspring. After she has laid her eggs she has completed her role in nature and dies of total exhaustion. She may have lived as a moth for only a few short days.

As a female silkworm comes out of either a ground burrow or a cocoon, she will emit into the air a chemical known as pheromone. This transmits a certain message to lonely males. From great distances they pick up the pheromone messages on their antennae and begin to fly in a systematic pattern, homing in on the female moth. And man thinks he created radar! When a male finds the female they mate; soon she is ready to lay eggs, and the cycle begins again.

When we are in need of help and call out to God, He will find us. If you desire Jesus to come and live in your life, ask Him this morning. He is listening for your call.

SUPERSEALS

Hast thou not known? hast thou not heard, that the everlasting God, the Lord, the Creator of the ends of the earth, fainteth not, neither is weary? there is no searching of his understanding. Isaiah 40:28.

Weddell (WED-ul) seals are remarkable creatures. They live the farthest south of any seal, in the Antarctic, and remain there the year round. They live under the Antarctic ice for months at a time. How do they get air? They keep breathing holes open by gnawing at the ice with their strong canine and incisor teeth, which are adapted for this purpose. The upper incisors extend forward and contact the ice before the canines.

During the summer the seals will go up on top of the ice, sun themselves, and give birth to their pups. This time in the sunshine is very limited, because the sun doesn't last very long in the Antarctic. In the winter, temperatures drop to about $-80°F.$ ($-62°C.$). If these seals stayed out in this temperature they would freeze, even with their fatty blubber insulation, so they live mostly under the ice where the water temperature is about $29°F.$ ($-2°C.$).

These creatures are called "superseals" because of their lifestyle in the areas where they live and survive.

Superseal pups have the shortest childhood of any large mammals. They are born from the mother seal right onto the ice. The pup begins to shiver, because the difference in temperature between the mother's body and the air is more than 60 degrees. The shivering not only shakes off the ice crystals that form on its body immediately, but also warms up the pup. Soon the pup begins to drink his mother's warm milk and grow. At six weeks the pup stops nursing and is shoved into the sea by his mother. She will swim near it and protect it, but soon it is on its own.

God has many secrets that man will probably never know or understand. There are many questions about the superseals that scientists have not found out. God knows the number of stars, and the number of hairs that we have on our head, because He is the Creator.

Thank God today for the knowledge He has allowed you to obtain and that you will obtain as you study.

BLUE-FOOTED BOOBY

To every thing there is a season, and a time to every purpose under the heaven. Ecclesiastes 3:1.

Blue-footed boobies are birds, very comical to any human watching. But of course to other boobies, they are perfectly normal. The blue-footed booby has large webbed feet that are light blue; that is how it gets its name.

There are six species of boobies. The blue-footed lives in colonies on islands, mostly along the Pacific coast of Central and South America. Boobies eat fish as their main food.

When there is an abundance of fish they begin their courtship dance. The males will point their long bills upward, extend their wings, and strut around. They will begin to dance a little. If a female becomes interested in a certain male she will join him in the dance, and then the courtship begins. Both of the boobies will stay close together and point their bills into the air, touch their bills, bow, and goose-step with their oversized blue feet. Those who have watched it say it is comical.

As the young hatch, the older boobies will catch fish and bring them to the babies. They will commonly fly about fifty feet or more above the water until they spot a fish, then they will fold their wings and dive into the water after the fish. They are so designed by God that just before they hit the water they can readjust their aim, arrange their wings in a streamlined fashion, and pierce the water like an arrow.

There is a time for everything. Boobies have a time for their courtship dance, and a time to fish. Many of us need to learn that there are certain times we do things and other times we don't. We must take time to survive spiritually every day, by taking some time with God's Word. Ask God to help you take time with His Word today.

215

KANGAROO RATS

And he said unto his disciples, Therefore I say unto you, Take no thought for your life, what ye shall eat; neither for the body, what ye shall put on. Luke 12:22.

The kangaroo rat doesn't worry about what he will drink, for he gets his water, just like all of the other pocket mice and rats, from the food he eats, which is mostly seeds. Kangaroo rats live in the Southwestern United States. They are basically hermits, in that they each have their own house away from other rats.

Kangaroo rats will build many tunnels in the ground and have as many as 12 entrances to their house. These rats will go out and gather up seeds, storing them in pouches in their cheeks. They may get hundreds of seeds before coming back and unloading. They unload the seeds in the tunnels, where they are continuously moved from place to place. The seeds are not only food but den humidifiers as well, both of which are necessary for survival.

These little creatures are about 15 inches long, more than half of which is tail. They have short front legs and long back legs like a kangaroo; that's where they get their name. Their tail is used to give balance as they jump. It has a nice bushy clump of hair on the tip. They have pale-yellow to dark-brown hair on top, with a white stripe along the side and down the tail, and a white underside.

The female will have her babies twice a year, and she will have from two to six in a litter. Naturalists say that the tunnel house becomes a nursery of infants, mewing like kittens. When they get angry they will thump the ground; that is a warning to stay away.

Kangaroo rats put most of their energy storing up food. God wants us not to worry about our physical needs. If our spiritual life is right with Him, He will take care of the rest, but most of us have so little faith that we don't want to trust Him that far. Tell God this morning that you want to trust Him. Then really and truly trust Him, and see what happens. You'll be surprised.

GLACIERS—RIVERS OF ICE

Out of the south cometh the whirlwind: and cold out of the north. Job 37:9.

I have always been fascinated by the glaciers in the mountains of North America. The Rocky Mountains in both the United States and Canada have some very large glaciers. As I walk out on them I have an uneasy feeling; I watch for cracks that are always present, somewhere. I don't want to fall into one.

A glacier is a interesting formation. It is usually in an area that has a lot of snow fall but a short melting period, such as at a high altitude. I wondered why those cracks or crevices were always present, and I found out. The ice of the glacier moves downhill. As it comes to uneven terrain the top of the glacier continues to move and the bottom slows down, so a split is formed. Scientists have discovered that the ice of the glacier moves faster in the center and slower on the edges.

As glaciers move downhill, they will flow at different speeds. When the glacier gets to a warmer zone, it melts completely and forms a creek or river. Since the weather is always cool where glaciers form and the summer short, the glacier doesn't usually disappear entirely. As the snow falls and builds up, the snow turns to ice, and this accumulates. Many of the North American glaciers may be between 200 and 300 feet deep. They usually form in valleys where they are protected, but they may spill down into open areas as they move and melt.

It is interesting that even in Bible times prophets wrote about the cold coming from the north. In the Northern Hemisphere, cold still comes from the north. The farther north you go, the colder it is. The farther south, the warmer it gets, until you get to the southern part of the Southern Hemisphere; then it gets cold again.

God's love for us is never cold or hot. It is always the same temperature, and He invites us to take advantage of His love. He will do much for us, because He loves us. Tell Him how much you love Him this morning, then show Him throughout the day, by the things you do, that you really do love Him.

RUBIES OF THE BOG

I pray for them: I pray not for the world, but for them which thou hast given me; for they are thine. John 17:9.

When the Puritan pilgrims landed on the eastern shores of North America in 1620, the Wampanoag Indians presented them with some small red berries as a goodwill gift. The pilgrims had no idea what these berries were called or how to use them, but they accepted them in good faith and planted them. In June of that year, the pilgrims noticed that the berry vines were covered with pale-pink flowers that made the vines look like they were sprinkled with powdered sugar. Up close, the flowers looked like the head of a bird called a crane. So the Pilgrims named the berries "crane-berries." It wasn't long until the name was shortened to cranberry, and that is what we call them today.

Cranberries need to grow in a sandy soil, with peat on the surface, where the sun does not get too hot and where some snow comes in winter to cover the vines and keep them from freezing. Unless the plants are well pollinated, they will not produce well. The growers discovered that by bringing in bees to pollinate the plants, they produced better. Of course, the bees liked the cranberry flowers and made good honey.

In the year 1816 Henry Hall began to take an active interest in farming the cranberries. From that point they really became famous. Many others started farming them, even in Oregon and Washington.

It wasn't until Jesus took a special interest in this world and decided to come here that we were given the hope of a new life. If He had not taken this special interest in the world, we wouldn't be here this morning. Thank God today in your prayer that Jesus took a special interest in you, so that you could have a new life for all eternity.

WATER MONITORS

Behold, I will bring it [Jerusalem] health and cure, and I will cure them, and will reveal unto them the abundance of peace and truth. Jeremiah 33:6.

In the countries of China and Malaysia, one of the food delicacies of the people is the water monitor, which is a lizard. The people like the meat; they broil, grill, stew, fry, smoke, and curry it. The skin is much desired for purses and other leather goods, as it is very fine and soft.

Drum heads and small stringed musical instruments similar to the banjo are also made from the skins. Some have been used by the tribal people for hundreds of years. The tonal quality of this lizard skin is considered to be very good—superior, in many cases.

These lizards are also used for medicinal purposes in witchcraft and other healings. People eat the meat because of the superstitious belief that "strength" and "heat" come from it. The gallbladder is dried, and a tea is made from it that is supposed to help with heart and liver ailments. The body fat is mixed with herbs and sold as a balm for a variety of illnesses. Because the monitors get few diseases and seem rather healthy most of the time, the natives believe that eating the meat can bring strength and health to them.

In the country of Sri Lanka, some people believe that one can be killed by administering a concoction of human blood and hair mixed with monitor oil and flesh.

We should be thankful today that God is a God of love and that He has given us the proper things with which to take care of our bodies. He has told us that our bodies are His temple and that we should take care of them. As Christians we need the love of Jesus. We don't get that power from eating meat but from "eating" His Word. Thank God today that there is power in His Word to give us health.

219

FLASHLIGHT FISH

But blessed are your eyes, for they see: and your ears, for they hear. Matthew 13:16.

In the Caribbean waters, between the United States and South America, there live among the coral rock, fish that have lights on their heads. These have been properly named "flashlight fish."

The first one of these fish was found in 1907, floating on the water near the island of Jamaica. The second one was found in 1972 by Mexican fishermen. Scuba divers reported that they had seen these from a distance, but no one came close to them in their natural habitat until 1978. At that time a team of four divers went down more than 200 feet in the Caribbean.

These divers dove at night, in total darkness. As they approached the 200-foot mark, they knew they would be able to stay that deep only about ten minutes. Suddenly they saw the headlights of a Caribbean flashlight fish. They immediately surrounded it. Using the fish's own tactics, they shown a light on it and began to take pictures.

The Caribbean flashlight fish are very timid. They live at depths of 100 to 600 feet. They can turn the light fixtures on their head off and on, as desired. If in danger they will zigzag through the water, turning on the lights when they "zig" and off when they "zag." The brightness of their lights is about that of a dull pen-sized flashlight.

In the Red Sea and Indo-Pacific area there are two other species of the flashlight fish. During the Six-Day War in 1967, an Israeli night plane spotted a green glow near the water's edge in the Red Sea. Thinking it was from underground Egyptian frogmen, they threw hand grenades into the water. The next morning there were dead flashlight fish all over the beach. A green glow still showed from their tiny eye pouches.

God has given us spiritual eyes as well as physical ones. He expects us to use these spiritual eyes to find His truth and all the counsel He has for us. Thank God today that He has given you spiritual eyes whereby you can see the "light of truth."

JUMPING KIDS

Let them [false gods] rise up and help you, and be your protection. Deuteronomy 32:38.

The Rocky Mountains, from Alaska southward, is home for the American mountain goat. These white-haired creatures live on the steepest slopes and precipices that exist anywhere. They do this for safety and security.

They generally move in herds, except during the birthing season. At that time a female, or nanny, will leave the herd and pick out a crevice to stay in. Within a day or two she will give birth to her kid. This little kid, about the size of a human baby, eight to nine pounds, will be up and around soon, trying to jump and frolic. The legs aren't that stable yet, but the kid will try, anyway. The nanny will stand between her kid and the edge of the cliff so that if it does something "stupid" she can be there to keep it from falling.

The kid will nurse at first, but on the second or third day it will try to join its mother in eating vegetation. In about a month it is weaned and eats only vegetation. After about two weeks from giving birth, the nanny is eager to join the herd. She will take her kid along with her. Meanwhile the kid has learned to jump from one jagged rock to another one but the nanny is always near to protect and help junior.

Sometimes the larger, older adults in the herd will try to push the younger ones out of the way. But for about ten or 11 months their mother is always nearby. During the winter's heavy snows about half the new kids will lose their lives, as the temperature and snows are too cold and too deep for them. They weigh only about 40 or 50 pounds, and have very little fat. The first winter is rough on the new kids.

In our text for today, Moses indicates that false gods cannot protect Israel. But God could. As the nanny protects her kid, so God will protect His "kids." He loves His family and will go all out to protect them from the enemy. Ask God this morning to protect you from your enemy, the devil, today.

221

MARVELOUS EYES

For since the creation of the world His invisible attributes,
His eternal power and divine nature, have been clearly seen, being
understood through what has been made. Romans 1:20, N.A.S.B.

Who could make something as complicated as a human eye?
Men have tried to duplicate it. A camera lens is similar to the
human eye. There are certain things that happen in an eye that
ophthalmologists (eye specialists) can repair, but they cannot
create a new eye. When an eye goes bad, many times it has to be
removed and a glass eye put in.

God did a masterful job in creating eyes. Sight can be broken
down into four parts: (1) ability to detect light from darkness,
(2) ability to detect movement, (3) ability to detect and make
out forms, and (4) color vision.

It is fascinating to note that not all creatures' eyes are the
same. An owl has very keen eyesight at night. That is when it
hunts for food. The earthworm has two eyespots for sensing
light. An amoeba senses only light and darkness. Spiders have
a simple eye structure that allows them to see objects at a close
distance. Flies have fantastic eyes, and dragonflies probably
have the most complex eyes in the animal kingdom. Reptiles see
well and have very keen vision. Birds have the keenest vision of
all creatures, as a whole. Some vultures can see a "meal" on the
ground from 4,000 feet in the air.

Dr. Les Thornburg, an optometrist from Durand, Wisconsin,
says, "We will probably never be sure of what other animals
see. . . . But one thing seems sure: . . . Every animal sees exactly
what it needs to see." That is just the way God created all of His
creatures, different for a purpose.

I'm glad we have a loving, caring God who created us with
tender loving care. He thought of everything. Thank Him in
your prayer this day for the way He made you and the life you
have from Him.

WARMTH FROM THE SUN

Ye have sown much, and bring in little; ye eat, but ye have not enough; ye drink, but ye are not filled with drink; ye clothe you, but there is none warm. Haggai 1:6.

Butterflies are interesting little creatures as they flutter, float, and glide from flower to flower and from tree to tree. Researchers tell us that the different kinds of butterflies react differently to the warmth of the sun's rays.

Most butterflies fold their wings straight up over the thorax (body) so that the wings almost touch, some hold their wings completely open, and other species hold them at various other angles. The butterflies bask in the sun to absorb the needed heat to be able to fly, and the angle controls the amount of heat they receive in the thorax.

The body temperature of butterflies cools off very rapidly. Some butterflies cannot fly more than about three feet without having to stop and get more heat. The larger butterflies can fly for greater distances because of the larger thorax, which does not cool down so soon. There are some that can fly in the shade, especially in the heat of the jungles of South America.

To be able to fly, all butterflies must have a temperature between 82° and 105°F. About 50 species need to have their bodies heated up to about 95°F.

I'm sure that many of you have gotten up on a cold morning and, still in your pajamas and with your teeth chattering, have gone over to a fireplace, stove, or heater, and rubbed your hands together and said, "This heat feels so good!" After a few minutes of warming you feel that you can function, so you get dressed and go to school.

The butterflies need the warmth of the sun to keep flying, and we as Christians need the warmth of God's love to function properly in our Christian life. This warmth is received by a close relationship with Christ, by studying God's Word, by praying to Him, and by sharing Him with others. Ask God to send the warmth of His love to you today.

SPIDERS

But glory, honour, and peace, to every man that worketh good. Romans 2:10.

Many of us react negatively to spiders because we are afraid of them and don't really understand them. Most spiders are harmless but helpful creatures. There are more than 30,000 species of spiders, only a few of them harmful. Spiders are useful in that they gobble up insects by the thousands. That saves our health, our crops, and maybe our dispositions.

Spiders are not insects, because they have eight legs and only two body parts. They all have "jaws" with fangs at the tip. Venom runs through the fangs into the victim's body to kill or paralyze. Most spiders have eight eyes, situated in two rows. Others have fewer eyes, and those living in caves have no eyes at all.

All spiders spin silk, which comes from glands in the abdomen. The fluid passes through little organs called "spinnerets" at the tail end of the creature and solidifies into tiny threads when in contact with the air. These threads have many uses. Some spiders weave webs to catch food. All spiders put out single strands of silk called draglines that are used as lifelines for the spiders to move from one place to another or escape from enemies. Many spiders make bags from their silk to deposit their eggs in until they hatch. Spider silk is used by some spiders as transportation. They will let a strand loose in the air until it bears them aloft, then hang from it and drift with the air currents from place to place. This is called "ballooning." One report said that a spider was seen floating on a silk strand more than 200 miles out at sea.

God created each of us different. Each of us has our way of doing things. I praise God for our individuality. There are characteristics that all spiders share, and there are characteristics that each of us has. You can be creative and, with the help of God's Spirit, develop your own way of growing spiritually. Ask God this morning to help you be creative in your life so you can be "you." He will help you and you will be surprised at how creative you can be in your religious experience.

GREAT THINGS
FROM SMALL BEGINNINGS

And the earth brought forth grass, and herb yielding seed after his kind, and the tree yielding fruit, whose seed was in itself, after his kind. Genesis 1:12.

Acorns are the fruit from more than 100 different varieties of oak trees in the United States. Historians tell us that up until the Middle Ages many Europeans ate acorns. There are still some Europeans who eat them today, but Americans rarely include them in their diet. The Europeans discerned that if the leaves of the oak tree had rounded lobes, which indicated that they were the white oaks, the acorns were sweet. If the leaf lobes were pointed, they belonged to the red or black oaks and the acorns were bitter.

Acorns come in many sizes from the size of a pea to about the size of a large purple grape. In some species, such as the over-cup and laurel-leaved Oak, the acorn can barely be seen in the cap, while in the California white oak the acorn protrudes out of the cap about one and a half inches, with the cap just barely covering the base.

Acorns are eaten by deer, squirrels, woodpeckers, raccoons, wood ducks, turkeys, and bears. Acorns have many nutrients in them that provide good food for the animals that eat them as the main part of their diet. There are so many animals and birds that eat acorns that most of them do not grow into trees.

God has put into the tiny acorn, the entire growth systems necessary for a large oak tree. The tiny acorn has the potential root, trunk, branch, and leaf systems in the embryonic state. God put everything necessary in the acorn for the seed to sprout and make a big tree.

God has equipped us with special senses to help us learn about Him and know Him better. He hopes we will use these senses to become strong Christians and not be detoured by Satan. Use your senses today to know God and learn more about Him. Remember, you, too, can grow into a big and powerful Christian with God's help.

MASKED BANDIT

Be ye all of one mind, having compassion one of another, love as brethren, be pitiful, be courteous: not rendering evil for evil, or railing for railing: but contrariwise blessing; knowing that ye are thereunto called, that ye should inherit a blessing. 1 Peter 3:8, 9.

In the world of nature our text this morning reminds us of the raccoon. Raccoons are playful little creatures. They have compassion one for the other and do not seem to be revengeful toward each other. They are mischievous, but not normally harmful.

Raccoons are found almost anyplace you go in the Americas. Although many raccoons have been killed for their skins, they seem to flourish anyway. In fact, they are in overabundance today. If there is anything that they can get into, they will. They can open doors, pull out drawers, get into refrigerators, and into just about anything to get at food or something else they want. Where we lived in Massachusetts, it was difficult to keep them out of our garbage cans. I would tie the lids on, and they would untie the rope and get in.

A female raccoon may have two to seven "kits" in her litter, but usually four. She will nurse them for a short time. She carries them by the back of their neck from place to place until they are able to go on their own. Raccoons may wet their food before eating it to wash off sand or grit or unpleasant skin secretions. A female coon will attack her enemies if they are out to bother her kits. Coons will eat eggs from nests; they will also look for crayfish and snails or other small animals and fruits. Sometimes they will playfully bat the food around with their paws before eating it.

God wants us to enjoy life, like the little raccoon. One way to do that is to be kind to one another. I know it is hard, when your brothers or sisters fuss at you and your schoolmates call you names, but try being kind to them and see if it doesn't pay off. Our text says that you will receive a blessing. Ask God to help you be kind today and see if you don't receive a blessing. It may not come immediately, but it will come.

DEEP-SEA TALK

And when they went, I heard the noise of their wings, like the noise of great waters, as the voice of the Almighty, the voice of speech, as the noise of an host; when they stood, they let down their wings. Ezekiel 1:24.

There are many voices and movements in the depths of the ocean communicating to other creatures a message. Some of these noises and movements are addressed to their own kind, and sometimes they form messages for other creatures.

Marine biologists have discovered that fish actually use vocal sounds or other noises to communicate. Soon after the start of World War II, the U.S. Navy developed a device that could pick up noises under the water; they wanted to use this for tracking German submarines. When they tested the device they heard a lot of snapping, barking, grunting, and clicking. It was discovered that these noises came from fish communicating with one another.

Fish do not have vocal cords but they are able to make a variety of noises by flexing the muscles attached to the swim bladders, causing them to resonate like a drum. The male damselfish makes a staccato chirplike noise in the courtship ritual. Groupers make a thundering sound as a warning.

Fish also have a way of communicating without making a noise. The way they dart or swim may be a message to other fish or intruders. Other fish make other movements and their neighbors know that it is "chow" time. Let's explain this one. Some fish are "cleaned" by other smaller creatures, such as the small wrasses and cleaner shrimp. When the big fish wants a cleaning, he gives a signal such as head down and tail up, or the other way around. It could also be by raising the left pectoral fin and holding it straight out, like the big fish wanted to make a left turn. At these signals, the different creatures rapidly swim to the motioning fish and begin to clean it by taking off the dead skin, cleaning out the teeth, and grooming off the parasites.

In our text this morning, the noise of the angels was heard by the prophet as he saw them in vision. We may not hear the words of Jesus audibly, but He does speak to us. Thank Him this morning that He is interested enough to speak to you through His Word.

PUPFISH

For ye are bought with a price: therefore glorify God in your body, and in your spirit, which are God's. 1 Corinthians 6:20.

"There is a delicate ecological experiment going on, and the fact that it is God's rather than ours is all the more reason to surround it with barbed wire." This was a statement by Pete Sanchez, a natural resources specialist with the U.S. Department of Interior. Mr. Sanchez was referring to the Devil's Hole pupfish, near Ashland, Nevada.

It seems that some small fish called pupfish were marooned since the Flood in a little spring-fed pool about 20 miles from Death Valley. These little creatures have had a difficult time surviving as they are in a very tiny pool. According to some ichthyologists (scientists who study fish), this species of pupfish has no commercial or aesthetic value. Because the species is found only in this small pool of water, it has been placed on the U.S. Government's endangered species list.

Mr. Sanchez has erected a chain-link fence around the pool to keep people out. At last count, in 1977, only 350 fish were found. They grow to a length of only about three quarters of an inch, and they have no pelvic fins.

A group of real estate developers wanted to develop this property and sell the lots, but they could not do so because the development would have destroyed the pools where these and other species of pupfish survive. If they had been destroyed it would have meant a year in jail for the developers. The U.S. Government has spent $5.5 million to develop a wildlife reserve to save these few hundred little pupfish because it was felt they were valuable. The developers had hoped to sell the lots marked out in the development for about $420 million. Imagine spending $5.5 million to save a few small fish!

There is a high value placed on our lives by Jesus. He gave His life, dying on the cross that you and I might be redeemed from sin. Thank Him today for that sacrifice that purchased you back for Him.

PRAIRIE, PAMPA, SAVANNA, STEPPE, VELDT

And I will send grass in thy fields for thy cattle, that thou mayest eat and be full. Deuteronomy 11:15.

What is nicer than a prairie, pampa, savanna, steppe, or veldt? What are all of these places? They are the same, just different names in various languages for an area that is a treeless grassland. Prairie is English, pampa is Spanish, savanna is African, steppe is Russian, and veldt is Dutch. The prairies are in the United States, the pampas in Argentina, the savannas in Africa and the veldts in South Africa, and the steppes in Russia.

People have asked the question for years, what makes a grassland? Why no trees? It is believed that the bison had much to do with there being no trees on the prairies of the United States. As the small tender shoots of trees came up, the bison ate them or trampled them into the ground, so they didn't grow. But though they ate the grass also, and trampled it, it continued to grow. Scientists think elephants are doing the same thing in Africa by pushing down trees to eat the foliage.

Grasslands are homes for many varieties of wildlife. Many birds live in the grasslands. Those that cannot nest in trees because there aren't any, use the grass or ground as nesting areas. Many rodents and other smaller animals live in the grasslands and burrow into the earth for their homes. Large animals and birds also live in some grasslands. They eat the grass as the main part of their diet. Hundreds of species of insects also claim the grasslands as their home. They live on the grass, in grass clumps, and in the ground. These creatures also provide food for the other inhabitants of the grasslands.

Jesus created the grass on the third day of Creation. It was to be for food and to beautify the earth. Can you imagine how ugly this world would be if it weren't for green grass? Thank God this morning for the beautiful grass that covers the ground.

PLATYPUS

Lift up your eyes on high, and behold who hath created these things, that bringeth out their host by number: he calleth them all by names by the greatness of his might, for that he is strong in power; not one faileth. Isaiah 40:26.

For years scientists spent time in categorizing different types of creatures so that the study of God's creation would be easier. They recognized categories such as birds, mammals, amphibians, fish, et cetera. When they thought that they had covered every area and had things well organized someone called their attention to a creature that lives in the streams of Australia and Tasmania. This creature defied all of their categories; they could not fit it into a group. The creature is called the *platypus* (PLAT-uh-pus); sometimes it is called a "duckbill."

Why is this creature so different? It has fur like a mammal, a snout and webbed feet like a duck, a flat tail like a beaver, and venomous sharp spurs like a rooster on the hind legs of the male. It barks like a dog but it lays eggs like a bird, instead of giving birth to live babies. Actually, the platypus is a mammal, because it does nurse its young with milk.

The leathery bill of the platypus is used to find crayfish, worms, and other small creatures at the bottom of the streams. Platypuses do not have teeth so they chew their food with two horny plates on each side of the jaw. They are about two feet long, including the tail.

When the eggs hatch, the mother platypus will use her tail to hold the young close to her, as they have no fur. This helps to protect them and she can nurse them at the same time. They will stay hidden in the nest for a period of several months. The male has the poison glands; as enemies approach, he will scratch with his spurs and poison them.

God created many varieties of things for our enjoyment. Thank Him today that He created you different from all of the other creatures. You were made in His image.

THE MYSTERIOUS WIND

The wind bloweth where it listeth, and thou hearest the sound thereof, but canst not tell whence it cometh, and whither it goeth. John 3:8.

Have you ever wondered where wind comes from? I did, for many years. In fact, I really never understood much about the wind or weather until I was studying to become a pilot. Then I learned that wind is caused by an uneven heating of the air around the earth by the sun.

Wind is still mysterious. We can feel it but we cannot see it. Even though it is somewhat mystical, it still is refreshing to humans and other creatures on a hot day. In its strongest force, wind can bring destruction.

No doubt at one time or another you have seen the destructive results of wind. Trees have been blown down, houses have been lifted off their foundations and moved to another spot, automobiles have been lifted up and taken off the street or highway, ships at sea have been turned over and sunk. Strong winds have caused high waves that have been very destructive to coastal areas. Wind has blown many airplanes off course, and if the pilot or navigator was not watching carefully, the plane may have missed its point of destination or hit against a mountain and crashed. Although wind has caused much damage, we can't control it.

In our spiritual lives we feel the winds of temptation blowing. They get stronger and stronger as the devil and his angels tempt us. Jesus invites us to come to Him. He will calm the troubled sea of our lives with His almighty hand. Ask Jesus in your prayers to be with you during this day, to help keep you in His love, away from the winds and storms of temptation. He's waiting; just ask Him.

LIVERWORTS

Behold, there is a people come out from Egypt: behold, they cover the face of the earth, and they abide over against me. Numbers 22:5.

There are plants that cover many areas of this earth that we call mosses, but actually they are liverworts. They are closely related to the mosses. The liverwort gets its name because in the early days people thought that since the small leaves looked like the human liver, the plants must be good as a cure for liver diseases.

The liverworts usually grow in cool, shady areas or near water. There are some varieties that actually grow in water. Liverworts are valuable to mankind, especially where there is bare soil, because they will take root and prevent soil erosion.

The main part of the plant is called the *thallus*. Underneath this leaflike part there are little rootlike projections that absorb water and minerals, which the liverwort needs to stay alive. These rootlets also hold the plant to the rocks and trees.

On the liverwort thallus, or gametophyte, there are male and female organs that help in one method of reproduction of the plant. The male cells are called antherozoids and the female cells are called eggs. The antherozoids swim through the moisture on the surface of the plant over to the eggs; as they meet, the egg is fertilized. The fertilized egg then grows into a tiny new structure called the sporophyte. This sporophyte lives on the thallus and in time begins to produce spores, which are the tiny seedlike bodies that make new plants. Thus, they alternate. The gametophyte produces sporophytes; the sporophyte produces gametophytes. As these tiny spores grow, more and more earth is covered.

As the liverworts cover the ground, so the children of Israel were covering the land of Moab, and King Balak was fearful. A day will come when the world will be fearful of God's remnant church and they will do what they can to destroy it. At that time, as always, you and I must be ready and faithful to stand up for our beliefs. Ask God to help you be ready every day until Jesus comes.

A TENTACLED
NEUROLOGY LABORATORY

*Let this mind be in you, which was also in Christ Jesus.
Philippians 2:5.*

In early June, as the sun begins to warm the coastal waters
around Cape Cod, Massachusetts, a group of Atlantic squid
arrive from out on the edge of the continental shelf. These squid
are about a foot to a foot and a half long. They swim in a darting
fashion. There are literally tons of these creatures.

At the same time about 50 scientists also arrive at Cape Cod,
to continue their research on the squid. Through scientific
investigation, scientists have discovered that the squid has a
central nervous system similar to that of higher orders of animals and of humans. These squid have nerve fibers that are
larger than any other creature, even man, and therefore they are
easy to dissect and study.

The researchers who study the nerve cells of the squid are
trying to find answers to many human nerve problems. Many
people are afflicted with one of two diseases of the central
nervous system, Alzheimer's disease and Lou Gehrig's disease.
Alzheimer's disease involves a progressive senility in which the
victim forgets, gets disoriented, and eventually loses the mind.
Lou Gehrig's disease involves the deterioration of the motor
nerve cells that serve the body's major muscles; the victims lose
control of their muscles.

Squid make an excellent resource for researchers who are
looking for cures to these two diseases. The researchers are able
to inject drugs and do many other things with the large nerve
fibers of the squid. By the time this project is finished, scientists will have studied axons from about 15,000 squid under
powerful electron microscopes in the laboratories at the Wood's
Hole Marine Biological Laboratory.

I hope that these scientists find a cure or treatment soon, as
I have had relatives and friends die from these diseases. God
wants us to have good, sharp, keen minds. Thank God this
morning that you have a good, keen mind.

CROSSBILLS

Your Father knoweth what things ye have need of, before ye ask him. Matthew 6:8.

Crossbills are a unique kind of bird. Do you know where they get their name? The bottom and top parts of the beak cross over each other. The bottom part curves upward and the top part curves downward; thus they cross each other. The two parts of the beak do not come together and match like they do on most nonpredatory birds.

The male crossbill is red like a cardinal, and the female is dull olive gray. They live in the northern part of the United States and Canada. These birds have a gizzard that is a special part of the bird's stomach. Hard foods, such as seeds, are ground up in the gizzard with the help of sand or gravel. A gizzard does the same job for the bird that our teeth and jaws do for us. It is necessary for birds to eat sand and small pieces of rock.

One person reported that a whole flock of crossbills came down onto the chimney on his house in Montana and began to peck away at the mortar between the rocks of his chimney. They may have been looking for sand for their digestion and calcium for their bones; most mortar has calcium in it. The ground was completely covered with snow and these crossbills probably couldn't find any sand or small gravel except in mortar.

How do these birds stay alive in winter? Fir, spruce, and pine have cones with nuts inside, and the crossbill with its special beak can pry out nuts that most other birds cannot.

God provides for the needs of the crossbills, and He will also provide for you and me. He has told us that He will supply all our needs. Tell God what you really need today in your life. Thank Him for His provisions to you thus far.

LARGE ANIMALS

Behold, God is mighty, and does not dispise any; he is mighty in strength of understanding. Job 36:5, R.S.V.

Probably all of you know about the elephant, rhinoceros, hippopotamus, cape buffalo, and lion. You may have thought that everything was great in their life in Africa, but that is not so today. All of these animals, except the lion, are herbivores. They eat plants and grasses. As the countries in Africa continue to develop and more people are added, the conflict grows between the people who want the land to live on and farm and these large animals that need so much land to eat from.

For example, an adult elephant eats more than 500 pounds of foliage a day, or about 80 tons a year. This elephant will need about one square mile of savanna to fill its need. In Kenya alone, the elephant population needs about 225,000 square miles to feed on. Rhinos also need a lot to eat. If farmers come into their area to farm, the rhino will tear up the crops and maybe even the farmer.

Then there are the hippos. They need about 130 pounds of foliage a day, yet they cannot be too far away from water because if they become overheated they will die. If a farmer comes into a hippo's territory, the hippo will just make himself at home on the farmer's crops. The cape buffalo also eats a lot of grass. One buffalo will eat about 50 pounds a day, or about nine tons a year. All in all, what these four large eaters need is space, and the humans are taking up that space. Some game preserves are now in existence but they cannot accommodate the large populations of these animals. What will the future hold?

We know who holds the future in His hands. In the New Earth God will have many animals and they will have no problems in finding food. Ask Him today to take care of the needs in your life. He will be glad to do it, if you ask Him.

HYDROTHERMAL VENTS

I know thy works, that thou art neither cold nor hot: I would thou wert cold or hot. Revelation 3:15.

A group of scientists were working on the Pacific Ocean near the Galágagos Islands, close to the west coast of South America. They were dragging through the water a camera and thermometer about 8,600 feet down. They were looking for hydrothermal vents, a place where hot water comes out of the ocean floor. They had heard of such but had never discovered any. All of a sudden the thermometer shot way up. The boat was stopped and three scientists went down in a little minisubmarine called *Alvin*. They found the hydrothermal vent, and around it strange-looking creatures called tube worms.

Apparently what happens, according to the scientists, is that the cool ocean water is sucked through openings in the ocean's floor. It passes over hot rocks near the earth's core and this hot water then comes streaming back up through other vents in the ocean's floor. The water takes on a black appearance and the hot stream is called a "black smoker," resembling the lava from a volcano.

As this water goes from cold to hot and goes through a portion of the earth, it picks up some chemicals and forms a chemical "soup." As it flows upward out of the earth this soup is affected by bacteria in a process called chemosynthesis. In the process the bacteria convert the compounds of the "soup" from carbon dioxide into the organic molecules that make up carbohydrates and sugars. Did you understand all that? It is just a process of making food by bacteria.

Scientists believe that there is heat inside this earth. "There is fire there," they say. God wants us as Christians to be on fire for Him so He can use us. Unfortunately many of us are cold and say nothing to anyone about our love for Jesus. Ask Jesus to help you be "hot" for Him today.

HALOPHYTES

Salt is good: but if the salt have lost his savour, wherewith shall it be seasoned? It is neither fit for the land, nor yet for the dunghill; but men cast it out. He that hath ears to hear, let him hear. Luke 14:34, 35.

Did you ever hear of "pickleweed," "Palmer's grass," and "saltwort"? I never had until I read about a research project that has been undertaken by the University of Arizona's Environmental Research Laboratory. Researchers there are trying to grow food plants in salt water or salty soil. Such plants are called halophytes.

In the United States about one twelfth of the land is unusable for agricultural purposes because of the high salt content in the soil or because there is salty water close to the surface of the soil.

There are many sandy and salty areas that could produce many varieties of halophytes. The researchers who are working on this project say that the output of these plants is from two to three times that of those that grow on regular farming soils.

Some halophytes exclude most of the salt at the roots by means of semipermeable membranes. Some plants absorb salty water and the salt is secreted by special salt glands on the leaves. Others absorb the salt and deposit it in the stems and leaves. But when the third type absorbs salt water, it clogs up the feeding system.

Pickleweeds can tolerate salt, but they grow better where it is less salty. Palmer's grass, which grows in the northern estuaries of the Gulf of Mexico, drops seeds that are eaten like peanuts; this grass does not absorb salt. Saltwort traps salt in the cells in the leaves so that it cannot escape. One good thing about halophytes is that their leaves are 14 percent protein, the same percentage as in alfalfa.

God wants us to be the salt of the earth so that we will season our environment with the sweet savor of His love. Ask Jesus this morning to help you season someone's life with the richness of your life, through the power of the Holy Spirit.

PLAYING AROUND

When I was a child, I spake as a child, I understood as a child, I thought as a child: but when I became a man, I put away childish things. 1 Corinthians 13:11.

Researchers are discovering that the younger creatures in many of the mammal and bird families play games. You have no doubt seen dogs, cats, and other animals play with each other. One pup will jump and play with another pup. One kitten will jump at and play with another kitten. In many instances, when they don't have one of their own kind to play with, they will play with another kind of animal.

A few years ago the youth camp I was directing was given a baby coyote and a baby raccoon. These two baby animals were raised in cages side by side. From time to time the nature director would take them out of the cages and put them together. They would jump, roll, and tumble, and bite each other, all in fun. They were real pals and had many friendly brawls. Shotgun, the coyote, and Ringo, the raccoon, grew up together and were not afraid of each other.

Monkeys run and chase each other. Little lambs run, jump, and twist their bodies. Horses run and kick up their hind legs. Even birds dive on each other and struggle. All of this play among the animals and birds, researchers tell us, is to help the animals and birds mature. As you boys and girls play games, you are learning how to get along with one another.

The apostle Paul, in our text today, is saying that when we grow up we put away childish things. As juniors you no longer act and play like a baby. Soon you will act like teenagers, and then like adults.

As we become more mature in our Christian life we are able to read and study more difficult Biblical passages. As our minds mature we understand and act differently.

Pray today that God will help you recognize the needs for your age, and that as you grow you will be more mature in your decisions for the Lord.

THE RIGHT WHALE

Now the Lord had prepared a great fish to swallow up Jonah.
And Jonah was in the belly of the fish three days and three nights.
Jonah 1:17.

In the Argentinean waters between Buenos Aires and Tierra del Fuego is an outpost called Patagonia. This is a great place for people to study whales. The whales that come here in most abundance are the right whales. Yes, this is their name. It is not just correct, it is "right." These whales grow up to sixty feet long and may weigh forty-five tons, or about 90,000 pounds.

Right whales come to the gulf waters of the Peninsula Valdes, where they mate and have their calves. Whale watchers have counted about 700 coming there year after year, but they have identified only about 500. These have individual characteristics so that they can be picked out as regular visitors each year. The identifying characteristics are color and irregular growth patterns on the head.

The whales begin to arrive in July or August. They just loaf around, swimming in the gulf, until the calves are born and they have mated again. The gestation period is 12 months for these whales. The whales will swim around the warm gulf waters of Patagonia until about December, and then they head out to sea. No one has been able to follow them so the scientists are not sure where they go, but they think that they may go down to the Antarctic waters.

These whales move with a gentle grace in the water. When they wish to rise to the surface of the water, they do so with such ease that they display neither speed nor strength. In musical terms, if the dolphin is the staccato (fast moving and lively), the right whale is the basso profundo (slow-moving and dignified).

God doesn't always move fast to display His speed or strength. He moves in His own way, in His own time, to do that which He knows is best for us. Thank God this morning that even though He may not move fast, yet He does show His strength to ward off Satan.

LIKE A MERMAID

And one of you say unto them, Depart in peace, be ye warmed and filled; not withstanding ye give them not those things which are needful to the body; what doth it profit? James 2:16.

Many years ago a strange creature surfaced in the water south of Florida and scared some fishermen. They could not imagine what type of animal or creature it was because it had its baby clutched to its chest. It had only one swimming flipper on each side, and its body tapered into a single large flat tail, with no hind legs or flippers. What the men were looking at was a manatee, a water mammal that lives in the warm waters from Florida to eastern South America. The fishermen said that it looked like a mermaid, and that is what many people have called the manatee.

Manatees are not harmful mammals. They can easily be trained but in the wild they don't like to be too close to humans. They have a long face that in some ways resembles a large dog, but their face is full. They have big cheeks, and whiskers growing out from them. They eat the flowers, vines, and other aquatic plants that grow so profusely they clog up the waterways in Florida. The manatee is a natural waterway cleaner.

Manatees seem lazy during the daytime. They just float in the water with their heads and tails down, only part of their backs showing. They eat mainly at night. The female gives birth to her baby right in the water. She then takes it to the surface for about 45 minutes. Then she will start to submerge it in the water a little at a time, until it gradually gets used to the water. Later, the baby will learn to eat and nap like the mother, with the head and tail in the water, and look for food at night. Adult manatees are from eight to 15 feet long and weigh from 500 to 1,300 pounds.

Like the manatees, who need warm water to stay warm, we need a close relationship with Jesus to stay warm. He wants us to have that relationship with Him, and to join each other in this delightful experience. Ask God this morning to help you feel the warmth of His love and those with whom you associate today.

PYGMY CHIMPS

So God created man in his own image, in the image of God created he him; male and female created he them. Genesis 1:27.

Pygmy chimpanzees are found in only one part of our world—the rain forests of Zaire. Researchers claim these small chimps are as close biologically to human beings as any animal can be.

Bonobos (bo-NO-bos, another name for pygmy chimps) are very playful. They are also intelligent and easily taught. In an experimental zoo close to Atlanta, Georgia, researchers are working with these chimps to teach them to "talk" by means of symbols. They make little grunts and noises, but it is impossible for them to talk.

Blood tests run on these pygmies show that they all have the same type of blood, Type A, like some humans. These chimps have genetic material that is 99 percent identical to humans.

Bonobos have rounder eyes, smaller ears, and less protruding jaws and brows than common chimps. They inhabit a rain forest in Zaire that is very difficult to get to; however, developers are starting to bring housing and industry to their habitat.

Pygmy chimps move through the trees with great ease, swinging, leaping, and diving from one branch to another with more acrobatic maneuvers than the common chimps. They are also more sociable. Pygmy chimps eat fruit and leaves as well as the stems from some plants. They like to share their food with each other. They don't seem to be "piggish" with their food. They are very protective of each other, especially of the young.

I am happy that in the beginning God created animals and man. I'm happy I know I didn't come from a chimp, but from the Creator's hand. Thank Him today He created you.

MIMICRY

And be not conformed to this world. Romans 12:2.

In southern Arabia, there is a butterfly called the milkweed butterfly or plain tiger. This butterfly resembles the common monarch butterfly that is seen in many parts of North and South America.

The milkweed butterfly has rich, honey-brown colored wings on top with jet black tips on the forewings, slashed by a prominent white bar. These colors and the slowness of flight that leave the wings open for easy visibility are a warning to birds not to eat it. Why? The milkweed butterfly is poisonous! In its caterpillar stage it feeds on milkweed plants, which to most other creatures are poisonous, but not to this caterpillar. As the caterpillar pupates and turns into a butterfly the poison from the milkweed plant remains in its body. Most birds, through God-given instinct, are aware of the poisonous nature of this butterfly and leave it alone.

A second butterfly in southern Arabia is called the eggfly butterfly or diadem. The male diadem has jet-black upper wings with white egg-shaped spots bordered by brilliant purple; the female is an almost perfect copy of the plain tiger butterfly. Although the diadem butterfly is not poisonous, the instinct of the birds tells them to keep away from it, because it resembles the poisonous plain tiger butterfly. This look-alike trait among animals is known as "mimicry."

Today it seems to be the "in" thing to live a lifestyle like the others in the world. Many young people are really not interested in being different; they want to live as their non-Christian friends do. After all, why be different? If your friends know you want to be a Christian, they will make fun of you or ignore you, so it is easier to mimic their language and lifestyle and not be different or made fun of.

As Christians we should be different! Our lifestyle is not to mimic the worldly lifestyle. People will be able to tell that we are different by our lifestyle, and when asked, we can tell them why. Ask God to help you not to conform to the world and its lifestyle but to follow Jesus and His lifestyle.

NATURE'S MURDERERS

Thou shalt not kill. Exodus 20:13.

As we look at God's natural world around us, we are saddened to see how it has been altered by sin. God's original plan was perfect but jealousy and selfishness have caused all of the problems that we have today. The root cause of many murders is jealousy.

Unfortunately, the natural world has not escaped this terrible ordeal. Many of the lovely creatures that God created have become murderers. This is not a very pleasant subject to talk about yet we must face the issue, as this is reality. For many years my wife has had a little cartoon on the refrigerator door. It shows a family with all kinds of problems. The caption says, "You can't switch channels; this is real life." So it is.

Except in the search for food, most animals are not killers, but there are a number that are. The reason is usually jealousness. Interestingly enough, in most cases it is the male of the species that does the dirty work.

What a sad state of affairs, that animals cannot be happy either. Some of the most docile animals, such as certain species of monkeys and baboons, will kill swiftly and fiercely. Jealousy is a real threatening situation for the males that have harems. Other males want to be "king" among the females, so they challenge and fight the dominant males.

God never intended His world to be so upset. All was created in peace and harmony. This world will not get to that state again until Jesus comes back to this earth. In your prayer this morning, ask God to help you make this world as nice a place as possible. Ask Him to help you not to be self-centered or jealous today, but to be a peaceful person. Show your friends what Jesus can do in the heart of one who invites Him to come and live within.

CALIFORNIA SEA LIONS

Look on every one that is proud, and bring him low; and tread down the wicked in their place. Job 40:12.

Just off the coast of southern California are some islands called the Channel Islands. For years these islands have been the special habitat for many thousands of species of ocean creatures. One of the animals that has survived well is the California sea lion. These creatures grow to about eight feet for the bulls and about six feet for the females. Adult bulls weigh about 500 pounds and the females about 300 pounds.

Every summer as the bulls come swimming into their island paradise, they stake off their territorial claim. Most of them want to be close to the water, so the early comers have the advantage and stake off the beach claims first. The reason that beach property is preferable is that as the females come swimming in the large bulls can get their early attention and a good choice of mates.

The bull sea lions fight with their large teeth. They try to tear the skin of the opponent and drive it away. They may bleed profusely, but usually they are not seriously hurt, because they have a lot of blubber under the skin. As these bulls fight, they raise their heads in the air. Scientists think that this is a special act. In experimenting with a sea lion, a scientist noticed that when he was lower than the sea lion, it attacked. When he stood up and was thus taller, the sea lion did not attack. It is evidently a matter of pride, a "status symbol," for the sea lion to hold his head as high or higher than that of his opponent.

Sea lions have very poor eyesight; they depend on smell and hearing for safety. When their calves are born the mothers start to bellow, in sea lion talk, and the others answer back. Mother sea lions will swim with their babies, and bellow to them as they swim. This is how the mother keeps the calf safely beside her.

Jesus doesn't want us to be proud of ourselves or our accomplishments, but He does want us to be proud that we are Christians. Ask God in your prayer to help you be proud to be a Christian today, as you talk with your friends.

OWLS

For he will render to every man according to his works: to those who by patience in well-doing seek for glory and honor and immortality, he will give eternal life. Romans 2:6, 7, R.S.V.

Owls are most active at night. They have eyes that allow them to see up to 100 times more effectively than a human can in dim light. They can also turn their heads nearly 270 degrees, which is three fourths of a circle, but they cannot move their eyes up and down or sideways in their sockets like you can. The owl has to move his head to see objects around it. A barn owl can hear sounds ten times fainter than you can, therefore it can easily catch a mouse in the barn in total darkness.

The flight feather of the owl's wing are soft, and the fringed edges of these feathers help the owl fly quietly to unsuspecting prey by muffling the noise of air passing through. An owl will attack a skunk from behind, sinking its razor-sharp talons into the head of the skunk. Thus the skunk will not have a chance to spray its smelly chemical on the owl. This smelly spray of the skunk wouldn't make any difference to the owl, anyway, since it doesn't smell very well.

There are about 250 different species of owls in the world. They range in size from the five-inch elf owl of Central and South America to the 30-inch great gray owl. Owls are good to humans in that they destroy many small pesty rodents that become problems to us in many ways. I enjoy hearing the hoot of an owl when I am out camping in the woods, because I know that a nightwatchman is on duty.

Jesus made the owls, as He did all of the other creatures, and He gave them instincts to know how to survive. God has given to each of us talents. Maybe we could use some of these talents to know and understand Him better. By sharing Jesus' love with our friends we are able to give the devil a "surprise attack." Ask God this morning to help you invite a friend to accept Jesus today as his or her personal Saviour.

TOY DEER

Fear not, little flock; for it is your Father's good pleasure to give you the kingdom. Luke 12:32.

Out on the Keys (small islands) off the coast of Florida lives a tiny deer called the toy deer or key deer. When fully grown, these deer are smaller than a Great Dane dog. A fawn's hoofprints are about the size of a human thumbprint. The only place where these small white-tailed deer can be found is on the Florida Keys.

The deer were being treated roughly by humans and were fast disappearing. An 11-year-old boy decided he would do something about it. In 1949 this lad, named Glenn Allen, wrote a letter to President Truman asking that land be set aside as a refuge to save these toy deer. He wrote to members of Congress and to newspaper editors asking for their help. Residents of the Keys didn't want to give up their "precious" land for deer, so they tried to block the establishment of a deer refuge.

Eight years later, when Glenn was 19, he really went to work on his project. He got others involved, and in 1957 Congress passed a bill creating the National Key Game Refuge. People who live on the Keys today are friendly to the little deer. There are only about 400 presently in existence.

When Columbus sailed to the New World for the fourth time, they landed on a Key, and one of the sailors went exploring. As he tramped through the thick tangle of palmettos he saw a small deer staring at him. In the ship's journal he described this toy deer as a "great wonder." Glenn Allen and his friends also saw these toy deer as a great wonder and were successful in preserving their lives.

Jesus has promised to give us a "refuge," too, as we are His little "great wonders." Thank Him for that promise He gave in our text today. Trust in Him; He'll never fail you.

SAHARA DESERT

The wilderness and the solitary place shall be glad for them;
and the desert shall rejoice, and blossom as the rose. Isaiah 35:1.

The Sahara Desert is famous for its great heat and dryness. From 2 to 3 million people inhabit this desert, which covers more than a third of the northern part of Africa. Water is very scarce, but in this great expanse of land there are some beautiful places called oases. Since each oasis can support only a few people, the men go into the northern cities and find jobs. With the money they earn they buy things and take them back to their homes in the oasis. Water comes from deep wells. The main source of power for pulling the water out of the wells is the donkey. When the water has been drawn it is put into animal-skin bags and taken to the house and stored.

In the month of July the sun passes directly overhead, dividing the day into two equal 12-hour periods. With the intense midday heat, the farmers go to their farms early in the morning and return about ten o'clock. Then they take a long siesta and rest until the late afternoon worship time.

The desert dwellers have to continually battle to keep the wind from piling up the sand in their oasis. Each family has a house that is made of mud and cement. The houses are built around a courtyard, which helps protect the people from the blowing sand. Each room has a door that opens into this central courtyard.

Most oases have date palms growing around them. The dates are eaten, and the wood is used for pole rafters in the houses. The dates are harvested once a year, and each tree may yield more than 100 pounds of dates. All of the water used to irrigate the date palms must be carried from the wells.

What a joyful event it will be when Jesus returns and remakes this earth. These barren and desolate places will be beautiful again, like they were before sin entered. Thank God this morning for His restorative power, and ask Him to help make you a kind and friendly person today.

TRILLIUMS

And after three months we departed in a ship of Alexandria, which had wintered in the isle. Acts 28:11.

Winter is a long drawn-out season to many people, especially those who live in the cold and snow. They have to fight it for many months. There are many winter sports enthusiasts who feel that winter is not long enough, but in many areas of the world, winter is not a welcome season of the year.

During the winter months there are many things that slow down and almost stop because of the cold. Many plants and animals become dormant during the winter, while some just slow down their activity. Others seem to prepare for the spring and summer that will come. There are many people like that, too.

One of the plants that I especially like to watch for as the snow begins to melt is the trillium. To me trilliums are some of the most beautiful flowers that exist, and they start to bloom as the snow leaves the ground. They have been preparing for this moment.

Trilliums belong to the lily family. I am aware of six or seven varieties of trilliums. The one that I was describing that comes out, even in the last remnants of snow, is the snow trillium. It has beautiful white petals. All trilliums bear single flowers with three petals, three sepals, and six stamens, and there are three whorled leaves on the stem.

The reflexed sepal and the sessile flower trilliums have purplish-brown petals. The large-flower variety has large white petals that turn pink with age. The Gleason's trillium has a long stem and bends down, but should not be confused with the nodding trillium. Walpole's trillium also is purplish, but has cream-colored stamens.

Paul and his fellow travelers waited out the winter in Malta, then proceeded on their journey. Trilliums wait out the winter, then perform in all their beauty, demonstrating God's love for life and beauty. Many times in our Christian experience, we run into a winter experience where all seems bleak and dreary. God invites us to come to Jesus; He will brighten and beautify our day. Ask Him this morning to bring the beautiful "spring" into your life, that you might radiate like the beautiful trillium.

CAPE BUFFALO

For what is a man advantaged, if he gain the whole world, and lose himself, or be cast away? Luke 9:25.

Although the Cape buffalo of Africa would like to graze or loll around, probably more hunters have been killed by this creature than any other animal in Africa. The Cape buffalo is a large animal and has never been tamed. The Cape buffalo has horns that start in the center of the forehead and take a downward swoop, then curl back up in a half circle.

These buffalo cannot exist more than two days without water, so they stay fairly close to water. They eat lots of grass, green or brown. In a herd of buffalo there will be several large dominant bulls. Occasionally a young bull will try to take a place in the herd. He will confront a dominant bull and there will be a lot of clashing of heads and horns, but it lasts only a short time. The loser will just quietly walk away. The females usually stay with a herd all their lives.

The buffalo calves are the beneficiaries of this communal society of the Cape buffalo because they grow up in the herd and stay with it generally throughout their lifetime. Male buffalo spend hours each day lying around soaking in the mud. They don't toss and move around like the hippos, elephants, or rhinos; they just lie there. They do a lot of their feeding at night and do not want to be disturbed. If danger approaches, the males will lie in wait and charge at the last minute. Because of this, many hunters have been killed. Lions have a hard time killing the Cape buffalo for food. It takes several lions to bring one down, and then they may not succeed.

Cape buffalo protect their own and act as though they own the whole world. Jesus has told us that we may gain the whole world and lose our own soul. Ask God to help you not to put your trust and hope in the world today, but in Him. Put your emphasis in God's kingdom and His righteousness.

249

THE INSECT WORLD

For I am not ashamed of the gospel of Christ: for it is the power of God unto salvation to every one that believeth. Romans 1:16.

There is good news and bad news about insects. Let's start with the bad news first. Insects bite, sting, invade clothes closets and eat clothing, eat wooden buildings, and eat wool carpets. They invade the food and flour bins, cookie and cracker boxes, and so many other things. They sound bad, right? Half right. The other half is good news.

Insects provide honey for us to eat, silk to make clothing from, wax for candles and polish, and shellac for wood finishing. They pollinate many crops, which provide nutritious food for our tables. Much of this would not happen without insects. They are also food for other creatures. Just by existing they help make our world more interesting and beautiful—some of them, that is.

More than 800,000 insects have been classified, and every year scientists tell us that they are still discovering thousands. Someone estimated that there are still from 2 to 5 million insects to classify.

Insects are different from other creatures in that they have six legs, three main parts to their body, antennae and many have wings of some sort. Spiders, ticks, centipedes, and mites do not fit into the insect category because they do not have the identifying characteristics. Insects have the head, thorax, and abdomen as the three body parts. The head has the antennae, eyes, and mouth parts. The thorax is where the six legs attach, as well as any wings. The tail section or abdomen is the digestion and reproduction center.

In our world there are millions of people, only a small part of whom have been classified as Christians. There are many in the world who need to be classified as Christians. They need someone who is not ashamed of the gospel to help them be identified as a Christian. Someone needs you to share God's love with him or her today. Why not ask God this very morning to help you identify a person in need today, and share God's love with that person.

LEECHES

For it is the life of all flesh; the blood of it is for the life thereof. Leviticus 17:14.

For years leeches have been charged as being bloodsuckers, and most of them are. But some of the 650 known species of leeches live on larvae of different insects, worms, and snails.

Leeches are found all over the world. Generally we think of them as living only in the warmer climates. But actually more leeches have been found in Antarctic waters than in the tropics. They are also found from sea level to more than 12,000 foot elevations.

Roy Sawyer, a research scientist from the University of California at Berkeley, was on an expedition in French Guiana. As he was stomping through the swamps looking for leeches, he found the kind he had been looking for: an 18-inch-long Haementeria brown leech. Ecstatic, he brought two back to the laboratory for experimentation. The researchers named one "Grandma Moses" because she produced 750 offspring in three years. These large leeches can lay up to 200 eggs three times a year.

In his research Sawyer has discovered that leeches are gluttons. They will fill themselves so full of blood at one sucking that they can live for four to six months without eating again. Four or five good-sized leeches can drain the life out of a rabbit in about 30 minutes. In the Middle East there is a species of leech that attaches itself inside the nostrils. When Napoleon's army entered the Sinai in 1815, they failed to heed the Jewish Talmud, which specifically warned about drinking water from open ponds. The lives of many of Napoleon's men were lost because of leeches attaching themselves to the nostrils of the soldiers. The British suffered the same fate in World War I, just 100 years later.

God has given us life through the blood that runs in our veins. Jesus gave His life that we might have a new life for all eternity. Thank Him for His life today.

GANNETS

In the Lord put I my trust: how say ye to my soul, Flee as a bird to your mountain? Psalm 11:1.

The gannets are interesting birds, considering their takeoff procedures and nesting habits. There are six North American colonies of the northern gannet, and twenty-four colonies in Great Britain, Iceland, and France.

The gannet is a beautiful white bird with black wing tips. The young adults have black specks on their wings until they reach about 4 or 5 years of age. These birds usually mate for life. When they arrive at the colony nesting grounds they become very excited as they seek their mate. They will dance around with their bills in the air and rub their bills and necks together. The neighbors are easily offended, and they peck the arrivals with their bills.

The gannets are skilled fishermen. Both of their eyes are on the front of their heads. They can see fish swimming in the water from more than 100 feet up, but the normal height that they fish from is about 50 feet. As they spot a fish, they make a dive, and when they hit the water, the water may spout up into the air in a ten-foot spray. For the gannet, the dive is cushioned by air-filled cells beneath the skin. These cells are mostly around the birds' necks and shoulders and are connected to and controlled by the lungs.

Gannets make their nests in the colony and will come back to the same nest year after year. After the single egg is laid, both the male and female will sit on the nest to incubate it. The male will probably spend more time than the female, though. When the egg hatches, after 42 days, both parents will fish and feed the youngster. As the parents come to the nest they will open their beaks and the young will stick their heads inside and eat the regurgitated fish.

As the young gannets put their trust in their parents, so we, like David, should put our trust in God. He will take care of us, even better than the parent gannets. Thank God this morning for His loving care and protection.

REAL FRUITS

Ye shall know them by their fruits. Do men gather grapes of thorns, or figs of thistles? Matthew 7:16.

One of the joys that we have here on this earth is to eat delicious, juicy fruits. Each fruit has its own flavor; it is very rare to have two fruits taste alike. Did you know that there are fruits that do taste alike but don't look alike?

In the large country of Brazil in South America, many types of bananas are grown. There is one banana that is called the *maçã* (ma-SAH) or apple banana. If you close your eyes and ignore the texture, thinking only of the taste, you would think you were eating an apple.

A few years ago our family had a reunion in the Hawaiian Islands. Thirteen of us traveled in two station wagons. As we were driving down the highway we came around a curve in the road. There before our eyes were large bushes with small white flowers on them. Mingled in with the small white flowers were big bunches of red flowers. I couldn't believe what I saw. I had never seen anything like that before. I slammed on the brakes of the station wagon and pulled to the side of the road. I jumped out and took some pictures with my camera. I wanted to take a closer look, so I went over to the big bushes to investigate. Guess what I saw? Someone had taken clumps of big red flowers from one bush and had wired them in among the small white flowers of another bush. What a letdown! But it was still pretty for the holiday season.

Jesus said that people would be known by their fruits. He meant that as people look at the life of another person they can tell if he or she is a Christian. If a person is a Christian he will be doing things that a Christian should do. He will not be going to places where he knows a Christian should not go. He will not use language he shouldn't use. He will not eat and drink things a Christian should not. He will not act like a person who doesn't follow Jesus. As your friends and teachers observe you today, will they know that you are a Christian? Ask Jesus right now to help you act and talk like a Christian today.

CHESTNUTS

For, behold, I create new heavens and a new earth: and the former shall not be remembered, nor come into mind. Isaiah 65:17.

For many years chestnuts were an important food, not only in the United States but in Japan and Europe. In the early 1900s chestnut wood was used in many industries in the United States.

Telephone poles and fence posts were made from chestnut trees because they were not only rot-resistant, they also grew tall and straight. Chestnut trees grew from 70 to 100 feet tall and three to four feet in diameter. The northeastern part of the United States was the most populous area for chestnut trees; more than 25 percent of all trees in that area were chestnuts.

It is presumed that in about 1904 a shipment of Oriental chestnuts may have contained a blight. The blight began to spread until most of the East Coast trees were contaminated. The blight later spread to Europe; it is believed that it arrived there aboard a shipment of mine timbers about the year 1917. It was not discovered in Italy until the 1930s; by that time a large portion of the trees there were already infected. Since then, Italian and American scientists have been working on trying to stop the blight.

The largest stand of chestnut trees is now in the State of Michigan, along the shores of Lake Michigan. The blight continues, but scientists and interested citizens are trying to keep it from spreading. It may be a losing battle, but they won't give up.

Sin has really made a mess of God's creation. Just think how good this world would have been without the blight of sin. Jesus has told us that He is preparing a new world that will be without sin. Ask God today to help you be faithful so you can see that new world, where everything will be beautiful and perfect.

CAMOUFLAGED

Thou shalt hide them in the secret of thy presence from the pride of man: thou shalt keep them secretly in a pavilion from the strife of tongues. Psalm 31:20.

For many little animals and birds, color is a means of survival. If God had not made them with the colors He did, they would not be able to live very long. God thought of everything as He created this earth, and I am amazed more and more as I continue to study His creation.

The variety of colors that God used was more than accidental. Camouflage was one purpose that God had in giving colors to some of His creatures. Let's look at a few this morning.

The ground-nesting American woodcock blends right into the dead leaves upon which it builds its nest, lays its eggs, and incubates them. It is very difficult to see the hen sitting on the nest. The eggs, and later the chicks, are also colored like the leaves. A perfect blend. The baby deer, as many of you know, has a light reddish-brown color and spots. As it lies down or meanders through the woods the colors and spots blend into the environment.

The American bittern has a long neck. As it stands among the cattails, stretching its neck and pointing the bill straight up, its coloration blends in with the cattails; neither predators nor the fish it eats can tell it is there. Some moths look like the leaves or bark of a tree. It is very difficult to tell them from the tree, they look so much a part of it. The same is true of some lizards and also a number of insects, such as the walking stick, which has the color and looks of a small twig.

God has planned that these creatures use their colors and shapes to camouflage themselves for life. God has promised to protect us from the enemy, too. I invite you this morning to kneel down and thank God for His protection, and ask Him for it especially today.

LEMURS

At the same time came the disciples unto Jesus, saying, Who is the greatest in the kingdom of heaven? And Jesus called a little child unto him, and set him in the midst of them. Matthew 18:1, 2.

A fascinating little tree creature that I want to introduce to you is the lemur. Lemurs are related to monkeys, and there are many species of them. The name means "ghost." They range in size from that of a rat to a medium-sized dog. They have faces that look like a raccoon or a fox and they all have a soft fur in various colors to mark the species. Some of them are white and black like a skunk; others are a reddish brown like that of a small fox, and others are like opposums, monkeys, and koalas. They also make a funny little "oink" like the pig.

These creatures are native to the large island of Madagascar. An unfortunate thing is happening there; the dense forests are being cut down for lumber and farms, and that is taking away the natural habitat of the lemurs. Basically they are tree creatures and eat leaves, fruits, insects, birds, eggs, reptiles, and other small forms of life. Some of them are active at night and others are active in the daytime.

The lemurs are family-oriented. As soon as the young are born, both the mother and father take care of them. They are very solicitous and guard them very carefully. To the parents, the baby lemur is very important. One writer said that the young are the center of their attention.

The disciples of Jesus wanted to know who was the greatest in the kingdom of heaven, because they were interested in having that position. The Bible says that Jesus took a little child and set him in the midst of them. That, my young friend, is what Jesus thinks of you. You are very important to Him and to your family, too.

Ask Jesus in your prayer today to help you be the kind of a young person that you know you should be. You might hurt Jesus in something you do today that He would not approve of, but He will still be by your side to help you when you stumble and fall into sin. Ask Him for help, and He will fulfill His promise.

NUDIBRANCHS

For the wrath of God is revealed from heaven against all ungodliness and wickedness of men who by their wickedness suppress the truth. Romans 1:18, R.S.V.

More than 2,500 species of nudibranchs, or nudibanks, commonly called sea slugs, are found in the ocean waters around the world. Although slow in movement, the nudibranchs can be vicious to their prey. They thrive in the sea world that is populated by faster, larger, and better-armed creatures. Nudibranchs are mollusks and are related to snails, oysters, and clams but they do not have a shell.

Ocean nudibranchs are not a dingy gray like their cousins found in your gardens and yards. They have bright and beautiful colors, and vary from species to species. Some of them are a bright orange, purple, red, and yellow. They have been nicknamed "butterflies of the sea."

All nudibranchs are predators. They feed on sponges, anemones, jellyfish, and sometimes on each other. As they attach themselves to a yellow or orange sponge, they take on the pigmentation color of the sponge. One species that eats jellyfish will attach itself to the body of the jellyfish and begin to turn blue or purple. It will eat away on the body of the jellyfish until it is all gone. Unlike most predators of the jellyfish, the nudibranch eats the stinging cells as well, and later may use these stinging cells, incorporated into the cells of the cerata, for its own defense against another predator. Scientists have not been able to understand how they do this and have no ill effect.

Jesus warned us not to spend too much time with people who are not good, for we might become like them. He wants us to be, not like other people but like Him. As His children we should show love and kindness toward others. Although the nudibranchs live to consume others, Jesus wants us to love and live to help others. Ask God this morning to help you not to be like the nudibranch, adapting to someone of the wrong type, but ask Him to help you be a good influence on others, with a Christlike attitude and character. It will work if you ask Him to help you.

HONEY ANTS

According as he hath chosen us in him before the foundation of the world, that we should be holy and without blame before him in love. Ephesians 1:4.

There is a species of ants called honey ants. These ants get their name because they collect a sweet nectar from galls. A gall is an enlarged ball that is caused by a wasp laying her eggs on a branch or in a crotch of the tree. Droplets from the galls ooze out and the honey ants greedily suck up this "gall sugar."

These ants have a "honey stomach" to carry this gall sugar back to their colony where it is stored by another amazing group of these ants called honeypots. These are special worker ants that are actually storage tanks for nectar that is brought in by the other worker honey ants. These special "tankers" hang from the ceiling and act as the "pantry" for the colony. Their abdomen stretches until they swell to about the size of a grape. Should they fall from the ceiling to the ground, which happens quite frequently, they burst as they hit.

When winter arrives and nectar is not available from the galls or yucca plants, the other ants will stroke the honeypots with their antennae and the honeypots spit up nectar, a little at a time, until they are empty.

Early Indians in the United States and Mexico used to dig down into the nests of ants, find the honeypots, and use the nectar for food and to treat diseases. In Australia the aborigines dig up the honeypots and bite off the nectar-filled abdomens for the sweet nectar.

No one knows how the "honey tankers" are chosen to be the nectar tanks. They are called for a very special task and they fulfill that task.

Jesus has called us to be His children. As all children have tasks at home, so He has given us a task—to share His love with others and to be loving. We have been chosen by Him. What a privilege to be chosen by Jesus. Thank Him today that He has chosen you to be His child.

MALLEE FOWL

Hide them in the dust together; and bind their faces in secret. Job 40:13.

One of the most bizarre creatures in Australia is the mallee fowl. These birds are ordinary-looking birds, but they are very different from any other bird. About the size of a chicken, the mallee fowl male will rake thousands of pounds of sand into a giant nest, which is probably among the largest of all nests. They are a wonder of the animal world.

In the Australian desert where the mallee fowl lives, the temperature may vary as much as 40 degrees between night and day. Therefore the mallee fowl must build a nest for the young that is well insulated because the eggs must be kept at a constant 90° to 96°F.

The mallee fowl male will dig a hole in the sand about three feet deep and six feet across. Leaves and sticks are raked into this hole, which will become an egg chamber. Next comes the insulating layer; thousands of pounds of sand, twigs, and leaves are scraped over the egg chamber. By the time the nest is built it may cover an area of about 16 feet across and be three feet high.

Although the nest is ready, the female has to wait for the right time. A tunnel has been made to the egg chamber but it is temporarily closed. Then the rain comes; the nest gets wet and begins to ferment, and the debris begins to heat up. The male will keep the female away until the temperature is just right. He has a heat-sensitive membrane in his beak. When all is right the female uses the tunnel to go inside and lay her eggs. The male watches over them to see that they are kept at the right temperature. Seven weeks later the eggs hatch. The chicks have to dig their way three feet up to the surface. They may never see their parents.

The wicked will be hid in the dust but God wants His children to live forever. He takes care of them, and at the right time He will come and get them and take them to heaven. Ask God in your prayer this morning to help you be ready for that "right time" when He will send Jesus back to this earth to get you and His other children.

WOLVES

And in thy seed shall all the nations of the earth be blessed; because thou hast obeyed my voice. Genesis 22:18.

A wolf howl may be a bloodcurdling sound that makes shivers go up and down your spine, but the howl is actually the wolves' way of communicating with each other. A howl is a song of the wolf. It may be a song of reunion, of membership in a pack, the wolf's family unit. The howl often assembles members of a pack before a hunt, provides communication during a hunt, and reassembles the group following a hunt. Howling also serves as a warning to outsiders that a specific area is being occupied by a wolf or pack.

Wolves are the largest member of the canid family. The average wolf weighs from 50 to 75 pounds. Some of the males may reach 100 pounds or more. The largest wolf ever reported was in Alaska and weighed 175 pounds. The males may stand two and one-half to three feet at the shoulder and be four and one-half to six feet long. Wolves live about ten to 12 years.

Wolves are highly intelligent and very sociable. They enjoy each other's company and at times they depend on each other to help hunt for food. Play activity is important to wolves. They will run together, tumble, "bite" lightly, and play tag.

In each pack there is an "alpha" male and female. These are the leaders; the other members of the pack submit to them. There is also a number two male, called the "beta" male. It assists the leader, leads the way on hunts, and breaks the trail through the deep snow in the winter. He is sort of the "field commander." The beta male leads the way in all activities.

Our conscience is like a "still small voice" telling us what we ought to do. Jesus talks to us through this still small voice. Do we listen to it and obey it? As the wolves listen to each other, we should listen to Jesus. Tell Jesus this morning that you are willing to listen to His voice as He guides you in your life. You'll be glad you did. As God blessed Abraham, He will bless you.

POPCORN

Thou visitest the earth, and waterest it: thou greatly enrichest it with the river of God, which is full of water: thou preparest them corn, when thou hast so provided for it. Psalm 65:9.

I don't read where the people of the Bible knew about popping corn, but the early settlers in the United States used all types of corn, and they may have even popped corn. Popcorn is different from ordinary corn. Each kernel has a very hard covering. When the kernel is heated this cover keeps moisture inside and it turns to steam. When the steam builds up to the right amount of pressure, it bursts, or "pops," and you have popcorn! Good kernels will enlarge from 30 to 35 times their original size. Growing and popping corn is big business today.

Popcorn, like apple pie and baseball, has become known as an American specialty. Back in the Depression days of America, the late 1920s and early 1930s, there were many people who had very little to eat. Some of them grew popcorn and ate it. They would use it for breakfast cereal and eat it with milk. Some used honey or molasses and made popcorn balls.

Popcorn is produced by the millions of tons in the United States and shipped all over the world. Popcorn experimentation has developed strains of popcorn that when popped leave very few "old maids" (unpopped kernels).

Popcorn is a Saturday night tradition in many homes. It has always been very popular, and probably always will be.

We should be thankful to our Creator as He thought of His created sons and daughters and created foods that we could really enjoy. Thank Him today for the good things He created for your enjoyment because "God saw that it was good."

COLOR CODE

And I said unto you, I am the Lord your God; fear not the gods of the Amorites, in whose land ye dwell: but ye have not obeyed my voice. Judges 6:10.

God talked to the Israelites, but at times they wouldn't listen because they wanted to do their own thing. God communicated with them time and time again, by voice and other signs, but often they ignored His communications.

God has given fish in the depths of the seas the ability to communicate, and one means of communication is by color. God has given some fish the power to manipulate their color pigments, just like some lizards do. Scientists have discovered that just under the transparent scales of certain fish there are color-bearing cells. These cells contain such color pigments as red, yellow, and orange. There are some cells that are black, and some other cells that have a greenish or yellowish color. When these colors are combined they may produce a silver, white, or iridescent color.

The small male Siamese fighting fish signals its preparation for battle by increasing its color intensity. When it is backing away defeated, it dims its color. A species of fish from India actually fights with color. These fish will square off with each other then "fire" with their color by brightening it. When one or the other acknowledges defeat, it dims its color to a very pale hue and swims away. Groupers can use so many different colors in their communication and change colors so quickly that the species are very difficult to identify. Some fish can use from eight to 12 different colors to declare anger, fright, show aggression, or court another fish.

Fish take note of the colors they see because they usually mean something. We can hear the voice of God to us through His Word. Do we heed that voice, or ignore it? Ask God this morning to help you heed His voice; you'll be a happier person today.

ANOTHER SOLAR SYSTEM?

I Jesus have sent mine angel to testify unto you these things in the churches. I am the root and the offspring of David, and the bright and morning star. Revelation 22:16.

Astronomers say they have discovered another solar system and that there may be others out there, too. They cannot explain the true origin of the heavenly bodies, yet they are finding out many new and interesting things.

Large telescopes such as the one on Mount Palomar are good, but now with the new IRAS (Infrared Astronomical Satellite) telescope, astronomers have discovered a large halo around Vega, which is believed by them to be the beginning of a new solar system.

The IRAS is sensitive to heat. Vega is twice as hot and about 60 times as luminous as the sun. But there was something about it that was puzzling. Then the scientists discovered that there is a halo around Vega that has a temperature of −300°F. They estimate this halo to be about 15 billion miles across. Vega is only 27 light-years away from earth, or about 162 trillion miles.

Scientists have used Vega as one of the "standard stars" to calibrate their instruments by, but this new discovery has bewildered them. They have said that they do not believe this pebbled halo mass will condense and form other planets, yet they feel there are now many other planetary systems in our galaxy.

Millions of dollars are being spent to investigate the world of space. Although the Bible does not tell us all about the universe, we know that God created it, a concept that many scientists do not accept. Newer and more interesting discoveries are being made about our universe, and men are becoming more knowledgeable. I thank God this morning that Jesus informed the world that He was "the bright and morning star." Our confidence can be placed in Him for He has all the answers. Place your confidence in Jesus today.

THE GREENHOUSE EFFECT

While the earth remaineth, seedtime and harvest, and cold and heat, and summer and winter, and day and night shall not cease. Genesis 8:22.

When God formed the earth during the Creation, He did so with a purpose. Everything in this world had a purpose. God was the master designer, and everything He made had a reason for existence. Scientists today are trying to figure out what some of those purposes are. They are doing all kinds of experiments to find out how and why.

Recently there has been much scientific investigation about what is called "the greenhouse effect." Scientists claim that the temperature of the earth is changing, and they believe that it is because of the burning of fossil fuels (coal, oil, natural gas). They claim that the burning of these fossil fuels is emitting into the earth's atmosphere a lot of carbon dioxide. As this goes into the air it helps cause clouds and these clouds are holding in the heat. Within the next thirty to forty years, some say the earth's temperature may be increased by about four degrees. What these scientists fear is that with an increase of temperature the ice in the polar regions would melt, thus raising the water level in the oceans. That would cause mass flooding and much damage.

Carbon dioxide and water vapor allow the visible light rays to pass but absorb the infrared radiation. This causes concern to some of the scientists and meteorologists. They foresee this heat causing changes in rainfall patterns, which could upset the crop raising regions as well as the rain forests and desert areas. What they are saying is that something is going to happen, and we don't know what.

We as Christians know that this old world is not going to last too much longer, and we know that God has control of it all. We need not fear if we have our faith and confidence in God. He will protect us and see us through. Thank Him this morning for the promises that He has made that He will be with us always.

LEAVING THEIR MARK

And thine ears shall hear a word behind thee, saying, This is the way, walk ye in it, when ye turn to the right hand, and when ye turn to the left. Isaiah 30:21.

If read properly, tracks in sand, mud, and snow can tell a story or a situation. Animal tracks are interesting to follow. No doubt you have at sometime seen tracks and asked, "I wonder what kind of tracks those are?" Or you may have seen some other types of markings that made you ask, "What did that?"

As you walk through the woods you may notice different animal tracks or signs of some creature's behavior. Holes in trees tell us that certain woodpeckers were there. A large pile of pinecone scales might indicate the presence of squirrels. Lower branches of trees that have been trimmed of leaves would indicate that deer had eaten heartily during the winter, and blackened, pealed-off aspen bark might indicate elk had been there, since they like aspen bark. Animal tracks can indicate if the creature that made them was alone, in a hurry, stalking another animal, or just meandering along.

You may have seen a sign in a park or forest that read, "Take only photographs and leave only footprints." That means, don't pick or take anything from the area, and don't leave any litter behind you.

Once after a heavy snow had fallen, I stepped onto the veranda of my cabin and observed prints. They were from a single animal. The prints stopped at one point and I could see where all four feet had been placed. Then the animal made a circle and came back by where it had stopped. Examining the prints, I discovered them to be prints of a dog. Those prints told me part of a story but not all.

Each one of us leaves our mark on this earth, more than just a footprint. People can tell that we have been around. People knew where Jesus was or had been because He went about doing good. He left His tracks by the miracles He performed and the people He healed. Jesus set an example for us. We can follow His example and leave our identifying marks by thinking of others and helping where it is possible. Thank Him for His example and ask God this morning to help you find someone today whom you can help or encourage. Your identifying mark may be left somewhere today.

265

BIOLOGICAL TRICKERY

In the midst of the street of it, and on either side of the river, was there the tree of life, which bare twelve manner of fruits, and yielded her fruit every month: and the leaves of the tree were for the healing of the nations. Revelation 22:2.

From what researchers are finding, God has given methods of defense not only to many species of animal life, but it appears that trees also have been given some form of defense. Some call it biological trickery, and others call it the silent battle. Whatever it is called, it is fascinating.

It has been noted that among groves of trees only a few trees in each area had suffered from the gypsy moth caterpillar. These caterpillars chew through every leaf in sight, and strip the boughs clean. Observing that many trees escaped damage, scientists began to restudy what was happening. It had been felt that only weather, predators, diseases, and parasites controlled these insects. Scientists are now discovering that many trees and some plants fight back with an arsenal of toxic chemicals. These chemicals make the foliage almost impossible to digest, or so toxic that it kills the insects outright.

Some plants contain as many as eight toxins. Others change their toxin from year to year. In some groves of trees in Washington and New Hampshire, scientists discovered, by examining the tree leaves every few days, that when one tree was being attacked by some insects, the other trees began to produce toxins in preparation for the insect attack. The researchers have almost begun to believe that there is some sort of silent communication that goes on among the trees and plants.

One researcher said that "the whole point for the trees, is to keep the insect zigging when it should be zagging." What kind of mystical sense did God give the trees and some plants for their protection?

God's tree of life is for His people in heaven. It will have a variety of fruits on it, the leaves will be for the healing of nations, and they won't produce a nasty toxin. No doubt, you'd like to have the opportunity to eat the special fruits from God's tree. Ask Him this morning to help you live a Christian life, and you will be able to eat that uncontaminated fruit.

BUILT-IN BABY CARRIER

He shall feed his flock like a shepherd: he shall gather the lambs with his arm, and carry them in his bosom, and shall gently lead those that are with young. Isaiah 40:11.

Animals with a built-in baby carrier are called marsupials. Most of these animals have a pouch to carry their young, but a few have large folds of skin that do the same job. The country of Australia has the greatest number and widest diversity of marsupial animals. There are some 250 species around the world. The opossum is the only marsupial native to North America.

Marsupials are born at a very early stage of development. Then they have to climb, without help, into the mother's pouch, which is quite a job for such a small creature. For example: a baby marsupial mouse is about the size of a grain of rice, a koala about the size of a bumblebee, and a kangaroo about one inch long. The rear legs of these tiny creatures are not yet developed. With the sense of smell to give direction, they must use the power in their front legs to make the trip to the mother's pouch. The kangaroo baby, known as a joey, usually will stay in the mother's pouch for a period of about seven months before it is weaned.

Marsupials range in size from a mouse, less than five inches long, to the seven-foot kangaroo. Marsupials that have large pouches include the kangaroos, koalas, and larger American opossums. The Australian mulgara (mouse) has folds of skin. The Latin American rat opossums and the ant-eating Australian numbat have no pouches at all.

Some of the more common marsupials in Australia are the kangaroo, Tasmanian wolf, marsupial mouse, tiger cat, wombat, and marsupial mole. They do not all move the same way, as their sizes and shapes are different. Marsupial doesn't mean they look and act alike, only that they have a means of carrying their young in a pouch or fold of skin.

Jesus is a lover of His children, and He will carry them through trials and temptations. He is anxious to help us in this world of sin. Thank God for His heavenly care for you today.

WORMS IN TENTS

I am come that they might have life, and that they might have it more abundantly. John 10:10.

If you have some cedar trees in your yard, you have probably seen some small pointed web bags covered with parts of leaves and twigs in the trees. These belong to the bagworms. The cedar tree is the favorite tree for bagworms to put up their tents, but they use other trees as well. The female bagworm has special built-in tubes through which she can spit out the silklike fiber that makes the tent. As this silk is spit out and comes in contact with the air, it hardens.

The female bagworm lays many little eggs in her tent. These little eggs are pale yellow in color. Each egg hangs by a silken cord inside the tent and is housed in a cocoon made of a silken fiber that is spun by the mother bagworm.

As the winter gets colder, the little bagworm eggs stay nice and warm in their cocoon. In the late spring the eggs hatch into tiny caterpillars that chew their way out of the silk tent and crawl down the tree and onto the ground. Then they invade other trees and begin to make their own little silk bag. As the wind blows, these little bags are blown from one tree to another.

As the fall comes, the bagworms attach their tents securely to a branch and seal up both ends. This is the time for them to change into an adult. After three weeks, the male bagworms turn into small beautiful brown moths with hairy bodies and clear patches on their wings. The female never becomes a moth. The male flies to seek out a female, which he will find from a scent she gives off. When he finds her tent, he puts his abdomen into her tent and they mate. After she lays her eggs in her cocoon, she drops to the ground. In a few days both parents die.

Jesus loves us and allows us to live a life full of many activities. The winds of strife come and blow us from place to place, but we can come back to Him and attach ourselves to Him for security. In your prayers today, thank Him for giving His life for you that you might have a more abundant life.

ALL-STAR CAST

And I will make thy seed to multiply as the stars of heaven, and will give unto thy seed all these countries; and in thy seed shall all the nations of the earth be blessed. Genesis 26:4.

Besides the stars in the heavens, there are other stars that are numerous. They have multiplied so that they are all over the bottom of the sea. They are called starfish. There are more than 1,800 species of these sea stars. They are somewhat similar to each other yet different. Some of these sea stars are very small, only a fraction of an inch across. Then there is the large Pacific sunflower star, which measures two feet across.

Most of the sea stars have five arms, but some species have as many as forty arms. Starfish anatomy is very simple. It includes a hinged armorlike skeleton that covers the outside of the body, light-sensitive eyespots, and tiny tube feet carried in each arm. These tiny tube feet are what the starfish uses to move itself over coral reefs and the bottom of the sea. Many species of sea stars were created with duplicate vital organs in each of the arms. If an arm becomes separated, the starfish can grow a new arm and the broken arm can grow a whole new body if part of the central disc remains.

This is also true of the 2,000 species of brittle stars. They have many arms. If one of these breaks off, they grow new arms and bodies. Someone has jokingly labeled this the "arms race." They not only grow new parts but they lay several million eggs into the water and these become starfish.

Some years ago a group of fishermen, trying to protect their abalone and shellfish beds against the invasion of starfish, which eat them, caught as many starfish as they could and cut them up into pieces to kill them and save their shellfishing grounds. The fishermen threw these scraps back into the water. Little did they know that each of these pieces produced another starfish.

God's promise to Abraham was real. Abraham's seed, God's people, were to go to all ends of the earth. Today we find God's people in all parts of the world. Thank God this morning that you are part of His family and that one day soon you will be with Him in heaven.

TRUMPETER SWANS

I will call upon the Lord, who is worthy to be praised: so shall I be saved from mine enemies. Psalm 18:3.

The trumpeter swan is North America's largest waterfowl. One of these birds will weigh up to thirty-five or forty pounds and have a wing span of up to eight feet. Once a plentiful species in North America, their native homeland, they became almost extinct in the early 1900s. The Migratory Bird Treaty of 1918 saved these birds. Today, there are about 1,500 in the contiguous United States and Canada, and 8,000 in Alaska.

The trumpeter swan gets its name from the low-pitched trumpeting call it makes. The swans trumpet as they battle over their territorial domain. Unlike many other birds, a pair of trumpeter swans, which mate for life, requires a 30-acre lake, but some of these creatures desire more area. They do not like to be in close proximity to other trumpeters, and this may cause more problems as they increase in number.

They prefer to construct their nests on clumps of reeds. If reeds cannot be found, they will pull up cattails stalk by stalk and lay them on the water until they have their floating home. The female will then lay her eggs and incubate them until her babies hatch. Baby trumpeter swans are called cygnets.

Many years ago the trumpeter swan was hunted for its meat and feathers. The skin was used for powder puffs and clothing. The swans were considered very valuable commercially. Now they are considered a valuable creature to be protected because they are not plentiful.

Today, Christians are in the minority on this earth. Seventh-day Adventist Christians are a very small group, considering the world as a whole. Our foundational doctrines are based on the Solid Rock, Jesus, and our relationship with Him must be for life.

Call upon Jesus this morning to help you to be true to Him in your actions today and ask Him to help you put more trust in Him.

PINE WILT

Think not that I am come to destroy the law, or the prophets: I am not come to destroy, but to fulfill. Matthew 5:17.

Since sin has entered the world, there are many things that destroy other things. About 35 years ago a pest called "blister rust" swept across the United States. It was caused by a fungus transported by a beetle that infested the pine trees and killed them. These insects were sustained during part of their life cycles by the wild gooseberry plants, so the Forest Service hired young men and women to go into the forest and pull up the gooseberry bushes, thus breaking the beetles' cycle.

Today there is a new pest, pine wilt, that is harming the pine trees of North America and Japan. Pine wilt has been a severe problem in Japan for many years but for only the past few years in North America. The pines actually wilt to the place where they die with the needles still on the trees. This is caused by a small parasite called the pine wilt nematode; it gets its name from the pine wilt disease in Japan. It was not known by American entomologists until a visiting Japanese plant pathologist suggested that they soak a piece of wood in water. They did so and hundreds of nematodes floated to the surface.

These little parasites attach themselves to the adult pine sawyer beetle, which is also called the roundheaded wood borer, by entering the breathing pores and moving up to the breathing tubes. When the beetle bores into the bark, the nematodes leave and enter the tree. They bore into the core of the tree and enter the oleoresin (pitch) and cut the flow of sap to the branches and trunk. When the weather turns warm they hatch and develop in five days. When enough of them eat the trunk lining where the pitch flows, they kill the tree.

The nematodes are in the destroying business, but Jesus said that He was not. He did not come to destroy things but to hold up and fulfill. His law, the Ten Commandments, will show us the way to life. God will help us develop these principles into our lifestyle if we so desire. Ask Him this morning to help you keep the commandments and keep your life in harmony with His will.

TROPICAL FROGS

And Aaron stretched out his hand over the waters of Egypt; and the frogs came up, and covered the land of Egypt. Exodus 8:6.

The Bible doesn't say what type of frogs these were that came up on the land of Egypt and covered everything. In South and Central America there are some of the most colorful frogs that exist today. These frogs may be found in various colors: red, white, yellow, pink, orange, and many shades of green.

Parenting among frogs is different in each species. There are about 2,000 known species of frogs, and about 10 percent of these frogs take special care in raising their young. The male Darwin's frog waits until the female has laid the eggs. He swallows them into a special vocal sac and there they remain until they are small froglets. Then they leave the father's vocal sac and exit through his mouth and begin life on their own. The male Fleishmann's frog will sit on the eggs for a period of 30 minutes every night, during which time it will wet on the eggs. Other males do not help in the incubation of the eggs but will guard them.

Poison dart frogs, named for their toxic skin secretions, which the Indians use on their hunting arrows, lay their eggs on damp ground. After the young hatch, the male will carry them piggyback to a leaf that is full of water, and there the female will lay other unfertilized eggs for food.

Another kind of frog is the midwife. The male midwife wraps the eggs around his legs and carries them wherever he goes until they hatch. Then he goes into the water and his tadpoles just swim away.

Don't you think that God must have enjoyed making frogs? He certainly made many varieties, and each one different. I would like to have seen all of the frogs that Aaron brought forth by raising his hands, although I am glad I didn't have to put up with them. God showed His power by using Aaron, and He can show His power through us, as people see we have a changed and different life. Ask God to help you today to get rid of one thing in your life that you know doesn't belong there. Let Him show His power in you.

PETE AND REPEAT

You are my friends if you obey me. John 15:14, T.L.B.

One summer before our youth camp season started, Dave, our nature director, came to me and asked if I'd like to have a couple of crows at camp. I told him it would be great, so he climbed up to the top of a large pine tree and took two baby crows out of a nest. He began to feed them and get them used to a "human mother." They were almost full-grown when Dave brought them to camp. He would work with them inside the cage as he fed them from day to day.

One day Dave came to me and said, "I think they will stay around camp. Is it all right if I let them out of the cage?" I agreed, and out of the cage came Pete and Repeat. The crows would fly and land on the head, shoulders, and arms of the campers as they held them out. The campers had fun with Pete and Repeat. In fact, these characters got so bold that at line call when all of the campers were lined up, the crows would come out to where we were and go down the line and untie some of the campers' shoestrings. They especially liked to untie my shoelaces.

We could depend on Pete and Repeat to be up to something mischievous all the time. Every morning about five-thirty to six, they would come to a tree close to my cabin and call me. I never needed an alarm clock while Pete and Repeat were around. Toward the end of camp, Repeat flew away to be with the wild crows. He would come back near the camp with them, but never again did he actually come down to be with us. Pete stayed around the camp for several months until the heavy snows came and very few people were around; then he finally went wild. We were happy that God had allowed these two birds to be friends with us during that summer.

Jesus wants to be our friend for a long time. He has been in this world and was a friend of many people, but He went back to heaven to be with His Father. Although we don't see Him anymore, He is still our friend. He wants us to talk to Him often, as we would to our earthly friends. Kneel down and talk to Him this morning. Then, throughout the day just talk to Him as you go from class to class, or walk around the playground, or walk home. He is a true friend.

ANIMALS IN ARMOR

Put on the whole armour of God, that ye may be able to stand against the wiles of the devil. Ephesians 6:11.

Armadillos are probably one of the oddest of the North American mammals. They have a head like a lizard, ears like a donkey, claws like a bear, and a tail like a rat. In addition, they have armor that covers the entire upper part of the body. There are twenty species of armadillos, most of them living in Central and South America. However, one species lives in the southern part of the United States, the nine-banded armadillo. The name armadillo comes from Spanish, meaning "little fellow in armor."

The nine-banded armadillo has a shoulder armor, then nine armor bands that cover the back, followed by a pelvic shield that covers the rear end. When armadillos cannot dig a hole to escape—and they are fast diggers—they will curl up into a ball and let the outside armor be their protection. Coyotes are their feared enemy. The coyote will sneak up on them (and that isn't hard, as armadillos hear and see very poorly; they depend mostly on smell to locate food) and flip them over and attack them in the armorless stomach region.

In giving birth, a female armadillo will usually have identical quadruplets—all the same sex. These four little creatures look just like mama but they have a soft armor that gets harder as they mature. They will be out foraging in a few days but they will nurse for about two months. Armadillos are mostly nocturnal creatures and can run quite rapidly, although a human can catch them. They make poor pets as they are always foraging in the yards and gardens for food tearing up the ground. They mostly eat fire ants, roaches, tarantulas, scorpions, grubs, grasshoppers, worms, and some berries. To cross a creek they will gulp air to inflate themselves and float across.

We are told to put on the "whole armour" of God, that we might be saved against the attacks of the enemy. Read verses 13 to 18 of this same chapter and find out what the "whole armour" is. God will help you with this armor, if you ask Him to.

THE NAZCA LINES

Whosoever therefore shall confess me before men, him will I confess also before my Father which is in heaven. Matthew 10:32.

For many years the Nazca lines in southern Peru have baffled scientists. These are lines in the earth and rock that go in all directions. They are very well drawn; surveyors are amazed at their precision. As one looks down on these lines from the air, they resemble enormous figures of a hummingbird, spider, monkey, and many other shapes. Who made these figures and why, on this barren terrain covering more than 30 miles, is really not known.

For almost 40 years, a German mathematician and astronomer, Maria Reiche, has studied these lines. She discovered that the lines in the ground match similar animal figures on Nazca Indian pottery. The lines that Maria has studied have been preserved in the gypsum soil, which has hardened like cement. The Peruvian Government has been so interested in her work that they have housed and fed her in the government hotel in Nazca, although she is very frugal in her lifestyle.

An expert on ancient irrigation systems was in the Nazca area in 1939, and discovered these lines. Later he got in touch with his friend Maria and asked her to come and study them. He had discovered that some lines formed a large bird when looked at from 400 feet up in the air. What began as a favor for a friend became a lifework for Maria Reiche. She dedicated herself to this work, receiving only a small salary from Germany.

What a different place this world would be if all of us as Christians were as dedicated to studying and telling others about our "find"—Jesus—as Maria Reiche was to her project.

Ask God in your prayer this morning to help you be willing to share what you know about Jesus with some friends today.

275

SUPERGRAVITY

But thou, O Daniel, shut up the words, and seal the book, even to the time of the end: many shall run to and fro, and knowledge shall be increased. Daniel 12:4.

Albert Einstein had a dream. As a physicist he wanted to discover a single theory that would explain the existence of all matter, all energy, and all forces in the universe. The day before his death in 1955 his calculations were still no closer to answering this puzzle than when he began. After his death other physicists began to study into what Einstein had been studying. They have come up with a new theory that they call *supergravity,* a set of mathematical equations.

Using the formula, they feel they can explain space, time, matter, and the manifestations of gravity and other natural forces. According to the scientists, supergravity explains the gap between gravity, which holds the macroscopic world, and quantum physics, which describes the microscopic world. Einstein studied mostly electromagnetism and gravity. Gravity, as we know, is the force that pulls toward the earth (when you jump up in the air, you come back down). One writer said that the reason that Einstein didn't succeed in the study of gravity is that he simply didn't keep up with the studies others were doing in the field of physics.

Scientists are still baffled by gravity. They really don't understand what it is all about. They know that it exists, but there is much to learn about it. Experimentation with gravity has been difficult, therefore it has been ignored by most physicists.

Although man cannot explain gravity, God can. Could it be said of us that the reason we do not understand God's love is because we haven't kept up with the reading of His Word? Pray this morning that even though you may not understand physics and the law of gravity, God will help you increase your knowledge about His great love toward you and give you the desire to read His Word.

LAPLAND

This same Jesus, Who was caught away and lifted up from among you into heaven, will return in . . . the same way in which you saw Him go into heaven. Acts 1:11, Amplified.

Far north of the countries of Norway, Sweden, Finland, and Russia in the Arctic Circle is an area called Lapland. Although the people who live in this area are citizens of the countries in which they live, they are called Lapps. In the area where they live the winters are nine months long and very cold.

The Lapps have some interesting customs in their culture. When a young man falls in love with a young woman and decides he wants to marry her, he will dress in his finest clothes, and get on his sleigh. Pulled by a reindeer, he will ride his sleigh to her house and circle it three times. If the young woman is interested in marrying him she will go out after the third circle. When he stops his sleigh she will go over and unhook the reindeer from the sleigh—and soon there will be a wedding!

The Laplanders depend much on the reindeer. They use them to pull their sleighs, they use their hides for carpets in their shelters, and their meat for food. Since they depend so much on the reindeer, they take good care of them. This includes migrating with the reindeer as they move in search of food. These migrations may take them far north, where the sun does not set for long periods of time and there are no trees. The whole family goes along. The younger boys and girls and women handle the sleighs; the men, older boys, and dogs go with the reindeer to keep them together. This is a long, hard trek (walk), but the Lapps enjoy it.

There is going to be a grand migration of God's children as we travel to heaven. God wants all to go along in that migration. We will carry no baggage or belongings, just our character. God has prepared a home for us. I want to be there, and I trust you do, too.

Pray today that God will help guide you into that migration.

PECCARIES OR JAVELINAS

And there was a good way off from them an herd of many swine feeding. So the devils besought him, saying, If thou cast us out, suffer us to go away into the herd of swine. And he said unto them, Go. Matthew 8:30–32.

We all remember the Bible story of the demoniacs, of how the devil spirits, at the command of Christ, went into the swine, which ran down into the lake and were drowned. I had the privilege of seeing that historical place; it was very barren.

In the Southern United States, and in Central and South America, there are wild pigs called peccaries. In the Southwestern States they call them javelinas. Whatever they are called, they are related to pigs. They have gray hair like a pig and a snout like a pig. The front foot has four toes and the back has three.

These creatures run in bands. When danger approaches they back into a circle, like the musk-ox, and defend themselves. They can tear a dog, coyote, or wolf apart with their long tusklike teeth.

The collared peccary that lives in the United States has a white collar around its shoulders; that is how it got its name. It has been suggested that it marks its trail as it travels with scent from a gland, called the musk gland, on its rump. This gland secretes a musky odor that may rub off onto the shrubs as it goes through them.

Peccaries eat all types of berries, fruits of prickly pear, herbs, acorns, roots, and beans from mesquite trees. When the piglets are born, there are generally two but there may be more. They are reddish-brown in color; within a few hours after birth they can outrun a man. The hide of the peccary makes good gloves and jackets.

On one occasion Jesus cursed the pig as unclean, and on another He allowed the evil spirits to go into the pigs so that they drowned. Thank God that He gave us instructions on what we should and should not eat. He knows best, because He created them.

278

SUPERPLANTS

Yet I have planted thee a noble vine, wholly a right seed: how then art thou turned into the degenerate plant of a strange vine unto me? Jeremiah 2:21.

Botanists (plant scientists) can graft trees so that they will produce bigger and better fruit. Now these researchers are saying that we need bigger and better plants so that we can have bigger and better vegetables. Better seeds bring forth better plants that produce better vegetables. How far can this process be carried?

A plant geneticist in Peru is collecting samples of tomatoes that are twice as meaty as the tomatoes most of us eat. They are ugly, green, and berrylike in appearance, yet they are resistant to disease. He has also collected tomato plants at elevations up to 12,000 feet. They don't need so much water for growth and are resistant to diseases and insects. What he and other scientists want to do is to transplant genes from these plants into tomato plants such as most of us are used to, and make a healthier, meatier tomato. Can it be done? Only God knows.

Other plant geneticists are experimenting with genetic engineering. They are trying to alter the present genetic structure of a plant and make it do something else. This has been done successfully in cloning, which is the growing of identical plants from single cells by a process biologists call tissue culturing. This is being done successfully in a few limited plants such as carrots, petunias, and tobacco. Important cereal grains and legumes (beans) haven't responded well yet to cloning.

Will man be able to improve plants by manipulating their genes? Only God knows that answer. Thank God today that He is an all-powerful God and that He has all of the answers to man's problems. We can trust Him.

MORAY EELS

O Lord our Lord, how excellent is thy name in all the earth! Psalm 8:9.

I have often wondered why God created some of the things that He did, but I must trust in Him and His judgment because I have seen so many wonderful things happen. I must praise Him, even though I don't know why He created the moray eel.

There are about 100 species of the moray eels. According to marine biologists, these eels are fish, but slightly different. Yes, they are slightly different. The moray eels have a mouth full of teeth and they are constantly displaying them. Some divers have thought that the eels were challenging them, and they may have been, but they may have been just breathing. The moray eel must open and close its mouth to be able to breathe, for it sucks water through the mouth, over the gills, and out through a small circular gill opening.

Moray eels have been known to attack divers, but only on rare occasions. They are very nearsighted but they have a powerful sense of smell; at times that is detrimental to them. In their hunt for food, eels generally do not go more than about ten feet from their hole in a coral reef. Many of them will remain in their hole; only a part of the body protrudes out, to grab fish, crabs, octopuses, or other food to eat.

Many species are beautifully colored and fit right in with their environment. They come speckled or in solid colors. They range in length from less than a foot to nearly ten feet. They range in weight from a few pounds to more than 75 pounds.

Very little scientific knowledge is available about the eels. Some divers have been bitten by a moray eel and become deathly sick. No one has yet proved that eels are poisonous, but some species may be.

Even though we may not understand why God created certain creatures, we can only trust Him and praise Him because He knew what He was doing. Tell Him this morning how much you love Him and trust Him as a God of love, understanding, and knowledge.

NATURE'S PINCUSHION ON LEGS

Above all, taking the shield of faith, wherewith ye shall be able to quench all the fiery darts of the wicked. Ephesians 6:16.

The porcupine has been equipped with a spiny pincushion shield. It works quite effectively against all animals except mountain lions, bobcats, and fishers. When the porcupine is attacked it will put its head down and stick up the quills, but mountain lions, bobcats, and fishers have learned how to roll it over, usually without harm to themselves, and attack it on the unprotected stomach side.

A mother porcupine will usually have only one baby at a time but sometimes she may have two. The quills on the new-born porcupine become hard and sharp as soon as they are dry. The baby can walk almost immediately, and will begin foraging soon. It will nurse for about seven weeks before it starts to go out on its own.

Porcupine quills are difficult to get out once they are in the skin. They have tiny barbs on them that continue to work their way in instead of out. With the movements of the muscles, the quills keep moving into the body, and have been known to pierce vital body organs. Some animals have had the quills work into the throat so that they could not eat, and they have starved to death.

Porcupines don't go around looking for trouble. They are principally night creatures and just look for food, but other creatures usually disturb their foraging process. Porcupines make nice pets and they will play with humans like puppies and kittens, but the porcupine has to initiate the play. They can be petted but they have to be stroked in the direction of the quill, not against the way they lie. Pet porcupines like to be petted and do not release the quills into their friends unless they are handled too roughly.

As God has given all creatures some type of protection against enemies, He has also given us a shield of faith. Faith is belief. Let us practice that in our lives, and ask God to help us have faith today.

FAMOUS KRAKATOA

Watch therefore, for ye know neither the day nor the hour wherein the Son of man cometh. Matthew 25:13.

You may not have heard of the small uninhabited island of Krakatoa. It is in the middle of the Sunda Strait, between the Indonesian islands of Sumatra and Java. Before May of 1883 the island of Krakatoa was just an uninhabited island, consisting of an old dormant volcano, ignored by most travelers. In that month, billowing clouds of smoke and booming thunder from the island caused a shiver of terror among the inhabitants of neighboring islands. People asked if the Krakatoa volcano was making a last gasp, but smoke continued to flow skyward every day. The islanders soon grew bored with this natural display and began to ignore it. On August 27, 1883, Krakatoa exploded with such force that the sound could be heard nearly 3,000 miles away.

Because of the explosion, the port cities of Java and Sumatra were hit by sea waves more than 100 feet high. Chaos reigned as the islands were blanketed by almost total darkness from the volcanic ash and the huge waves. When the fury ceased over 36,000 people had lost their lives. Although the volcano eruption was not the largest in earth's history, the tsunami waves it created are recorded as the worst in history. Two thirds of the five-mile-long island of Krakatoa had disappeared under the sea.

This volcanic explosion that happened more than 100 years ago in Indonesia may not seem to mean much to us today, but it does have a significant lesson. Jesus has given us warnings all along that His coming is soon. He has given us prophecies in the Bible to clue us in on what will happen. But many of us, like the Indonesians in Java and Sumatra, get bored with the signals and we begin to ignore them. The coming of Jesus will catch many unawares and sudden destruction shall come upon them. Pray today that God will help you heed the promises so you will not be taken unawares when Jesus comes back to this earth again.

282

PRONGHORN ANTELOPE

So he will hoist a signal to a nation far away, he will whistle to call them from the end of the earth; and see, they come, speedy and swift. Isaiah 5:26, N.E.B.

The fastest of all the North American mammals is the pronghorn antelope. Not a true antelope, it is the only species in its family. The pronghorns have ranged from southern Canada to northern Mexico but were almost wiped out many years ago. Today they are staging a comeback because they are on the protected list, although some States now allow some hunting of them.

Male pronghorns have horns that go up and curve to the back. These pronged horns consist of permanent bony cores covered with a sheath that is shed each year. Female pronghorns have smaller horns. The males will weigh about 115 pounds and the females about 90 pounds. They are a light tan, with a white rump, undersides, and stripes on the throat. They have very keen eyesight and smell. Their diet consists of sagebrush, grasses, and other vegetation, which may vary from place to place.

The hair on the pronghorn's body is hollow and serves as insulation. That helps the pronghorns because they range in areas where the temperature may be as hot as $100°F.$ or $-50°F.$ The hair grows thicker as the weather cools, and thinner as it warms. The pronghorns have muscles attached to the hairs so they can raise them or lower them, depending on the temperature. When they get frightened they will raise the white hairs on the rump, which can be seen for one to two miles away, as a warning to the others that danger is near. God gave these creatures great speed; they can run up to 60 miles an hour at times.

God will also allow His message of love to go with great speed to those in this world that want to accept it. That day is soon coming when His message of hope and love will go very rapidly to others. Ask Him this morning to allow you to be one of those who take this message of love and hope to others.

BLOOMING MEAT EATERS

Beware lest any man spoil you through philosophy and vain deceit, after the tradition of men, after the rudiments of the world, and not after Christ. Colossians 2:8.

Insects are attracted to the amazing pitcher plants. These plants are usually found in swamps and bogs in the eastern part of the United States and Canada. They have modified, tubular-shaped leaves that look like upside-down, half-closed umbrellas. Each has a pool of liquid at the bottom containing digestive enzymes and slippery inner walls. Insects are usually attracted by the odor of decay within the "pitchers." The nectar that causes this slippery coating is very attractive to insects. As the insect lands on the pitcher, down it goes, sliding to the bottom of the pitcher. There the creature is stuck, its retreat upward prevented by sharp, hairlike bristles on the walls that point downwards. The plant's digestive juices then break down the body of the creature and decompose it, and it is absorbed for food.

There are several creatures that are not affected by any of the ten species of pitcher plants. The pitcher plant mosquito lives in the plant and moves around it like a helicopter laying its eggs in the pools in the leaves. The Sarcophaga fly lays its larvae in the plants. When they hatch they secrete antienzymes that resist the chemical reaction of the plant. They feed on the remains of less fortunate prey found down in the plant. This harms neither the plant nor these flies. But the Exyra moth lays its eggs at the mouth of the plant and when they hatch and crawl into the plant, they spin a web that shuts off insects from being caught in the plant. The pitcher plant starves to death and dries up. It then becomes a special hibernating cavity for the moth.

As the pitcher plant attracts insects and then eats them, the Bible says Satan goes around seeking whom he may devour. He uses deception, and sometimes that is in the form of false doctrine—not according to the Bible. Paul tells us to beware and know what is true by studying the Bible. Thank Jesus today that He cared enough for you to give you this type of counsel.

PONY PENNING

Let both grow together until the harvest: and in the time of harvest I will say to the reapers, Gather ye together first the tares, and bind them in bundles to burn them: but gather the wheat into my barn. Matthew 13:30.

Just off the coast of the State of Virginia is a small island named Assateague (ASS-uh-teeg), which is inhabited with wild ponies. It is believed that the ancestors of these animals swam to this island from a ship that wrecked near there many years ago. The ponies breed and multiply on the island. Each year during the last week of July the people from the island of Chincoteague (SHING-kuh-teeg) invade Assateague where the wild ponies are, and drive them from Assateague to Chincoteague. The water is not very deep and the distance is not far, so the ponies can make this short trip through the water. All along the route are small boats loaded with people who encourage the ponies along or just observe.

This roundup has the longest history of any in the East, and it is called Pony Penning. After the ponies have reached the island of Chincoteague, they are allowed to rest. Then they are driven down the main street of town where thousands of people watch the "wild horse parade" as they are herded into a large corral, where hay is awaiting them to eat. As the ponies are eating some men will move on foot into the herd and begin separating the colts from their mothers, and putting them into separate pens.

The following day the colts are auctioned off. The highest bidders take them home. The proceeds from this annual event are used to buy firefighting equipment for Chincoteague and also for the care of the ponies on Assateague. When the colts are all auctioned off, the rest of the herd is taken back to Assateague where they are watched over very carefully by the Chincoteague islanders during the year.

Jesus said that the sinful people will be separated from the righteous, and only the righteous will go into heaven. Ask God to help you be in the group that will enjoy eternity.

THE SELFISH SEA CUCUMBER

It is more blessed to give than to receive. Acts 20:35.

One of the most interesting sea creatures I have observed is the sea cucumber. It is called by this name because it has the shape of a garden cucumber. It belongs to the same group of sea creatures as the sea lilies, starfish, and sea urchins but it has a body that is leathery and elastic. Because its body is mainly muscle, it can stretch out quite a ways or pull back to a small size.

The sea cucumber is an adaptable creature. There are species that live in shallow water and others in depths down to 30,000 feet. It eats plankton (small ocean organisms); it is able to eat up to about 100 pounds of these microscopic sea creatures in a year. Sea cucumbers may be black, dark brown, sky blue, or orange in color. It is reported that there are about 500 different species. The sea cucumber usually burrows into the sand, making an arch with the body and allowing only the head and tail to be exposed. Its mouth is located at the head end of the body; it may have from ten or more branching tentacles to eat with. As the tentacles float in the water, the plankton are caught like flies on fly paper. The tentacles are then put into the mouth one by one, and the plankton are cleaned from the tentacles and eaten by the sea cucumber. This is a continual process. The sea cucumber is always eating. It has a selfishness about it in that it constantly takes in but never seems to give anything away.

We can observe these creatures and learn from their habits so that we can have a life that is more meaningful and worthwhile. The sea cucumber reminds me of some Christians who only want help from God but are not willing to give up their desires and their will to Him and let Him lead and guide in their lives. They are selfish and refuse to help anyone else. I hope that you will follow the thought of our text today and not be like the sea cucumber. Truly, "It is more blessed to give than to receive." There are many people who need a helping hand. You could be just the one to help them out and cheer them up.

THE PROUD COCK

Wherefore let him that thinketh he standeth take heed lest he fall. 1 Corinthians 10:12.

One of the most beautiful birds that I have ever seen was in the jungles of South America. It is called the cock of the rock. The male bird has bright-orange feathers all over the body and the comb. The wings are covered with black and white feathers. The female is a dark color with no orange feathers. The cock of the rock received its name because the male has a comb like that of the rooster, and the female raises her young in sheltered rock niches.

Many Indians in the jungles of South America depend on bird meat to supplement their diet, and the cock of the rock is one of those birds that is hunted and eaten. After the Indians have killed a male bird, they skin the body, eat the meat, and dry the skin with the beautiful feathers. They use these to decorate the large pod necklaces they wear, or they hang them in their houses for decoration.

The cock of the rock is about the size of a pigeon and an interesting creature. At mating time, the males expand the tail feathers and strut around in a very proud fashion, trying to "show off" to the females. Once a mate is chosen, a female will continue to come back to the same male year after year, in most instances. Having mated, the female will build her nest, lay her eggs (usually two), and incubate them with no help from the male. The female feeds and raises her young alone, also. All the cock does is strut around.

In today's text it tells us not to be proud, like that strutting cock. We are to put our faith and trust in Jesus, not in ourselves.

I invite you to pray this morning, asking God to come into your life and help you not to be a proud and boastful person. He will help you to be a thoughtful and helpful Christian who thinks of others, as He did when He was here on this earth. He awaits to help you this morning. Ask Him now, believing you will receive the answer to your prayer.

GOLDENROD

Judge not, that ye be not judged. Matthew 7:1.

Toward the end of the summer many fields begin to turn yellow, and people who are allergic to pollen begin to sneeze. They often blame the yellow flowers called goldenrod. They think that these plants, which are in such abundance in some areas, are what makes them sneeze and wheeze. But the goldenrod is probably not the cause of all this discomfort. The poor goldenrod gets blamed for what its cousin the ragweed is doing. Have you ever been blamed for doing something that someone else did? I'm sure that all of us have. Well, that is what has happened to the goldenrod, because it and the ragweed bloom at about the same time toward the end of the summer.

There are more than 100 varieties of goldenrods in North America, and they are quite useful to the total environment. During the Revolutionary War George Washington and his troops sipped a substitute tea made from the goldenrod. The States of Nebraska and Kentucky have chosen the goldenrod as their State flower. Related to the daisies, goldenrods are called *composites,* because each plant's flowering heads are made up of many tiny disk flowers in the center with ray flowers around the outside. There is one species, the silverrod, that has a white ray flowers instead of yellow.

More than 1,000 kinds of bees, beetles, flies, butterflies, and moths feed on the goldenrod. On crisp, cool nights many of the creatures will take refuge in the feathery fruit heads, which have absorbed the warmth of the afternoon sun. The pollen of the goldenrod does not fly into the air, because it is a heavy sticky type and is spread only by insects. Goldenrod belong to the genus *Solidago,* which means "to heal or make whole."

Many times we may think bad thoughts about a person when really we don't know him or her. We may see someone do something and we immediately judge his or her actions. Jesus tells us not to judge because we might be in error and be judged ourselves. Remember the innocent goldenrod, which is blamed for another's faults. Ask God today to help you not judge or criticize anyone.

THREE WORLDS, ONE COUNTRY

In the mountains, and in the valleys, and in the plains, and in the springs, and in the wilderness, and in the south country. Joshua 12:8.

The children of Israel settled in a land that encompassed all types of terrain. When I had the opportunity of visiting Israel, I saw all these types of terrain and I thought how interesting it must have been to have lived back there in those days. However, I did have the opportunity of living in another country that has similarly diverse terrain, except that the mountains are higher. Let me tell you about it.

The South American country of Peru is unusual in that within its boundaries there are actually three different worlds— the coast, jungle, and highlands. My family and I had the privilege of living in two of these worlds. The people are friendly, loving, and kind in all areas, but in their own distinct manner.

Along the 1,400-mile coast line of Peru, which is on the Pacific Ocean, there is a long narrow desert area. For a long time, until the Peruvians began to irrigate these sand dunes, they were considered good for nothing. But the Peruvians have begun to irrigate them and plant gardens. Some of the most tasty and beautiful vegetables that I have ever eaten grow there. The people grow squash so large it takes three or four men to carry one. Sugar cane plantations are very abundant along the coast, too. Irrigation has to be used because for more than 200 years it has never rained on the coast of Peru.

Lima, the capital city, is about in the middle of this coastline. It is a very prosperous and bustling city. The majority of the people in Lima have come from other sectors of the country. They have a mixture of Indian, Spanish, and European ancestry.

God provides for all His children wherever they live. He has made provision for our physical needs. While all countries do not have the same kind of food, there is food provided to eat. Thank God this morning for His provisions for you.

OCELOTS

Thou art weighed in the balances, and art found wanting.
Daniel 5:27.

Around the world are small wild cats called ocelots. While they are young they are adorable but after they grow older they usually do not make good pets. I have seen these little creatures turn on their master. The governor of the state where my family lived in Peru had one for a while, but he had to get rid of it.

In most countries today it is against the law to kill ocelots. Their fur, which is similar to that of a leopard, is very valuable. In Europe an ocelot fur coat may cost as much as $40,000. It is against the law to bring the fur into the United States and into many South American countries.

In the southwestern part of the United States, in Texas, Arizona, and New Mexico, ocelots used to be very plentiful. Now they are almost extinct. A few have been trapped and equipped with radio collars to help in the study of their habits. But those studying them have not learned as much as they need to know about their nocturnal activities and eating habits. Ocelots do not like to be near people. In Texas they hide as much as possible in the vegetation during the day and hunt at night. Ocelots require a territory of from 500 to 800 acres to provide food for themselves. They even may go beyond that in order to obtain food.

Just as the ocelots are fading from existence, some so-called Christians are letting their faith fade away. When Jesus comes there will be many who will perish because they have not had faith in Him. Pray this morning that He will help you have faith and that you will not be in the group who are found wanting at the second coming of Jesus.

SINS UNDER WATER

Thou wilt cast all their sins into the depths of the sea. Micah 7:19.

A camp counselor was desirous of teaching his campers a spiritual lesson about God's great forgiving love. He loaded his unit of boys into several canoes and they paddled out into the lake to a spot where he had been told the lake was the deepest. He asked the boys to put the points of their canoes into a circle right over that spot. After the boys brought the points of their canoes to the place where their counselor was, he began his worship talk.

"Fellows, we are over the deepest part of this lake. I am told it is about 60 feet deep here. You know, I read that in the Mariana Trench near Guam there is a spot nearly seven miles deep. That is almost 37,000 feet. The Bible tells us that God will cast our sins into the depths of the sea. Just think, if God would literally cast our sins into the deepest hole in the ocean, they'd be under 37,000 feet of water. Isn't that neat? Now, I hold a rock here in my hand. Let's pretend this rock is our sins. I invite you fellows to confess to God a sin that you'd like to get rid of from your life. Then we'll ask God to take away these sins, according to 1 John 1:9: 'If we confess our sins, he is faithful and just to forgive us our sins, and to cleanse us from all unrighteousness.' We'll drop this rock, representing our confessed sins, into this lake and it will drop 60 feet." Each of the boys confessed a sin or two he wanted to get rid of and, after prayer, the rock was dropped. It soon reached the bottom.

"Can you see the rock, boys?" "No," came the reply. "That, fellows, is what the text means in Micah 7:19."

When we have sins in our life that we want to get rid of, all we have to do is to take them to God in prayer, asking Him to forgive us of those sins, and He will clean them out of our life. God does not want to see the forgiven sins anymore, so it is as though He throws them into the depths of the sea where they cannot be seen. God wants to forget the forgiven sins. If you have anything in your life that you'd like to get rid of, take it to God this morning in your prayer and ask Him to take it from you, and He will.

291

HOT-BLOODED PLANTS

Every plant, which my heavenly Father hath not planted, shall be rooted up. Matthew 15:13.

People burn fat in their bodies, and birds burn fat. But plants burn carbohydrates, which are sugars and starches that are manufactured from water, sunlight, and carbon dioxide. Plants also have fat cells called lipid cells. These lipids must be converted to carbohydrates, which is done in the cells, where some structures called glyoxysomes provide the enzymes necessary for the chemical change before they can be used by the plant.

Skunk cabbage is a plant that takes advantage of turning the lipids to carbohydrates by heat-producing cells. No one has yet determined how skunk cabbage and some of its cousins regulate their "floral furnaces." Apparently they are operated by some kind of thermostat. Imagine there is snow on the ground and the weather is cold. Yet during the months of February to April, skunk cabbage will poke its head up through the snow into the cold air, and bloom. The bloom will last for about two weeks. During that time the temperature inside the center of the blossoms and plant is 72° F.

The spikelike bloom of the skunk cabbage is called a spadix; it is shrouded by an insulating hood called a spathe. This spathe is what helps maintain the temperature inside the plant. The heat intensifies the aroma of the blossoms; which attracts flies and beetles that carry the pollen from flower to flower.

Why would God be so interested in a little skunk cabbage that blooms for only two weeks, that He should put a heater inside it? I can't answer this question.

Jesus used many outdoor illustrations. In our text today, He is referring to people as plants; those not of God will not last in the end. God does take care of the plants, and He will take care of us. Thank Him this morning that He is a God of love, and ask Him to guide and take care of you through the day.

WEEVILS SPOIL EVERYTHING

The angel of the Lord encampeth round about them that fear him, and delivereth them. Psalm 34:7.

Someone once said that the nosiest creatures in the world are weevils, because they always have their noses into something you don't want their noses in. There are more than 100,000 different species in the family. Scientists have said that there are more kinds of weevils than there are kinds of fish, reptiles, amphibians, birds, and mammals put together. That is a lot of weevils! These little creatures have invaded almost every type of plant there is.

In the Southern United States and in other warm areas, much cotton is grown. The cotton boll weevil is a real pest to the cotton farmer. They get inside the cotton bolls and lay their eggs. The larvae will feed on the cotton seeds and destroy that cotton plant.

Other weevils get into grains and lay their eggs inside. The larvae eat the heart out of the grain. There are fruit weevils that damage lovely and tasty fruits. Some farmers have said there is no good weevil—they are all "evil weevils."

Even weevils have a defense from their enemies. Peru has a weevil that looks like a fast-moving fly, so the birds and lizards don't even try to catch it. Other weevils in South America look like bird droppings, so are left alone. Still other weevils look like the tree bark that they feed on; they are so well camouflaged that they are not eaten. On the African Kalahari Desert there is a slow-moving weevil that curls up and plays dead. African women make necklaces of these weevils.

Satan is into everything, just like the weevils. Wherever you go, or whatever you do on this earth, Satan is there. He is there to ruin everything, although, like the acorn weevil, you never know he is around. He is sneaky and tries to spoil all of the good things God has given to us. Pray that God will help you beware of the devil, and that He will send His angels to be with you today.

A COMBINATION OF OTHERS— AARDVARK

Thou art the God that doest wonders: thou hast declared thy strength among the people. Psalm 77:14.

An exciting, little-known nocturnal animal that I want to introduce to you is the South African aardvark. These animals combine many of the features of other animals. As I've said before, God must have had a great time in creating the animals in this world.

Imagine a 140-pound animal with a long snout and stout body like a pig, the long ears of a donkey, the thick haunches and long sturdy tail of a kangaroo, and a foot-long tongue. The Boer settlers in South Africa discovered this creature centuries ago. They named it the aardvark, which is "earth pig" in Afrikaans.

The long tongue of the aardvark has a sticky substance on it that picks up ants, termites, and small insects, similarly to the anteater. Aardvarks live in large holes and burrows in the ground. The holes are usually hidden in patches of vegetation. As people ride horses through these areas, the horses frequently fall into these burrows, throwing both horse and rider to the ground.

Female aardvarks give birth to their young in these burrows. To avoid danger, they will move their young every seven or eight days to a new burrow. The babies' skin is so loose when they are born that it is about five or six sizes too large. Very "baggy britches." But they grow into their skin in a few weeks. The young will stay with their mothers for about six months, then dig their own burrow a short distance away from mama. Aardvarks use their feet for digging; they can dig more rapidly than three or four men together. The holes and tunnels are entwined and there may be eight or ten access holes to more than 500 square yards of tunnels, some of them down to 20 feet deep.

We serve a God that created animals with many amazing abilities. Ask Him today to teach you more of the things you can do for Him.

BIRDS KNOW THEIR WAY

Great and marvellous are thy works, Lord God Almighty. Revelation 15:3.

One of the mysteries that scientific researchers have not been able to fully comprehend is the migration of birds. It has been estimated that about 20 million birds migrate from the colder climates of the North to the warmer climates of the South during the migration time. Birds as tiny as the small hummingbird and as large as the red-tailed hawk participate in the migration.

Some of these mysteries that these scientists cannot answer are such questions as these: How do the birds know which direction to go? How do they stay on course as they travel? How do they find the same spot year after year? How do pigeons adjust their course and fly according to the position of the moon, during the day when the moon cannot be seen? Do some birds recognize landmarks such as mountains? Do others navigate according to the direction of ocean waves? Some researchers even feel that birds navigate by smell and others by hearing. How do birds know when to take off and migrate? Can they tell time with their internal clocks?

Researchers also discovered that pigeons and white-crowned sparrows can be confused by transmissions from a radio tower. They found that these birds have a sort of magnetic detector in their neck that evidently helps them to fly like a pilot using instruments in an airplane. Birds such as loons, cranes, gulls, pelicans, swallows, swifts, geese, and certain ducks travel during the day. Hawks, vultures, and eagles soar on updrafts created by solar heat, so they also travel by day. Smaller birds such as flycatchers, sparrows, orioles, warblers, thrushes, and vireos travel at night.

God is a great Creator, and we can put our trust in Him. He created not only the marvelous human body but each creature, with mysteries that we cannot understand. Thank God today for the world He created for you to enjoy.

PERU, LAND OF CONTRASTS

And I say unto you, That many shall come from the east and west, and shall sit down with Abraham, and Isaac, and Jacob, in the kingdom of heaven. Matthew 8:11.

Going east a few miles from the coast of Peru, the traveler begins to climb into the Andes Mountains. The roads are winding and narrow. Mostly Indian people live in this area, in small pueblos (towns). The folks in these pueblos make you feel at home. There are no hotels or restaurants, so you eat and sleep with the local people. They are basically from the Aymara and Quechua Indian tribes. They shear their sheep, roll their own wool, and knit their own blankets. Since their homes are not heated, except for cooking stoves, they will use up to eight or ten blankets at night, which are so heavy one can hardly move. Their diet is principally meat, rice, beans, and potatoes. They do have a few other vegetables, and they raise chickens, llamas, and some cows.

On the eastern or "oriente" side of the Andes, there is much jungle. There are many pueblos in the jungle, and the people represent some 100 different tribes of Indians. Many of these people out in the jungle live off of their little *chacra*, a small cleared area where they plant their gardens. The jungle people hunt and fish, as well as work in their chacras, for a living. The Indians in the jungle usually will give fruits and vegetables for their church offerings and tithe, as they have no cash. They are a very happy and contented people, not spoiled by the materialism of this world.

Even though there are three separate worlds in this beautiful country—the desert, the Andes, and the jungle—when the people are brought together for general church meetings they come in harmony because they all belong to the family of God on earth, and they rejoice in that fact.

Although members of the Seventh-day Adventist Church are scattered all over the world, we consider ourselves part of the family of God. Thank God that you can know Him this morning, wherever you are. He's with you.

WHORTLEBERRIES

O taste and see that the Lord is good: blessed is the man that trusteth in him. Psalm 34:8.

"I wanta go up to blueberry hill" were words from many of my summer campers at Camp Winnekeag in northern Massachusetts. The campers knew that about the middle of July the hill back of the camp would be loaded with sweet little blueberries. They would eat all they could, then pick more and bring them down to the cook for muffins and pancakes. She never disappointed them. She would get up every morning with her staff and bake blueberry muffins for the campers. The campers looked forward to breakfast.

Blueberries were first eaten by the American Indians. Besides eating fresh berries, they would also put them out to dry. When Lewis Cass saw his first blueberries in 1831 outside the Indian lodges he called them whortleberries. The deep blue of the berries has a powdery coating called bloom; that is why they look rather whitish.

There are two basic kinds of blueberries, the wild and the cultivated. The cultivated are larger and not as sweet as the wild berries. The State of Michigan, where we now live, is the largest producer of blueberries in the United States, producing about 50 million pounds each year.

Many people like blueberries the first time they taste them, but others have to acquire a taste. A person does not know if he likes blueberries until he has tasted them, but once one likes their flavor, he is "hooked." Blueberries are made into pies, syrups, fritters, fruit soup, pudding, muffins, pancakes, and other desserts. When frozen, they are fun to pop in the mouth and suck. They are good to the taste.

David invites us to "taste" Jesus. He will be sweet and good. When we trust in Jesus and He has all of our confidence, we will benefit from His wonderful sweetness. He is a God of love, and that love is ready to be poured out on each of us. Ask God to pour out His sweet love on you today.

THE ETERNAL DIGGER

For out of the heart proceed evil thoughts, murders, adulteries, fornications, thefts, false witness, blasphemies. Matthew 15:19.

The badger has been called the eternal digger because it always seems to be digging. Badgers are nocturnal animals. They live in underground tunnels with chambers nicely lined with grass or leaves. These tunnels are from five to 30 feet long and the nest chamber is two to eight feet deep in the ground. When the nests at the end of the tunnel becomes too old or disturbed, the badger will take out the old lining and put in fresh. They are very neat housekeepers.

In the early days in North America the settlers cleared the land and built houses. Along with their settlements they created cemeteries. As badgers would burrow into the ground, many times they would chew through the pine coffins and get their teeth caught in the clothes of the dead person. They would sometimes come to the surface and be seen with pieces of cloth in their teeth. So they were nicknamed the "grave diggers," or so I am told.

Badgers are about the size of a Boston bulldog. They weigh about 13 to 24 pounds and grow to about two feet long. The badger has powerful front legs with long claws that enable it to dig tunnels where it lives and raises its young. The badgers in the far north will hibernate during part of the winter in the tunnel, but elsewhere they are active all year. In May or June the babies are born, usually two to five in a litter. In late summer the babies are taken out to hunt; shortly thereafter they are put on their own. In fall and winter each badger lives alone.

Many people are cruel to others. They fight, hunt down those they think are weaker, and then chew them to pieces — talk about them. They appear to be a clean person — clean from sin when seen on the outside, but they are actually not clean. This kind of people doesn't want others to know the kind of lifestyle they live, so they do things at times when others cannot see them.

I would like to invite you today to pray that God will help you to be the kind of a person who is the same all the time.

298

CRABS LIVE IN ANOTHER'S SHELL

They shall not build, and another inhabit. Isaiah 65:22.

You have heard of the hermit crab, haven't you? These are the little crabs that live in the shells of other creatures. As the shells are discarded by their original inhabitants, the little hermit crabs find one about their size and climb into it. As they grow and the shells get tight for them, they look for larger shells to live in.

The coconut crab picks up fallen coconuts for food on many tropical islands. Some say it is a cousin to the hermit crab, but it is not a true hermit crab. However, during the first stages of its life it lives like a hermit crab.

As the mother coconut crab gives birth to her larvae, they look much like plankton. A month later the coconut crab larvae settle down to the bottom of the ocean and look like the hermit crab larvae. After a period of further maturation and growth, they look for small snail shells and inhabit them like the hermit crab. When the small coconut crab has grown to about an inch, it discards the shell and goes on its own without a shell. It is now a land creature with a tough, armored abdomen of its own. It looks for small burrows to live in, because it no longer has protection of the shell to shield it from the hot drying sun. As the coconut crab grows it looks for larger burrows.

The coconut crab can defend itself against any predator. It is reported that it has no known enemies except man. Men put out coconuts for the crabs to eat and as the crabs come out at night to eat, the men capture them. Coconut crabs not only eat coconuts, they eat each other. They are cannibals.

As the coconut crab matures and leaves the protection of the shell, it takes on more responsibility for its own defense. When we are small we need protection, too, which is provided for us by our parents. As we grow older and are more responsible, we need a relationship with Jesus. He wants to be our Protector and keep us from falling into Satan's traps.

Jesus has gone to prepare a home for us, and He wants us to be there with Him throughout eternity. Through His Holy Spirit, He wants to live within our hearts. Invite Him in right now.

LION'S TOOTH

And he said unto them, Go ye into all the world, and preach the gospel to every creature. Mark 16:15.

If someone came up to you and asked you if you would be interested in eating a pot of lion's tooth greens, you would probably wonder if he were crazy. But in reality there are many people who eat not only the leaves of the lion's tooth but also the roots and the flower. Have you guessed what a lion's tooth is? It is the plain old dandelion. In French the name is *dent de lion,* or the "tooth of the lion." That name comes from the toothlike leaves. "Dandelion" is the English form of the French name.

There is hardly a place in the world where there are no dandelions, because they can grow in almost any soil. Rich in vitamins A, B, and C, the leaves are cooked like spinach, used in salads, or cooked in soup. The taproot, which may be more than a foot long, may be dried, roasted, and ground to make an herb coffee. The Indians named the taproot "strong root." The coffee made from the toasted taproot was drunk to relieve heartburn.

In Europe and England the dandelion was regarded as a medicinal plant. The milky latex was used as a diuretic (to take water from the body) to stimulate the heart and kidneys, thus aiding in digestion and purifying the blood. A paste was made from the leaves and bread dough to heal bruises and skin disorders. The milky substance from the stalk was applied to pimples and warts, supposedly to aid in removing them. A concoction made from the leaves was believed to soothe troubled eyes and strengthen tooth enamel. It seems that the dandelion is good for many things.

Jesus is the answer to our problems. A close relationship with Him is also fun. As we reflect Him in our lives, others will note we are Christians. God wants us to be all over the earth like the dandelions are, so that we may be useful to those in need. Christians can bring Jesus' love to many, and that will change the whole world. Ask Jesus to help you to be beneficial to someone today by demonstrating His love.

WATER, WATER, EVERYWHERE

*And the spirit of God moved upon the face of the waters.
Genesis 1:2.*

When God created the earth, water was a very important part of His creation. It is difficult to have life as we know it without water.

Water is probably the most common substance on this earth. A large portion of this earth is covered with water. Water is all around us—in lakes, streams, oceans, under the ground, and in the clouds. Even our bodies are 70 percent water.

Water is very necessary in our world. Just about every living creature needs it. Water helps keep the earth's climate from getting excessively hot or cold. Man uses water for irrigation, power, drinking, cleaning and bathing, recreation, and industry, to name a few uses. Many of us enjoy water for swimming, boating, waterskiing, and just plain getting wet. It is very refreshing to us as well as a cleansing agent.

The average person in America uses from 50 to 70 gallons of water per day, either in himself or to grow the food he eats. Water has a natural recycling process. The clouds carry the water, it rains onto the earth, the water is absorbed into the ground, it filters down underground, and finds its way to lakes, ponds, streams, and wells. From the open bodies of water it evaporates into the sky by the warmth of the sun's rays, and as it cools, clouds are formed, and the cycle begins all over again.

Water can be a solid, liquid, or gas. As a solid, we call it ice. As a liquid it is known as water, and as a gas it is called vapor, sometimes steam. There is no other substance that can appear in all three of these natural states. You've heard of H_2O, haven't you? Well, water is made up of a lot of tiny molecules, and each molecule is made up of tiny particles called atoms. When two hydrogen gas atoms meet one oxygen gas atom, they form a water molecule. That is how it gets the name H_2O.

God blessed this earth when He made water, and we should thank Him for it and take care of it because we are dependent upon it.

THE "LONE" COYOTE

The heavens are thine, the earth also is thine; as for the world and the fulness thereof, thou hast founded them. Psalm 89:11.

The coyote is a very smart animal, but it has been misunderstood and labeled as a killer. At times it kills stray sheep and calves, but according to wildlife experts, the coyote does not kill for the fun of it. They explain that the coyote is probably more useful than harmful, but ranchers and sheep raisers will probably dispute that statement. Coyotes eat a lot of small animals such as gophers, rats, rabbits, and other smaller animals.

Coyotes are very family-oriented and sociable creatures. They are not the loners that many people believe them to be. They may be seen alone at times as they hunt for food, but they are not loners. Several females will help one another when taking care of a litter of pups, and at times a couple of females may even share a den with their pups. Other coyotes will help to take care of and defend these pups, too. They are very solicitous of each other's families.

When I lived in the State of Kansas I would often be out at our youth camp at night. The coyotes made a howling noise, and it sounded like they would soon be upon us, as they might have our scent. I enjoyed listening to the coyotes bark and howl at night, but I was glad they were not nearby.

God created the coyote and He created you, but He created each with a different purpose. God loves you because you are made in His image, after His likeness. Jesus died for you, and that is reason enough for you to feel a closeness toward Him. God doesn't want you to be a loner. He wants you as part of His family. There is a song that says, "I'm so glad I'm a part of the family of God." I *am* glad, are you?

Thank Him today that He does not want you to be a loner. He wants you to be part of His family. You can be part of His family by accepting Him as your heavenly Father.

LAKE TITICACA

And they came to him, and awoke him, saying, Master, master, we perish. Then he arose, and rebuked the wind and the raging of the water: and they ceased, and there was a calm. Luke 8:24.

Lake Titicaca is a most unusual sight. I have stood in awe looking over this lake in the highlands of Peru and Bolivia. It is, according to my understanding, the highest navigable lake in the world, about 12,500 feet above sea level. I have had the opportunity of crossing this lake in a boat during the night. We left Puno, Peru, about eight in the evening, and the next morning we arrived in Bolivia at seven.

This lake has beautiful blue water that is very clear. You can see down into the water for a long ways, if the vegetation is not obstructing the view. A giant reed grass grows in the lake. In one area where this grass is prevalent the Uro Indians have mashed the reeds down and made islands. On top of these islands they have constructed reed houses. They also construct reed boats that they use for transportation. For many years the Seventh-day Adventist Church wanted to work among the Uros, but it was impossible as they didn't want any outsiders around. But one day they put confidence in some of our people and permitted us to build a nice metal schoolhouse among their little "islands."

Lake Titicaca has some very large fish in its waters. The water is very cold but the fish flourish. Probably the best known is a rainbow trout. These are a large fish, the flesh is a bright orangish-red. When people prepare these fish for eating, they cut them into large steaks. In many instances one steak will almost fill a regular-sized dinner plate. The bones are quite large, also.

Because Lake Titicaca is so large, the winds can blow up some tremendous waves. Many lives have been lost from the storms that occur on this lake. Jesus will calm the storms in our lives if we will just ask Him. The disciples did, why don't we? Ask God this morning to calm your life and make it one of peace today.

NANOOK

O sing unto the Lord a new song; for he hath done marvellous things. Psalm 98:1.

A picturesque sight in the arctic area is a giant polar bear on an ice field. The polar bears, known to the Eskimos as "Nanook," used to flourish by the thousands but they have been hunted for their hides.

A female will not mate until she is 3 or 4 years old. Once she begins mating, she will have cubs only every two years. She may have one cub or twins, but twins are most common. When the female is ready to have her cubs she will build her den in a snow bank, opposite from the way the wind blows. It is estimated the temperature inside the den is 40 degrees warmer than outside. She will deliver her cubs in the den, and these little one-and-a-half-pound creatures will cuddle into their mother's warm furry coat to keep warm and drink her milk. The cubs are usually born in December or January.

What keeps the polar bear warm in the cold Arctic? Researchers say that the polar bear has a thick layer of insulating fat and an extremely dense, oily, water-repellent wool, covered with a coat of long hairs. As researchers looked at polar bear hair under powerful electron microscopes, they discovered that the hairs are hollow, transparent, and have a reflective inner surface. They speculate that the hair can transmit solar energy to the polar bear's black skin and thereby keep it warm. Did God create the polar bear with a solar heating system? Our guess is Yes.

God is a great Creator. We find out that He thought of everything. You and I would certainly not have thought of putting a solar heating system in the polar bear, if we could create one, but God did. This is another reason why it will be so fantastic in heaven. We can learn about all He did at Creation that we don't know now.

Thank God today that He took such great care in creating not only creatures, but you. Give thanks to Him, as you begin this day, for His marvelous works.

FIDDLER CRABS

Bless the Lord, all his works in all places of his dominion: bless the Lord, O my soul. Psalm 103:22.

There are some 65 species of fiddler crabs found along the coasts of the United States. These little creatures are only about two or three inches across. The name *fiddler* comes from the fact that the male has a big claw, which is many times the size of the other claw. This tiny crab holds this claw under its chin, much the way a violinist holds a violin. During mating season the claw is moved back and forth like a bow in a movement called *waving*.

Summertime is the mating season, and the fiddler males stand at the doorways of their burrows, waving their large claw, inviting the females to come. At night a male may beat his claw against the sand, making a thumping noise, to call the females. Each species of fiddler crab has a different sound that it makes. The females will listen for their males' sound and then head in that direction.

These little fiddler females are amazing. They have an internal biological clock producing "endogenous rhythms." This tells them about the tides so the female can time the laying of her eggs to the cycle of the tides. Scientists haven't yet found out how this "clock" works. Once the eggs are laid and safely tucked under the female's abdomen, the male leaves the burrow. The female will remain there in the burrow for about two weeks, while the egg embryos mature.

At high tide, under cover of night, the female fiddler will dig herself out of the burrow and briefly enter the brimming water. On contact with the water the eggs rupture and hundreds of little microscopic fiddler larvae float away into the marsh, wetlands, or estuary. For the next three weeks they just float and drift through the water, eating while they float.

Jesus wants to come and dwell in our lives. We can invite Him into our heart. He will be happy to be there, so ask Him in this morning.

ARABIAN ORYX

And she shall bring forth a son, and thou shalt call his name Jesus: for he shall save his people from their sins. Matthew 1:21.

One of the finest stories that I have heard about how people and organizations have rallied to the preservation of animals concerns the Arabian oryx. In the 1940s there was an abundance of these antelopes in Arabian countries. By the 1960s hunters had practically killed them all off; the last ones in the wild were killed in Oman in 1972. Before the last ones were killed, though, a group of people interested in preserving God's creatures captured a few of them and sent them to zoos in the United States and Europe. Those that were sent to the United States were put out on the desert of Arizona. In 1980 some of these antelope were crated and airshipped back to Oman, where the people wanted to begin to repopulate the area with the oryx. The first group was sent to Yalooni, where the Harasis people pledged to watch over them and protect them from hunters. Rangers were given radios, and several of the antelope wore transmitters around their necks, enabling the rangers to know where they were at all times.

The Harasis people are a very conservative people, and will not even cut down a living tree. They will use only dead wood for fuel. (They would make good Pathfinders, right?)

Millions of dollars were spent to set up and preserve a special fenced area, so that the oryx would be protected. The watching and guarding went on for two years, then the first baby oryx was born out there in the new habitat. At that time the scientists said, "The birth of this calf is very important to us, because we feel now that they are beginning a new life, and we feel it will be a prosperous one."

When a baby was born in a stable almost 2,000 years ago, in Bethlehem, a difference was not felt by the human race. But when He grew up and went to the cross and died for man's sins, many people knew that something was different in this life. His death and resurrection have given us a new life. His birth on this earth made it all possible. Thank God this morning for Jesus.

306

JAPANESE CRANE

And Adam said, This is now bone of my bones, and flesh of my flesh: she shall be called Woman, because she was taken out of Man. Genesis 2:23.

The Japanese crane, one of 14 different cranes, symbolizes for the Japanese people happiness, longevity, and marital fidelity, because the birds usually mate for life. It is a symbol of love. These cranes have a red crown on the head that makes them outstanding. They also inhabit portions of China, Siberia, Korea, and the eastern section of Hokkaido.

These cranes stand about five feet tall and weigh about 22 pounds. Some winter in Hokkaido, spending several cold months there. The temperatures will go down to about −4°F. In order to keep their long slender legs warm, the cranes stand on one leg while keeping the other one tucked up under a wing. When the leg they are standing on gets cold, they switch legs. If it is very cold, they also put their head under a wing.

In the early spring the male will fly to his mate and begin to court her by jumping and flapping his wings. She joins in the act and does the same things. If there are other cranes around, they will join in and do the aerial dance. This "lover's leap" lifts the crane high above his mate on the ground. As one jumps into the air the other mate circles on the ground with wings outstretched. When they are finished with their dance the male will stand tall by his mate and stretch out his wings as though to say, "I did it. Now you belong to me," and she does.

To fly they will flap their wings and run on the ground for about 30 to 40 feet before they get up enough lift to be airborne. Every two years the cranes will molt their large flying feathers. During that time they will have to remain on the ground for about two months.

The cranes have a call that the Japanese refer to as, "the voice of the crane." It is a call of authority, saying, "This is our territory, do not bother us." Jesus has made us His property; we belong to Him. He has told us how we are to live, both male and female. Thank God this morning for the rules that He has given for us to live by, because you are His property.

WEASELS AND MINKS

For even hereunto were ye called: because Christ also suffered for us, leaving us an example, that ye should follow his steps: who did no sin, neither was guile found in his mouth. 1 Peter 2:21, 22.

The two creatures for today's consideration are not the kind of creature that our text talks about. These two little creatures are examples of how Christians should not act; that is why I've chosen them to talk about this morning.

One naturalist said that the weasel is the "symbol of slaughter." It is probably the most bloodthirsty of all animals. With a reckless courage weasels will attack anything that comes in their way. They take as their motto, someone said, "Never Say Die." They will fight animals many times their size, and usually win. They seem to enjoy picking fights.

Most are brown in the spring and summer months, and turn white in the winter. Their skins have been hunted and used for the royal robes of kings, queens, and judges. It is estimated that more than 50,000 of these pelts have been used in British coronation robes.

For a woman, a mink coat is the height of luxury. The disposition of the mink has no effect on its fur. If it did, women might not want their coat of this fur. Minks have about the same disposition as the weasel, but that has been overlooked because their fur is so valuable for coats and other uses. It takes from 65 to 100 pelts for one fur coat. Mink coats now come in many colors—black, browns, pastels, white, and even lavender.

In the wild, minks usually live along the river banks in muskrat holes, hollow logs, tree-root cavities, or old stumps. They feed mainly on small game or water creatures. A baby mink weighs only about a fifth of an ounce when born, but grows to about two pounds.

Jesus was not one who went around looking for trouble. He went around looking for people whom He could help. He is our example, and He recommends this lifestyle to us. What a different world this would be if we were all trying to help someone else instead of trying to "get," just for ourselves. We are not weasels or minks, but Christians. Christians follow Jesus. Tell Him that you want to follow Him and His example today.

FLICKA

And ye shall be betrayed both by parents, and brethren, and kinsfolks, and friends; and some of you shall they cause to be put to death. Luke 21:16.

When I first saw Flicka, she was a bundle of black and brown fur. She was only 6 weeks old, the cutest little German shepherd pup. We had wanted a dog, and my wife, Millie, had the opportunity of getting this pup, so we took her and named her Flicka.

We fenced in the yard so she could not get out and then we began to train her. As she grew, she became a real friend to both of our children, because she was a family dog.

One day we decided that she should have obedience lessons. My wife volunteered to take her to the lessons, then she would come home and tell me what she learned. I would "work out" with Flicka and train her to do the things that a dog is trained to do in obedience class. She was a very smart dog, and learned very fast. I was happy for her progress.

The night of the final examination came, and I was to take her through her training procedures. We arrived at the park, entered the enclosed tennis court area, and along with the other dogs and owners began the "graduation" exercise. Flicka was doing great. When the other dogs were running around she was still and obedient. All was going well, and we were proud of Flicka. Then we were told to have the dogs "stand" while we left them. Flicka stood as the instructor went from dog to dog. When he got to Flicka something seemed to spook her and she took off running. It was a good thing we had a closed in tennis court or she might still be running. She let me down and failed her "graduation."

There will be many who will be let down by their parents, friends, and other family members, because they have become Christians. Jesus says that at this time we are to remain true to Him. He will never let us down or disappoint us, and we who are faithful will obtain the crown of life. Ask Jesus this morning to help you be a faithful friend to Him, because He will remain faithful to you and never let you down.

CHEMICAL WARFARE

Bless them that curse you, and pray for them which dispitefully use you. Luke 6:28.

We hear much in the world about "chemical warfare" and how we should be against it, but in God's natural world there is much chemical warfare going on everyday. We have discussed the trees and their leaves, and how they protect themselves against insects. One researcher said that when we see a tree being taken over by insects it is because the tree is not growing in good ground and getting proper nutrients.

We do not generally think of the plants as being aggressors in combat, but in many instances they are. They will go right after the avenger, and usually win. Bay leaves and cucumbers send cockroaches scurrying for the exits. Goldenrod, mushrooms, and marigold plants produce light-activated chemicals that actually burn holes in the insects' cell walls.

In the Caribbean Sea there are some seaweed plants that emit a chemical that makes seaweed-eating fish sick, or kills them. Leaves and roots of black walnut trees, sunflowers, creosote bushes, and wild cherries secrete toxic chemicals that sometimes poison neighboring plants and make room for their own seedlings. We have talked about the pitcher plants. There are other insect-eating plants, but the bladderwort is unique. It has underwater "trapdoors" that are open when a small pond animal, such as a water flea, nudges it. As this door opens, the water flowing in takes the small creature with it, and the door slams shut. The Venus's-flytrap has leaves that look like an open clam. As the insect lands on it, the plants send electrical impulses that stimulate the leaf cells. This causes the cells to enlarge and with a sudden growth expansion, the trapdoor closes, all in a matter of seconds.

How God created all of these wonders we may never know, but we can be sure that He is a God of love. He counsels us to love our enemies, not eat them up. Ask God today in your prayer to help you be a lovable Christian today, and not "eat up" your enemies with gossip.

WAPITI

If any be blameless, the husband of one wife, having faithful children not accused of riot or unruly. Titus 1:6.

Probably the most polygamous (having many wives) of the deer-type animals in North America is the American elk, or wapiti. The second name was given to these animals by the Shawnee Indians. The English who came over to America called them elk because they looked similar to those that they had in Europe. (I have often wondered what happened to the names that Adam gave to all of the animals.)

Like most in the deer family, the elk loses his antlers each fall and grows new ones in the spring. The bull elk will stand about five feet tall at the shoulders. He will have about five feet of antlers, so he is a very striking animal. During rutting season the big bulls let out a big bellow that sounds like *a-a-a-a-ai-e-eeeee-eough! e-uh! e-uh! e-uh!* When that bellow is heard, another bull usually answers back a challenge. They will meet shortly and battle until one is driven away. The winner walks away with the females.

Elk have tremendously strong bodies, as though they were made of steel. They have a grayish-brown coat, and a small whitish tail in the center of a yellowish patch on the rump. When the baby elk is born it weighs about 35 to 40 pounds, but as it nurses and grows it reaches 700 to 800 pounds. The wapiti or elk can run at speeds of up to 35 miles an hour, and they are quite quick in a turn. There is one species living in North America.

God told us that men were to have only one wife apiece. They were not to have many, such as the animals do. Man has altered God's plan since the Garden of Eden, and because of sin, we all suffer. Tell God this morning that you want to follow His instructions and not have your own way in things. You'll be a lot happier if you follow God's instructions, as He knows what is best.

311

TOM WAS A STRAY

For I was an hungred, and ye gave me meat: I was thirsty, and ye gave me drink: I was a stranger, and ye took me in. Matthew 25:35.

Some years ago, when we lived in Topeka, Kansas, my wife, Millie, was asked to be the Investment leader for the local church. She accepted the challenge and began to work with her committee to lay plans for the projects to raise funds for Investment. They wanted to encourage the church members to choose Investment projects.

They planned an investment auction. The date arrived and the church members and their friends and neighbors arrived, and the auctioneers began. A stray cat had come to someone's house, so they brought it to the auction. No one was bidding on the cat so Millie decided that to start the bidding she would bid $2.50. Everyone laughed but no one else bid, so Millie brought the cat home. Millie and our daughter Jackie kept calling it a "she," so in order to help them remember that it was a male, I named him Tom.

Tom lived with us for several years and was a good cat. He loved attention and petting. When friends came to visit us they couldn't understand why he behaved the way he did. He was a model of good behavior.

Later we moved to southern New England and Tom went with us. He settled right into the new house and was right at home. He never wandered very far; when we would come home from work, there was Tom awaiting our arrival. He wanted some attention and he usually got what he wanted. Eventually Tom died and two of our neighbors said to Millie, "Let's have a funeral for Tom, because he was a good cat," so they had a little funeral in the backyard where he was buried among the trees.

Tom was a stray, and we took him in and gave him love, and he responded. This also happens when we take in humans or help them when they are in need. We have taken in some needy young women, and a close bond developed between us as they lived in our home. Jesus invites us to help those who are not as fortunate as we are. Ask Jesus to help you find others today who need your help. You'll feel good about helping them.

NATURE'S GLIDER

Oh that I had wings like a dove! for then would I fly away, and be at rest. Psalm 55:6.

The flying squirrel does not have wings like a dove, but it has flaps of fur that it extends like wings when it wants to go from one tree to another one, or from the tree to the ground. As you would expect, flying squirrels live in trees, usually in hollowed-out trees, so they can hide for safety and care for their young.

The flying squirrel is not a large creature. Two of them would fit in the palm of your hand. They can adapt to humans and become very good pets. They have a soft brownish gray fur on the top and a white fur underneath. As the flying squirrel glides through the air the extended legs and fur act like wings and the tail as a rudder. Just before the squirrel lands the tail makes an upward swing. The squirrel guides itself by raising or lowering its legs.

Flying squirrels are mainly nocturnal creatures; they sleep most of the day. They eat mainly nuts and some insects for food. Acorns are their favorite food, and they enjoy the little grubworms in the acorns. They do not hibernate but will remain in their hollow tree den for long periods of time, especially if the weather is rainy or cold. They will usually have acorns inside, laid up for their meals in bad weather.

The female will have from two to six babies at a time and she will nurse them for five weeks or more, for they develop very slowly. If alarmed, the mother will grab the babies with her teeth and take them to safety. She may have two litters a year in the southern part of their range. They are probably the most docile creatures, among the smaller ones, that exist. It is too bad that we don't see more of them.

One of these days we will be able to fly away and "be at rest," as the psalmist says. That will be a great experience; at this time we cannot even imagine it with our finite minds. Jesus will return and take His children home and they will travel to other worlds. I want that privilege, don't you? Ask God to help you keep your life in harmony with His will, and you will have that privilege.

HEAVENS

When I consider thy heavens, the work of thy fingers, the moon and the stars, which thou hast ordained; what is man, that thou art mindful of him? Psalm 8:3, 4.

As astronomers search through the heavens with their telescopes, trying to understand what space and its celestial bodies are all about, they are making some very interesting discoveries. God could probably look down at us and say, "Ever since this people of Earth began exploring their planetary neighborhood, they have been surprised and awed at what I have created," and He would be right.

First, man looked at the heavens with unaided eyes. Then he built some small telescopes, and later, larger ones. One day he decided that to understand the heavens better he must put some satellites in space that could carry instruments and cameras. Using the spacecrafts Explorer, Mariner, Pioneer, and Voyager, men have learned much about the solar system. When men went to the moon, landed on it, and walked about on its surface, they learned more about God's creation.

Using telescopes, scientists discovered a giant canyon on Mars, which they have named Valles Marineris. This canyon, which is 2,800 miles long and four miles deep, is about four times deeper and ten times longer than the famous Grand Canyon in Arizona. Scientists discovered that Saturn has some very complex celestial rings around it that are intriguing and need more study. Scientists also see a faint celestial ring around distant Uranus. In the ring are frozen moons, three of which are named Ariel, Umbriel and Miranda. Astronomers also note that another moon orbiting Uranus, called Titania, has a totally frozen surface—solid ice.

As we consider the marvelous things that God has created, and especially the heavens, we can only marvel, as did David. God is to be praised for what He has created. He had a purpose in everything He created, so thank Him this morning for His creation, because *you* are a part of it.

SHIPS OF THE DESERT

Therefore take no thought, saying, What shall we eat? or, What shall we drink? or, Wherewithal shall we be clothed? Matthew 6:31.

One of the most versatile creatures living on this earth is the camel. There are two types of camels, the Arabian dromedary and the bactrian. This morning we'll talk about the dromedary.

Dromedaries provide food, shelter, transportation, clothing, and revenue for their owners. These animals provide a very nutritious milk; it is said that this milk provides all the nutrients a person needs to live on. I have heard that if travelers crossing the dry and hot deserts run out of food or water and come to a Bedouin camp, they are allowed to milk a camel for nourishment. In preparation for such an emergency, they carry a little bowl wrapped in a cloth on their heads, whereby they can milk a camel to satisfy their thirst. Camels, on the other hand, can go for several days without drinking water. They get water from the plants that they eat but they do not store water in their hump, as some legends say. They have such a keen sense of smell that they can smell water a mile away, if the wind is blowing in the right direction.

For years the best way to travel in the desert was by camel. Freight was carried mostly by the camels, so they became known as "ships of the desert." The dromedary does the work its owner requires of it, and does not seem to worry where its water will come from. The camel relies on its owner to care for it. The owners will not neglect their camels because they depend on them for service.

God has told us not to worry about our needs for the future. He will be more faithful to take care of us than the camel owner. We not only belong to God because He created us but we are part of His family. He will not neglect us.

I invite you not to worry about your future, but to ask God to take care of your needs. He has promised and He will keep His promise.

MUSHROOMS

For the earth which drinketh in the rain that cometh oft upon it, and bringeth forth herbs meet for them by whom it is dressed, receiveth blessing from God. Hebrews 6:7.

Mushrooms need a lot of moisture to grow. Most of the moisture they need comes from rainfall. There are about 5,000 known species of mushrooms in North America. About 100 of them are poisonous, but only about a dozen of these are deadly. The others can make you so sick you might think you are going to die, but you probably won't. Our advice is, don't eat any mushroom unless you are sure it is edible.

The science of studying mushrooms has become popular. Those who study them are called mycologists. They are constantly on the lookout for more mushrooms, which are classified as fungi.

Mushrooms come in many sizes, shapes, and colors. The colors include red, yellow, blue, green, orange, brown, black, and violet. They range in size from about the size of your little finger to one that will fill a shopping cart. They look variously like umbrellas, cups, bowls, balls, brains, coral, and other objects. Mushrooms spread and reproduce by means of spores. The large puffball mushroom has the capacity of spreading several trillion spores. One mycologist said that if every spore of the mushrooms took seed and grew, we might suffocate in fungi.

As I mentioned above, use caution in picking mushrooms to eat. Be sure you have correctly identified them and know that they are safe for eating.

God has given us many good things but Satan has added some counterfeits. Whether it is in the food you eat or in the ideas you entertain, be certain they are genuine and beneficial. Read your Bible regularly and carefully, that you will not be deceived with wrong ideas or thoughts. Pray that God will help you distinguish between a happy life and one filled with sadness.

SILVERFISH

Lay not up for yourselves treasures upon earth, where moth and rust doth corrupt, and where thieves break through and steal: but lay up for yourselves treasures in heaven, where neither moth nor rust doth corrupt, and where thieves do not break through nor steal: for where your treasure is, there will your heart be also. Matthew 6:19–21.

It is not a very happy sight when you go to the closet to get a suit or dress and find some holes eaten in the fabric. Most of the time we blame them on moths, and many times that may be the case, but there is another silent night creature that eats holes in starched clothes, and that is the silverfish. You may have seen them scampering across the floor, or a wall, or the ceiling, as you turn the light on. They work in the darkness. They have six legs, a long, slender body with scales on it, and three-parted tails.

Most of the time silverfish like to live behind the baseboards in your house or in dark areas such as cupboards or down under the refrigerator or stove. For the most part they like cool, damp areas. There is one species that likes hot temperatures.

Silverfish lay their eggs behind the baseboards and they will hatch there and grow into adults. As the baby silverfish grow they will molt at least three times, then they get scales like their parents. They will continue to molt throughout life, even after they have become adults; the only insect that does this. They may molt up to fifty times after reaching adulthood. That is a lot of changing of skin, especially since they grow to be only about one-half inch long.

Jesus said that we should be preparing our treasures in heaven where moths and rust do not affect it. But too many of us are excited by and attached to the things of this world, as though they had eternal value. Jesus offers us a life forever, where nothing will threaten the peaceful lifestyle and no silverfish will eat away at our clothes. Talk to God this morning and thank Him for the counsel He has given you, and tell Him of your desire to put your treasures in heaven for eternity.

SLOTH

He also that is slothful in his work is brother to him that is a great waster. Proverbs 18:9.

One of the most interesting animals that I have seen is the sloth. In the countries of Brazil and Peru, where we lived for many years, we found that there were two types of sloths, the two-toed and the three-toed sloths. These creatures move so slowly that you have to really watch carefully to see them move; averaging about six feet per minute. However, they can make a rapid slash with the front foot. Equipped with long, curved claws, they can tear flesh wide open as with a sharp knife.

Sloths live in trees, especially one kind of tree, the trumpet tree, and they eat the leaves for food. What most people are not aware of is that the sloth that hangs upside down from the limbs of trees most of the time are themselves the equivalent of hanging zoos. In the thick fur of the sloth live many different creatures. Someone said that sloths are "bugged." In their fur can be found nine species of moths, four species of scarab beetles, six species of ticks, and six or seven species of mites. Two species of mites live on the sloth's skin while the others hitchhike on the backs of beetles. As many as 978 beetles have been found on one sloth. Some green algae is also found on the sloth; it may give a greenish color to the natural light tan color of the fur.

The sloth needs to make a weekly trip down to the ground for a toilet ritual. It digs a hole to bury its feces. While it is doing this, the piggyback creatures drop off its fur and lay their eggs in the loose soil.

We have been admonished by the inspired Bible writer to not be as the sloth. They do nothing, and it takes them forever to do that. God doesn't want His people to be like sloths, so slow in what they do that they actually do nothing. He wants His people to be active, to show that there is really some life in them, and that this life comes from the Creator. Thank God for your life today and show others that you are "alive."

THE WHITE WHALE
WAITED TOO LONG

Therefore be ye also ready: for in such an hour as ye think not the Son of man cometh. Matthew 24:44.

It is estimated that the white whale population of North America is about 50,000. Only the Eskimos are allowed to hunt and use them for food. The Eskimos are fond of the thick blubber of the white whale, and the oil is used for lamps—it produces a white flame.

The white whale is a singer. It has a large variety of sounds and is the most vocal of all whales. The sailors used to call white whales "sea canaries." They make noises similar to the grinding of teeth, the grunting of pigs, bird calls, the bellow of a bull, the shrill scream of a woman, a squeaky snore, a baby's cry, a rusty hinge, and a horse whinny. They chirp, click, cluck, gurgle, grunt, groan, snort, squeak, moo, trill, yap, and mew. They make all these sounds through their nose, which is a crescent-shaped spiracle at the top of their head.

The male adults grow to a length of eighteen feet and weigh about 3,000 pounds. The female is slightly smaller and lighter. When the white whale calf is born, it is about five feet long and weighs about 170 pounds. At birth the calf is pink; soon it turns a mottled brown, then yellowish, and at about 4 or 5 years of age a glossy white. At about 30 years of age, the white whale turns a mellow yellow color.

An unfortunate thing about white whales is that many times they get trapped behind fast-forming ice in the Arctic and cannot get out to sea, because they want to stay in the warmer bay waters as long as possible. Those trapped, die or are killed by the Eskimos.

Many people want to enjoy the pleasures of this world; they say, "When I've had my fun and get older, then I'll be a Christian, because it is too hard being a Christian when you're young." This is one of Satan's traps. Let us not delay our decision for Jesus, like the white whale delays its departure to colder water. Ask Jesus to help you not get caught in Satan's trap.

THE PEEPERS

Ye shall know them by their fruits. Matthew 7:16.

The peeper is a frog so small that one will fit on the thumbnail of an adult human. It is one of the smallest frogs in existence—about an inch long. You may have heard some peepers sound off. These little creatures have a bell-like sound. When many of them are in concert they sound like sleigh bells and can be heard up to half a mile away.

New England folklore states that whatever you are doing when you hear the first peeper, that is what you will be doing when you die. Another folk belief is that when the first peeper is heard in the spring, there will be three more freezes that season. Interesting how people try to determine the future by the habits of various wild creatures.

When the peeper makes his noise, his mouth and nostrils are closed. The peeper inflates a large vocal sac, which acts as a resonator in the throat of the peeper. As the peeper passes air back and forth from the lungs to the mouth and over the vocal cords, the vocal sac resonates the sound.

Another interesting feature of the peeper is an X-shaped cross on its back. This helped it get the species name of "crucifer."

Although they belong to the tree-frog family, peepers are not found in trees. They live in low plants along the water's edge, and when a noise disturbs them, they shut right up or dive under the water. They can color themselves according to their surroundings like a chameleon. They change their coloration in response to variations in temperature, light, or humidity, but the process may take as long as an hour. This coloration process helps the little frogs escape from their enemies—herons, snakes, and larger frogs. A female may lay up to 1,000 eggs in the water. These frogs have special suction pads at the tips of their toes that enable them to climb.

As these frogs are known by their noise, so we as Christians should be known by our lifestyle. I suggest this morning that you ask God to help you pattern your life after Jesus' life, so people will know you are a Christian by your lifestyle.

RABIES

Their poison is like the poison of a serpent: they are like the deaf adder that stoppeth her ear. Psalm 58:4.

I'm sure that all of you have heard of rabies. It is a terrible disease that makes animals go mad. They carry the germs of the disease in their saliva, and when they bite another animal or human, the germs are transmitted to the victim. Rabies can be a fatal disease. In order to save the life of the person bitten, it is necessary that several things be done. First, the animal that did the biting is captured, if possible, and put under surveillance. If proven not to have rabies after ten days, the animal is turned loose. If it has rabies, it is put to sleep.

If rabies is suspected, the person who has been bitten must start a series of shots. The shots hurt, but the victim must have them, just in case. If it is proved that the animal does not have rabies, then the shots can be stopped.

During the past few years not many dogs and cats have been found with rabies, because they have been treated with immunization shots. The upswing of the disease now is among wild animals. Skunks, even pet skunks, seem to be the most common carriers of rabies. Bats, raccoons, some foxes, and coyotes carry rabies, too. It was once thought that rodents were great carriers of rabies, but it has been found that they are not. Some squirrels may have it, but very few. Most people who get it from wild animals are getting it from skunks.

Authorities tell us that even though rabies is not common among dogs and cats today, they must still be vaccinated so as to keep the disease out of circulation as much as possible. If a person is bitten, the wound should be cleaned out with much soap and water. (One physician said that that was almost as important as the rabies vaccine.) Then, of course, a doctor should be consulted. The incubation period of rabies is rarely less than 15 days and may be several months, so it is very important that it be treated immediately.

David, speaking about wicked, unconverted folk, talked about their poisonous influence. Ask God to protect you today from the poisonous influence of those who are not Christians.

A RARE SPECIES

Whosoever shall confess me before men, him shall the Son of man also confess before the angels of God: but he that denieth me before men shall be denied before the angels of God. Luke 12:8, 9.

The black-footed ferret is a cousin to the weasel. These little creatures are considered to be the rarest mammals in North America. They were never very plentiful, but as poison has been put out to kill off the abundant prairie dogs, the ferret has largely disappeared, because the prairie dogs are the chief source of food for the ferret.

The black-footed ferret used to range from Canada to Texas, especially in the central part of the United States, where there were a lot of prairie dogs. The only place that they are known to be now is in Meeteetse, Wyoming. They are protected there. These little mammals are only about 20 to 24 inches long and weigh about one and a half pounds.

The black-footed ferret usually comes out only at night. It is rarely seen, except in the wintertime when there is snow. It is buffy in color, with a mask on the face similar to the raccoon, and it has black feet. By the summer of 1983, about 22 had been seen in the colony in Wyoming. Six of these were caught and radio transmitters were attached to them to help researchers study their habits.

There is a group of people called Seventh-day Adventists that is small in number, compared to the population of the world. Other people would really like to know more about Seventh-day Adventists, but they are not able to find us. Do you go around hiding, ashamed to let people know who you are, or do you let people know you are a Seventh-day Adventist Christian?

Jesus said that He would confess us if we confess Him. He will be willing to represent us in heaven if we will represent Him here on earth. What will be your response? Ask Him today to help you be willing to be His representative here on earth. What a thrill to be the representative of the King of the universe!

GOING, GOING, GONE

The wolf and the lamb shall feed together, and the lion shall eat straw like the bullock: and dust shall be the serpent's meat. They shall not hurt nor destroy in all my holy mountain, saith the Lord. Isaiah 65:25.

Almost every day on the radio and television news we hear about some part of our environment that is in danger of being damaged or destroyed, or that some wild animal or plant is in danger of extinction. For many years the Federal Government has had an endangered species list; it is against the law to harass, capture, or kill any plant or animal on that list.

The list was updated in 1983. Two kinds of Great Lakes fish and one bird that had been on the list were no longer on it—the blue pike and the long-jaw cisco, and the Santa Barbara song sparrow, of California. Evidently they are extinct. We are told that the Florida cougar is almost extinct. Only 20 or 30 are left in the State.

We have mentioned other creatures that have almost been wiped out for one reason or another, such as the black-footed ferret. We could go on down the list of species whose numbers are dwindling for various reasons. Most of these creatures are becoming endangered, because of man. Hunting, poisoning, trapping, and acid rain are some of the reasons that they are becoming extinct.

I enjoy going outdoors and observing what God created. Whether it is in the mountains, on the beach, in the desert, or in the woods, there is beauty everywhere. The world was originally created for our enjoyment. We can't enjoy some of the creation if we don't have it, can we?

From our text today we know that there will be animals in heaven. I am happy that God has chosen to have wildlife in heaven. Can you imagine what it would be like if there were no wildlife to observe or play with? God has given us the opportunity to enjoy and take care of His creation now. Ask Him to help you enjoy it more.

LICORICE

Woe unto you, scribes and Pharisees, hypocrites! for ye pay tithe of mint and anise and cummin, and have omitted the weightier matters of the law, judgment, mercy, and faith: these ought ye to have done, and not to leave the other undone. Matthew 23:23.

I was happy to note that in His talks to people Jesus mentioned anise, a licorice-flavored plant. Of all the candies, licorice is my favorite. When I was a boy there were several licorice-smelling plants where my family lived, and I enjoyed chewing on their stems.

There are four licorice smell- and taste-related plants, but licorice stands alone. The other three are related, and used extensively in cooking for the flavor. Anise, fennel, and star anise are the other licorice-smelling and -tasting plants. Licorice is an herb from the legume family. It is claimed that pieces of the licorice root were found in King Tut's tomb. The licorice root is very sweet, and it is reported that even when it is diluted in water, 20,000 times its volume, it can still be tasted.

Fennel and anise are members of the carrot family, which includes other plants that are rich in essential oils: dill, parsley, celery, coriander, and caraway. Fennel and anise have been used for a long time as flavorings. Star anise was discovered by some British sailors; they introduced it into candy making. The Chinese use it heavily in making candy. They also use it to flavor many of their meats—chicken, beef, ham, cold cuts, and even nuts. The substance called anethole is what gives the taste of licorice to these different plants.

Jesus was talking to the people of His day about doing some things and not others. He told them it was good that they should tithe (returning to God one tenth of our earnings), but that they should not forget to be just and merciful. Tell God this morning that you are willing to tithe your income and to be merciful to your fellows.

HUMPBACK WHALES

And he said, It is not the voice of them that shout for mastery, neither is it the voice of them that cry for being overcome: but the noise of them that sing do I hear. Exodus 32:18.

As I stood on the porch of the condominium where my family was staying on the island of Maui, in the Hawaiian Islands, I saw several big humpback whales come up out of the water. I could not understand why they were coming up out of the ocean and splashing back down. I have since learned that even scientists do not know why the humpbacks do this "breaching." Some have speculated that it may be a form of communication, or an attempt to dislodge the barnacles or crustaceans that live on the whales' flippers and undersides. Whatever the reason, when one does it several may follow, and it is an interesting sight to watch. One report records a humpback breaching forty times in a row.

Humpback whales are singers, and their underwater songs have been recorded. It is the males that sing, and they all follow a similar pattern. They perform alone, within 150 feet of the surface of the water. When they sing the head is down, flippers are outstretched, and the body is inclined to a 45-degree angle. After a while they stop singing and swim to join the other whales.

Several groups of scientists have been studying humpback whales by taking tape recordings of their singing and at the same time taking pictures of their bodies. The scientists then relate the pictures and the tapes. It has been found that the whales of Baja California go to southern Alaska for the summer and the humpbacks of Hawaii go to the Aleutian Islands.

Joshua and Moses were listening to the sound of people, and Moses recognized it as singing. God wants us to be happy people. Singing is one way of not only showing our happiness but of communicating a message. This is why it is so important to make sure that we sing and listen to good music that is uplifting and inspiring. Our music should not be human-centered but Christ-centered. We can communicate with God through music. Why not try that today? Ask God to help you choose good music so you can communicate with Him.

BLUEFIN TUNA

Go ye therefore, and teach all nations, baptizing them in the name of the Father, and of the Son, and of the Holy Ghost: teaching them to observe all things whatsoever I have commanded you: and, lo, I am with you alway, even unto the end of the world. Matthew 28:19, 20.

One of the largest of fish in the ocean is the bluefin tuna. It is also one of the fastest fish, capable of bursts of speed up to 55 miles an hour. It is built for speed, as three fourths of the body is pure muscle. It has ramjet ventilation and a strong heart, and it is hydrodynamically designed. No predators except the killer whale and mako shark can catch it. Tuna glide through the water like a bird glides through the air.

Some say that their name in the Greek language means "rush," and that is just what they do. Their fins are set into grooves in the body so that they can glide through the water without any resistance. They cannot stop swimming and must keep their mouth open all the time in order to get oxygen, as sea water contains only about 2.5 percent as much oxygen as the air we breathe. The bluefin takes in water and forces it through the gills to remove the oxygen in a procedure called "ramjet ventilation."

The bluefin has an exceptionally muscular heart, which pumps a large volume of blood. The bluefin tuna has the ability to conserve and regulate heat to the extent that it can feed in the northern seas, where the temperature is 40°F., and spawn in the tropical waters, where the temperature is 85°F. Their muscle temperatures will average about 88°F.

Many bluefin have been tagged and later found all over the world. They are great long-distance travelers. When they are caught by fishermen they are shipped all over the world for special meals, which are very expensive.

Jesus wants us as Christians to be found all over the world spreading the good news of His salvation and love. Ask Him this morning in your prayer to help you, right where you live and go to school, to share the gospel with others today.

BABIRUSA

And the swine, though he divide the hoof, and be clovenfooted,
yet he cheweth not the cud; he is unclean to you. Leviticus 11:7.

The domestic pig has been declared unclean by God, unfit for food. However, on the Indonesian island of Sulawesi, and on a few smaller surrounding islands, there lives a piglike creature called the babirusa. This name means "deer hog," because it eats leaves and other foliage like a deer. It not only has divided hoofs, it also chews its cud. The babirusa has a long snout; growing from that snout are curved tusks.

The babirusa is attracting much attention because it eats cellulose-heavy foods such as leaves, which a real pig cannot. The babirusa has an extra sac that resembles the stomach of the sheep. Scientists are not quite sure of the function of this sac, but they speculate that it acts like the extra stomach that cows and sheep have. Another word for chewing the cud is *rumination,* a form of food processing in which the animal eats the food and swallows it, then at a later time the food is regurgitated and chewed again for digestion.

These 200-pound animals are rugged and seemingly resistant to diseases. According to naturalists, this would make the animal a welcome creature in the tropical areas of the world where there is much disease, especially since they eat vegetation and not expensive grain.

God has given us the instructions as to what is all right to eat and what is forbidden. God had His reasons, and today scientists are finding out that creatures such as the pig are unfit to eat. Could the babirusa be fit to eat? Scientists are not sure about that yet. God has given us many good things to eat that we can get "firsthand." We don't need "secondhand" food, such as meat. Thank God for providing for your physical needs when He created the earth.

BIRDS THAT WALK ON WATER

And he said, Come. And when Peter was come down out of the ship, he walked on the water, to go to Jesus. Matthew 14:29.

The western grebe is about the size of a mallard duck. When one grebe meets another grebe, they perform a ceremony called "rushing," walking on top of the water at great speed. They will do this for a while then they will dive down into the water. If it is a male and female doing this with each other, they may come back up out of the water with some reeds in their beaks. They perform another little ritual with their beaks in the air and the reeds hanging from them. They will then paddle toward each other, bump breasts, and swim off to a clump of reeds and begin to build their nest.

The male will help the female stamp down the reeds for the nest. The male is very faithful to the female and the family during the time the young are being raised. He will help the female incubate the eggs, which are a pale bluish white. As these three or four chicks hatch, the baby chicks will climb up onto the backs of the parents into a feather pouch that is between the wing and the body. It is usually the female that carries them; as she swims out of the bulrushes with her brood, the male will swim on ahead. He will spear or catch some fish and feed it to his offspring.

Grebes have calls for each other. The male or female will pick out their mate's call from among many calls and swim toward it, even if it is coming from a tape recorder.

Jesus gave Peter the invitation to walk on the water, and Peter accepted the opportunity. Peter got along fine until he took his eyes off Jesus, and then he began to sink into the water. Jesus invites us to come to Him. He may not invite us to walk on the water to come to Him, but He does invite us to come in other ways. This morning in your prayer to God, tell Him that you will be happy to accept His invitation and go to Him.

PRAIRIE DOGS

For I [Paul] long to see you, that I may impart unto you some spiritual gift, to the end ye may be established. Romans 1:11.

If you study all of the breeds of dogs that there are in the world, you will not find among them the prairie dog, because it is not a dog; it is a squirrel. The early American Indians heard the shrill barks of the prairie dogs and thought they were dogs—that's how they got their name. Lewis and Clark, in their reports about the explorations of the West, called them "barking squirrels."

Prairie dogs do not live in trees like many other squirrels, but in holes in the ground. Their burrows go down ten feet or more and then run horizontally. The entrance tunnel drops straight down but it may have a small ledge just below the ground surface. The prairie dog can go there and listen for danger, just before exiting.

These little "dogs" of the plains are about a foot long and yellowish brown in color. A town may consist of a group of mounds each a foot or two high and 25 to 75 feet apart. It is reported that one such town stretched almost 240 miles long and 100 miles wide and contained about 400 million prairie dogs. Can you imagine the noise they must have made when they started barking?

Several "sentries" are stationed at their respective holes to watch for danger. When they see an owl, hawk, coyote, or other enemy approaching, they sound the alarm with a bark or series of barks up to 40 times a minute. All of the residents of the town scurry to their holes for safety. When the danger is gone the sentries will sound the "all clear" bark.

As Christians we need to let our friends know of the dangers of sin and try to help save them from the enemy, if possible. Jesus told us to love and care for one another. You may have a friend today who needs your help. Ask Jesus to help you be a good sentry and sound the alarm for your friend when you see that he or she is approaching the danger of sinning. Jesus will give you the knowledge you need as to what to do or say. Just ask Him this morning.

SUNFLOWERS

And I will make thy seed as the dust of the earth: so that if a man can number the dust of the earth, then shall thy seed also be numbered. Genesis 13:16.

When I was a boy going to school I used to stop by a little store and purchase some bags of sunflower seeds. I liked to crack the seeds open with my teeth, spit out the hull, and eat the inner part. Now I can buy these seeds already shelled and salted.

Sunflowers are an interesting plant. The State of Kansas is called the Sunflower State. Many sunflowers are grown throughout the central part of the United States. The early Indians discovered that they could boil the seeds from the sunflower plants and skim off oil that they could use in cooking. This process has been passed down to us; some of the oil that is used by housewives is sunflower oil. It is used as cooking and salad oil and in margarine and paints.

The sunflower plant grows to a height of nearly 15 feet. A radio station in one of the cities where we lived sponsors a sunflower-growing contest every year. The radio station will supply sunflower seeds to the people who request them; the contest is to see who can grow the tallest plant. I think the record for the tallest was about 19 feet. The plant produces a very large head, about 12 to 15 inches across. This is filled with the seeds, some of which are made into oil and ground into meal for cattle feed, and some seeds are processed for human food. It is very nutritious.

The Russians claim to have developed the first commercial processing of sunflower seed for oil; they have increased production of the oil content by 45 percent through research. Bees are the principal pollinator of the sunflowers plants.

God told Abraham that his descendants would be numberless as the dust of the earth. The seeds of the sunflowers are also very plentiful and are almost impossible to count. God made a promise to Abraham, which He kept. His promises are still valid today. He will keep His promises, so claim a promise this morning and ask God to fulfill it in your life. He will, just for the asking.

GEOTHERMAL ENERGY

Then Nebuchadnezzar flew into a rage with Shadrach, Meshach and Abednego, and his face was distorted with anger. He gave orders that the furnace should be heated up to seven times its usual heat. Daniel 3:19, N.E.B.

Can you imagine the anger that King Nebuchadnezzar had against these three young men, because they wouldn't follow his orders? The heat of that furnace must have really been great to kill those who threw the three youths into the fire.

In Iceland there are some important volcanoes that have been put to good use by the people there. Put a volcano to good use, you ask? Yes, that is right. Many years ago some of the people there discovered that if they poured water on the smoldering volcanoes, it produced steam. So a system was invented whereby sea water was brought in and dumped on the smoldering volcanic fires. The steam was trapped and piped into the cities, where it was used to heat houses. There are also some underground hot springs from which water is piped. There are about 28 cities in Iceland that use this hot water for heat. In the capital city of Reykjavik, one half of the island's population (237,000) use hot water from hot springs.

The government has gone to a lot of expense to pipe this water into the homes as well as greenhouses where vegetables are raised. This "geothermal energy," as they call it, is not only used for heat but it is also used to make electricity and power industrial plants. Some companies have even started mining the residue that comes up with the steam and hot water from the volcanoes.

Down through the years men have learned to do many things with the natural resources that are found on this earth. Heat has been a very important need. Gas, coal, oil, and other resources have been used to produce heat. God will use heat and fire to cleanse this earth for the new world that He will bring into being here. Ask Him this morning to help you be a citizen in that new clean world. He'll help you.

SHREWS

But the tongue can no man tame; it is an unruly evil, full of deadly poison. James 3:8.

There are only two mammals known that poison their prey, the platypus and some shrews. There are about 30 species of shrews in North America. These are little mouse-sized creatures, feisty and afraid of almost nothing. They will tackle a rat or other rodent almost twice their size, and usually win.

A shrew must eat more than its own body weight daily, just to stay alive. Shrews have a very high metabolic rate. Their heart beats at a rate ranging from 700 beats a minute when calm, to 1,200 beats a minute when frightened. One species is reported to breathe 850 times a minute. Because shrews are so small, they need to breathe more rapidly to keep their body temperature up, as they have no fat. Some shrews can starve to death in about seven hours if they don't have food. They are constantly eating insects, rodents, frogs, worms, mollusks, and some small amphibians.

Shrews are rarely seen by humans. They are active both during the day and at night. During the winter months they are usually under leaves or in burrows made by other animals. They have very poor eyesight so they have to depend on their keen senses of touch and smell. Shrews are really their own worst enemy, although they do fall prey to other predators occasionally. They may become frightened from a clap of thunder and drop dead. Shrews are constantly looking for something to eat, which usually means killing.

The apostle James has told us that our tongue can be like poison. It may not kill but it surely can hurt. God gave us tongues to help us eat and enjoy our food, and to talk. Ask God to help you use your tongue nicely today as you visit with your friends. They will appreciate your not "cutting" them down. God will help you; just ask Him. You'll be glad you did.

DIGGING IN TO SURVIVE

For in the time of trouble he shall hide me in his pavilion: in the secret of his tabernacle shall he hide me; he shall set me up upon a rock. Psalm 27:5.

The great Mojave Desert in California is a most fascinating place. So many things happen on this desert that it is a paradise for those interested in studying God's created world. The temperature may change as much as 80 degrees in a day. Rain may fall suddenly and cause flash flooding. Beautiful flowers may adorn certain areas while adjacent areas show no signs of life. And there are hundreds, if not thousands, of creatures that make the desert their home.

The burly tortoise is one of these creatures. Tortoises don't live on the desert as much as they live in it. They are a very hefty and hardy species, able to survive the changes in temperature, the torrential rains, and all of the other natural changes that occur. They dig burrows or tunnels and live in them most of the year. During the winter months they will hibernate in their tunnel, living off the fat that their bodies have stored up.

Although there is not much water available to these tortoises, they do drink deeply when water is available and they get some water from the foliage they eat, some of which is stored in their bladder. You have noticed, I am sure, that turtles or tortoises have a hard leatherlike skin. This helps them retain water in the body and protects against evaporation.

The tortoise has a hard shell to protect it from its enemies, but David knew that his ONLY protection from Satan was Jesus. So he put himself into Jesus' hands and allowed Him to take care of him. Like David, we need Jesus to hide us under His almighty arms of protection. If you want Jesus to hide you from the devil today, just kneel down and ask Him to hide you, and He will.

SNOWSHOE HARE

Therefore if any man be in Christ, he is a new creature: old things are passed away; behold, all things are become new. 2 Corinthians 5:17.

Another marvel of nature is the snowshoe hare. This little creature is unusual in that it changes its color of hair twice a year. It has brown hair for the spring, summer, and fall, and snow-white hair for the winter when snow is on the ground. The snowshoe hare lives in the northern parts of North America, where there is usually a lot of snow.

Some have thought that the snowshoe hare turned white because of the amount of snow. This is not true. As the rays of the sun pass through the eyes of the hare, they activate the pituitary gland, which regulates the amount of pigment that goes into the hare's new coat. Over a period of about a month, small patches of white begin to appear among the brown. Eventually the hare is all white, except the black tips of its ears. The change of color is usually affected by the length of daylight.

These creatures have long back legs; they can run at speeds up to about 25 miles an hour and jump as much as ten feet in distance. When running, they have the ability of zigzagging. Sometimes they can throw a predator off their trail by the amount of zigging and zagging they do. However, this is generally not enough to escape, and many of these little creatures fall prey to larger animals, especially the lynx. During the winter months the snowshoe hare has extra hair on its feet. This allows it to walk on top of soft snow; few other animals, including the lynx, can do that without sinking in.

As the Lord has provided the wherewithal for the snowshoe hare to change his fur color, God has given us the wherewithal to change our lifestyle. When we come to Him He will change our lives and we can be a new creature. Ask God to change your life today as it may need to be changed.

LOOKING FOR A COMET

He telleth the number of the stars; he calleth them all by their names. Psalm 147:4.

No one had seen the famous Halley's comet since 1910. Astronomers had been looking into the heavens and studying them, year after year, looking for a trace of Halley's comet and any other celestial body that might be of interest to them. From the latter part of 1982 there was a race on to find Halley's comet.

A group of astronomers at the McDonald Observatory in Texas slept in the daytime and worked at night, searching for some evidence of Halley's comet. They would set the large telescope by the computer, then begin to search the heavens. When they would find something they thought might be the comet they would take pictures of it, then move the telescope a slight bit and take more pictures. They would then develop the photos and examine them to see if they really had Halley's comet on film. They were not quite sure.

Halley's comet was named after a British astronomer named Edmund Halley who calculated that the comet would return to visibility from earth every seventy-six years. The next expected sighting was in November, 1985, for the Northern Hemisphere, and April, 1986, for the Southern Hemisphere. Perhaps you have already seen it, although it may not be visible to the naked eye.

Some astronomers do not give God the credit for creating the heavens. They believe that things just happened. They are trying to put the pieces of their theories together and they always come up empty-handed. It is not until men realize that God created the heavens and the earth that much of what they see will make sense.

Men will not know all about the stars because God is the one who created them. He knows all about them; and even knows their number. I trust that you will put your confidence in God, knowing that He knows all. Thank Him this morning for knowledge about the heavens.

MOOSE

For thou art an holy people unto the Lord thy God, and the Lord hath chosen thee to be a peculiar people unto himself, above all the nations that are upon the earth. Deuteronomy 14:2.

Moose are among the beautiful animals of the forest, meadows, and water. They belong to the deer family and are the largest animal in that family. Even though they are large, they are very fleet-footed. They can run at good speed through shallow water and can swim quite rapidly in deep water.

Moose can make themselves at home in alpine meadows, dense forests, frozen tundra, and sprawling marshlands. Usually where they live, in the northern latitude from Maine to Washington and Wyoming to Alaska, springs are brief, summers are short, and winters are harsh.

Throughout the winter the young calves may stay with their mother but when spring comes she chases them off in preparation for new calves. Since the winters are so harsh and foliage is scarce, the moose become very malnourished. But as spring comes and the snow melts, the moose eat a lot. A large bull will eat from 50 to 60 pounds of food a day. Young calves, which weigh about twenty-five pounds at birth, will gain in weight to about 150 pounds in one season. Moose do not have any upper incisors; they have to use their lower teeth and upper lip to take foliage from trees and eat grass.

As spring approaches the bulls begin to grow their large antlers again, as they have lost them in the winter. By the end of the summer they have rubbed off the velvet from the antlers, and as fall approaches they begin the rutting season, (fighting for territory and females).

As moose are quite different from the rest of the deer family, so God's family is to be different from the rest of the world. God wants His own special people, and those who accept Him and follow Him are His chosen and special people. Thank God this morning that you have been chosen by Him as part of His special people.

BALANCED ROCKS

And Jesus said unto them, See ye not all these things? verily I say unto you, There shall not be left here one stone upon another, that shall not be thrown down. Matthew 24:2.

Naturally balanced rocks have been found in many places in the world. It has been a marvel to millions of people as to how these rocks got the way they did, and what keeps them from falling. Geologists explain that in most cases, the under rock has been worn away by glaciers, wind, or running water, leaving a harder rock in place above.

In the country of Zimbabwe on the African Continent, just south of the capital city of Salisbury is a very famous pair of balancing rocks called the Rocks of Epworth. According to history, these two rocks have been balancing there for centuries and are among the oldest of the balancing rocks. These rocks appear to be an easy "pushover"; many tourists and others have visited these rocks and have tried to push them over, but in vain. The rocks teeter back and forth but that is all. They seem to have a perfect balance, and no one has been able to move them off of their perch.

In England there are the famous balancing rocks, the Dartmoor; in Australia, the Yellowdine; in Argentina, the Tandil; in the United States there are many, including the Red Rocks of Colorado, the Garden of the Gods in Colorado, Monument Valley in Arizona and Utah, and elsewhere.

As people admire these rocks, they stand in awe. "How did it happen?" they ask.

As Jesus was talking about the beautiful Temple in Jerusalem, He told the people of trouble coming when not one stone would be left standing upon another one. He linked that time with the end of the world and His second coming. I hope you are looking forward to Jesus' return, and that you will ask Him just now to help you be in His heavenly family.

BROOK LAMPREY

The people which sat in darkness saw great light; and to them which sat in the region and shadow of death light is sprung up. Matthew 4:16.

While living in the Commonwealth of Massachusetts some years ago, I heard about a fish that wasn't really a fish. There had been discovered in the inland waters a species of lamprey, different from the kind found in the coastal tributary waters. The inland lamprey is the brook lamprey; the coastal one the sea lamprey.

With an electric shocking mechanism, the researchers were able to catch a few of the brook lamprey. Very few of them had been seen so not much was known about them. They discovered that the brook lamprey is not a true fish. It has a primitive skeleton of cartilage but no jaws, ribs, shoulder girdle, pelvic girdle, or paired fins.

These brook lampreys have a life span of about five to six years. They reach a length of about six to eight inches but are not parasites as are the larger sea lampreys. The brook lampreys are blind, toothless, and have a fleshy hood over the mouth. They spend most of their life in the bottom mud and muck of the streams and come out from the muck only when they mature, when they are about 5 years old.

When the adult females spawn they make nests of gravel for their eggs. (They get their name from the Latin *lampetra*, which means "sucker of rocks.") After laying their eggs they die and the new generation takes over in the muck of the streams. The eggs will hatch in five days and the larvae burrow into the silt and muck where they live for the next five years of their life.

As the brook lampreys live in darkness, so those who continue to sin are constantly in spiritual darkness. Jesus does not want any to sit in the darkness of sin. Matthew says that those who were sitting in darkness received light when Jesus came. Those who invite Jesus into their life will have a life of light, not darkness. Invite Jesus to come into your life this morning, so you don't have to live a life in darkness, like the lampreys.

THE NAMIB DESERT

But I scattered them with a whirlwind among all the nations whom they knew not. Thus the land was desolate after them, that no man passed through nor returned: for they laid the pleasant land desolate. Zechariah 7:14.

As I have traveled in the area of Israel that this verse talks about, I can see that it is very desolate country. There are other desolate areas in the world, also. One of these is the Namib Desert, on the southwestern tip of the continent of Africa, in what is now known as Namibia.

It doesn't rain in this desert very often. Marks that have been made by humans passing through the area remain for many years, as they are not erased easily. Tracks made by the smaller creatures that live here stay for a long time. This desert is about 1,200 miles long.

Creatures of the Namib have learned to adapt to the situation of no rain and hot weather. The temperature may go as high as 150°F. in the hot part of the day. Two kinds of beetles have learned to survive in this barren desert, the head-stander beetle and the button beetle.

The head-stander beetles will crawl up to the top of the sand dunes and wait for the heavy fog that comes about 60 times a year. They point their abdomen into the air and as the fog condenses on their shell, the moisture runs down and they catch it with the mouth. The button beetle has a different method. It digs furrows in the sand, parallel to the top of the sand dune. As the heavy fog settles it goes into these furrows and they get wetter than the rest of the sand. The button beetles then go under the sand and drink the water there.

There is very little vegetation, so most creatures live on the water and seeds, with the predators living on the smaller creatures. Apparently there are no large animals living in this area, due to the lack of food and water.

Although God scattered the Israelites into desolate areas, He is planning a beautiful home for His faithful children. Ask God this morning to help you be in His heavenly family. Plan for that today; it will be a beautiful life.

FIRE BLIGHT

The Lord of hosts hath purposed it, to stain the pride of all glory, and to bring into contempt all the honourable of the earth. Isaiah 23:9.

Fire blight is not known to many people; it is basically pear farmers and other agricultural people who are aware of the blight and the damage it does. When the early settlers came to the United States, they brought from Europe some very fine pear, apple, and quince trees. These had produced well for them in the Old World so they decided to try them in their new homeland.

The trees grew fine for the first several years, then they started to show black splotches on the leaves, trunk, and fruit. It was discovered, after years of wondering what was happening, that the cause of this black stain was a bacterial infection to the tree. The disease was named fire blight because the blossoms, young fruit, and shoots wither up and drop off, blackened as though they had been in a fire.

Most of the pear trees on the east and west coasts of the United States have been wiped out by this blight. Most of the pear crops now being produced are in the midwestern areas of the United States. The colder climate keeps the bacteria from spreading very fast, and in some areas it actually kills them off.

These little bacteria are so tiny that when their image is enlarged about 30,000 times by an electron microscope they appear only about an inch long. Under the magnification of the microscope there can be seen hairlike flagella, which propel the bacteria. One of the effective carriers of this bacteria is the honeybee. The bees land on the flower to take out the sweet nectar and then go to another tree. They pollinate the trees in this way, which is a must, but they also carry the bacteria from tree to tree.

The lives of those people who deny Christ will be stained by the blight of sin. That will cause them to lose their life. Pray to God this morning, asking Him to purify your life so that it will not be stained by the blight of sin.

340

MY HORSE BACH

Whatsoever thy hand findeth to do, do it with thy might; for there is no work, nor device, nor knowledge, nor wisdom, in the grave, whither thou goest. Ecclesiastes 9:10.

Ever since I was a small boy I had wanted a horse, but my family always lived where there was no place to keep one. Finally we moved to a small farm near Boulder, Colorado, and we had a place to keep a horse. I kept reminding my dad that I wanted a horse, but Dad always said, "We just can't afford one, son."

One day I was riding with one of my friends on his horse. We happened to pass one of our bachelor neighbors who was working in his garden beside the road. As he saw us boys come riding by on the one horse, he looked up and said, "Hey, I have a horse I'd like to sell. Maybe you could buy him. His name is Bach. I want only $10 for him." I told him I'd tell my dad. You can be assured that when Dad came home that night I told him about Bach. Well, Dad thought we might be able to afford that, so we drove over to our neighbor's house. Not only did we buy Bach but we bought two sets of harnesses, a harrow, a small walking plow, and a couple of other items, all for $20.

I was excited as I put the bridle on Bach and began to ride him home. The only problem was that Bach had one stiff front knee. Naturally he couldn't run. I was happy, anyway, to have "my horse." Even though Bach was not perfect, I took care of him as though he were. He was a work horse, not a saddle horse, but that didn't make any difference to me. Dad would put the harness on him and hook him up to the plow or harrow, and Bach would work right along as best he could. He was a good horse, only a little lame. Whatever job Dad had for him, he would do it, but not as fast as a good horse.

Although just a horse, Bach taught me many lessons. The one he taught me that has meant the most was to do my job well, whatever I was asked to do. My dad helped instill that lesson in me, too. This is counsel from God, to do well whatever we do. Ask Him this morning to help you do well whatever you need to do today.

341

NATURAL ARCHES

Hearken to me, ye that follow after righteousness, ye that seek the Lord: look unto the rock whence ye are hewn, and to the hole of the pit whence ye are digged. Isaiah 51:1.

Among the many interesting natural phenomena around the world are the natural arches. Some of them disappear after many years, due to erosion, but others still withstand the weathering of time.

There is one national park in Utah that is set aside just for the purpose of preserving natural arches; it is called the Arches National Park. In this park is the famous Landscape Arch, the world's longest natural arch. It measures 291 feet. In Panama City there is another natural arch, the flattest natural arch in the world. Israel has a number of natural arches, too. In the State of Virginia there is the famous limestone Natural Bridge. Natural arches are found where there is a lot of sandstone, as this type of rock lends itself to the making of natural arches.

Natural arches and bridges seem to abound where there is pink-tinted sandstone. This rock takes its color from minute particles of quartz and makes a very beautiful sight. In the Arches National Park a famous arch is the Delicate Arch. It looks so fragile people wonder why it doesn't fall, but it is quite solid. There is also one section in the park called the window section. People can look through at the arches and give them their own name. The tall Courthouse Towers and Fiery Furnace are named as such because of their soil color and formation.

While in Hawaii some years ago, we saw along the ocean a beautiful natural arch and I took pictures of it. Two years later when we returned, the arch was gone. The ocean water had washed away all the sandstone and it had collapsed. We could see only where it had been.

Paul says Jesus is our Rock of salvation; we are made in His image. Thank Him today that He made you and that He is the solid Rock of your salvation.

THE MIGHTY AMAZON RIVER

And a river went out of Eden to water the garden; and from thence it was parted, and became into four heads. Genesis 2:10.

The Amazon River is one of the natural wonders of this earth. I was happy to have had the opportunity to live on the bank of the Amazon in both Brazil and Peru. The Amazon is not the longest river; that distinction belongs to the Nile River. But the Nile is not much longer than the Amazon. The Amazon River is about 4,000 miles long and is the biggest of all the rivers in the world. It is said that it would make about 12 Mississippi Rivers.

The Amazon begins up in the Andes of Peru, just about 100 miles from the Pacific Ocean. Little trickles run down through the small valleys, then pick up more water, get larger and continue to grow until in Peru the Ucayali and Maranon (mar-RAN-yon) rivers are formed. These join up just east of the city of Iquitos, where we lived for six years. Flowing another 500 miles, this "Amazon River," called as such by the Peruvians, meets other rivers from Colombia and forms the Solimões (sol-LEE-moings) River until it reaches the Brazilian city of Manaus (man-OUS). Just south of Manaus the Solimoes runs into the Rio Negro ("black river") and the two form the "Brazilian" Amazon. From the point where the two rivers come together, there is a line between the muddy and the black waters that continues for many miles downriver until they finally merge in the muddy Amazon.

Since the Amazon does not have much fall to it, the ocean tides from the Atlantic Ocean affect the height of the Amazon River upstream for more than 600 miles. The waters from the Amazon empty into the Atlantic Ocean, so the water in the Atlantic is "sweet" for many miles out.

God created a river to water the Garden of Eden. He divided it into four heads, but the Amazon with all of its water flows from many heads and goes into one. We who are God's children are many, but we are united in Jesus. Thank Jesus today that you belong to a united family. Tell Him that you want to stay under His guiding hand.

AUSTRALIAN SINKHOLES

They that dwell under his shadow shall return; they shall revive as the corn, and grow as the vine. Hosea 14:7.

In the southeastern part of Australia are underground caverns called sinkholes. It is not a very glamorous name for them, but in essence that is what they are. There is a large cavern, filled with water, that goes down almost 200 feet, called Picaninnie Chasm. This chasm is located in the largest sinkhole, called Picaninnie Pond. The water is very clear and presents divers with a beautiful picture of the underground world. One diver said that swimming in that water reminded her of just floating in space. It was almost like flying.

The rock is all limestone. It is suggested that if you could cut a slice of this out like you would cut off a piece of cake, it would look like a piece of Swiss cheese. There are about 20,000 sinkholes in this region of Australia, although many of them are dry.

Many divers have lost their lives in these sinkholes, therefore it is necessary now for all divers to obtain diving permits and use special equipment. Some of the older divers, who actually discovered many of the sinkholes, cannot now dive, due to the new regulations.

In the sinkholes named Ewens Ponds, there are lovely green plants. Water comes in through springs at the bottom at the rate of about 36,000 gallons a minute, which creates quite a current; however, the plants are not disturbed. Water cress and other edible plants abound in these ponds. A person could make a giant salad with all of the greens that grow there. The rapid movement of water prohibits stagnation, and the amount of plant growth on the bottom prevents silt from muddying up the water.

From "down under" comes the lesson to us that when we are prepared properly, and under the shadow of guidelines and regulations, life will be safer. The same is true under the guidelines and care of Jesus. Thank Him today for the guidelines He has given us for our safety and future life.

NATURAL HOUSES

The holy portion of the land shall be for the priests the ministers of the sanctuary, which shall come near to minister unto the Lord: and it shall be a place for their houses, and an holy place for the sanctuary. Ezekiel 45:4.

Sandstone has been a favorite building material for many because it can be easily worked. There are many beautiful buildings made of sandstone blocks of varying colors. Around the world, people have made houses of sandstone, but we'll talk about only two of these this morning.

In the central part of Turkey, the city of Urgup, which is about 150 miles southeast of the capital city of Ankara, has some unique houses. Many years ago the people noticed the sandstone columns of the area and decided that they would make good houses, so they began to carve into them. These houses are still in use today. In the larger columns churches were carved, and the people worshiped in them. More than 300 churches have been found.

In the State of Colorado is another interesting sight. The Pueblo Indians built themselves villages and communities under large overhanging rocks, actually part of a large open cave. These rocks were so large and flat they were named *Mesa Verde,* Spanish for "green table."

The Indians cut out the sandstone, formed blocks, and built their dwellings in the cliffs, under the overhanging rocks. This is the largest assemblage of Indian ruins anyplace in the United States. This mesa is about 20 miles long and 15 miles wide.

Instructions were given as to how the people in Israel should build and locate their houses and the sanctuary. No doubt some of their technology has come down through their descendants to our day. Provisions were made in every community for some type of religious services.

God is preparing a home for us in heaven, and we will worship our God throughout all eternity. I want to be there to do that, how about you? If that is what you want, tell God this morning in your prayer.

345

QUEENEY THE COW

And he said, Who art thou, Lord? And the Lord said, I am Jesus whom thou persecutest: it is hard for thee to kick against the pricks. Acts 9:5.

When I was a boy I lived with my parents in Boulder, Colorado. We had a little farm, and Dad bought quite a few head of milk cows so that we would have milk and so that we could sell some to help support us.

Dad would go out and buy the cows and bring them back one or two at a time in a trailer and unload them into our corral. I would help him, and it was fun—until he brought home Queeney. When Dad and I unloaded her from the trailer she went immediately to the feed trough. Shortly she whirled around, saw me, and made a straight line toward me. I ran and jumped up on the corral fence; she stopped just short of me.

That scared me; after that I would take care not to get in her way. But when she saw me coming toward the corral she would come toward me, and as I had the fence between us, I would tease her. Evidently that is what had happened to her at her previous home, too, and she didn't like little boys.

Some months later, my dad, who was a truck driver at the time, suffered an accident. A load of pipe rolled off the truck and pinned him to the ground, breaking his ankle. His ankle was put into a cast and he had to stay off of it. This meant that Mother, Grandpa, and I had to do the milking. We put hobbles (chains around the legs) on Queeney, and Mother would milk her in the morning and I was supposed to milk her in the evening. I moved in between the cows and sat on my stool and began to milk Queeney. She noticed by the pull that there was a different milker. She looked around and saw me and kicked like crazy, even with the hobbles on. I went sailing under two cows. Boy, could she kick! I was happy I was not hurt. Mother finished out the milking of Queeney.

Saul was persecuting the Christians but God finally stopped him on the road and asked him why he was doing it. He told Saul that he shouldn't kick against Him. We can't kick against God, either. Queeney could kick against me, because I was human. God invites us, as He did Saul, to come to Him. Accept His invitation this morning.

346

COCOONS

The Lord is good unto them that wait for him, to the soul that seeketh him. It is good that a man should both hope and quietly wait for the salvation of the Lord. Lamentations 3:25, 26.

Cocoons are most fascinating objects to me. It is astonishing to know that a little caterpillar can change its whole life in a short time, inside one of these cocoons.

No doubt most of you have seen a cocoon. It all begins by a butterfly or moth laying some eggs. After a certain period of time the eggs hatch, and out of each egg crawls a caterpillar. The caterpillar feeds on a certain type of leaf, depending on its species, as each has its own kind of food. As the caterpillar grows and gets fat, it comes to a time in its life, again designated by species, when it begins to spin its cocoon. The caterpillar has some glands that secrete a liquid that hardens in the air. The caterpillar wraps this silky substance around itself. The caterpillar will work until it has itself completely enclosed and sealed off from the outside world.

The caterpillar becomes an immobile pupa inside its cocoon. Through the process of metamorphosis, its entire body is changed into that of a beautiful butterfly or moth. When it is time for the newly formed butterfly to come out of the cocoon it chews open a hole and tries to get out. It will struggle and struggle, and all the while it is struggling, it is developing its strength to fly. It eventually gets out, unfolds its wings, lets them dry, and flies off.

God has a developing plan for each of us, and each of us is developing in a different way. Some of us see our friends developing faster, and we want to develop faster too, but that is not God's plan for us. We need to accept God's plan and be patient and wait for the Lord. There is a reward for those who wait on the Lord. He knows no haste nor delay. Ask Him this morning to help you be patient in your life, and wait on Him.

347

EUROPEAN ALPS

Then they shall begin to say to the mountains, Fall on us; and to the hills, Cover us. Luke 23:30.

The Alps of Europe extend in an arc through the seven countries of France, Italy, Switzerland, Austria, West Germany, Yugoslavia, and Liechtenstein. These mountains are high and rugged; the Flood and subsequent geological forces were really active in this part of the world. Those geologists who do not believe in anything relating to Creation or God have said it took more than 180 million years for the Alps to form. Fortunately, the Bible tells us the truth about the Flood.

These mountains are about 750 miles long and contain some of the most beautiful sights in the world. The Matterhorn, the Jungfrau, and Mont Blanc are some of the famous peaks in the Alps. Two famous glaciers, the Aletsch and the Gorner, provide water for the croplands below. Famous rivers such as the Danube, Rhine, Po, and Rhone have their headwaters in the Alps.

The Alps form a climatic barrier between the warmer airs of the Mediterranean and the colder temperatures of Northern Europe. They are the highest in the west and south, and slope off to the east and north. Climbers have looked up at those tall peaks for many years. In the year 1786 two men, both Frenchmen, succeeded in climbing Mont Blanc for the first time. It is the tallest peak, at 15,781 feet. Tourism is very popular now in the Alps, as people want to vacation amid the beautiful scenery.

The day is soon approaching when Jesus will be coming back to this earth. There are many people who will not want to see Him come, because their lives are not in harmony with what He taught. The light shining from Jesus when He comes will be blinding; the people who are not His followers will not be able to stand it and will call for the rocks and mountains to fall on them. Pray this morning that you will not be in that group. Ask God to help you be in the group that awaits and looks forward to His coming.

WALLEYE FISH

Now he that ministereth seed to the sower both minister bread for your food, and multiply your seed sown, and increase the fruits of your righteousness. 2 Corinthians 9:10.

One of the biggest fish management programs in many Midwestern and Northern States is the stocking of streams and lakes with walleye. When I was a boy, I heard much about trout and bass and other fish, which I used to fish for, but I had never heard of walleye until I was a grown man. Walleye are one of the fisherman's dream fish today. They are not really strong fighters but they put up some resistance. They are a fleshy fish, and may weigh up to 20 pounds.

One of the reasons that the state departments of natural resources like these fish is that they help keep the lakes and streams clean. They are not scavengers like catfish but they are a predatory fish and help to keep nature in balance. With all of the pollutants in the water now, the walleye help manage the streams and lakes in a remarkable way.

State natural resources personnel continuously catch female and male walleyes in their spawning run. They milk the "ripe" females of their eggs and fertilize them with male milt. This has to be done in 60 to 90 seconds, so as to produce more small fry. Literally hundreds of millions of these walleye "fry" are returned into the streams. Many of the fry are eaten by fish or other creatures, so the large amount of fry placed in the water does not necessarily mean a large population of walleye adults.

A single female walleye may lay as many as 20,000 eggs at a time. These hatch in 12 to 16 days. As the little fry hatch out, they eat on their egg sack for several days, and then with enough strength, they begin to look for food on their own. Neither parent will look after them, once the eggs are laid.

We have a God who is interested in us; He will not just let us go and develop as we can. He is willing to be by our side through the Holy Spirit and help us develop in the right way, if we want Him there. Pray this morning and ask God to send the Holy Spirit to be by your side, along with your angel, to keep you from falling prey to the enemy today.

PELICANS

The same dealt subtilly with our kindred, and evil entreated our fathers, so that they cast out their young children, to the end they might not live. Acts 7:19.

Pelicans are interesting birds. They are among the largest of the flying birds. An adult is between four and five feet long and weighs up to 16 pounds. The brown pelicans that people in the United States are familiar with are maritime birds. They are well insulated against cold weather as they have heavy, thickly feathered bodies and numerous air spaces beneath the skin and also in the bones.

They are tremendous fliers and can soar to great heights by using thermal currents, or updrafts of warmer air. When migrating or looking for fishing grounds, they will usually do so in flocks. By using the thermal currents they will arrive at their destination with a minimum of effort.

Pelicans are sustained almost altogether by the eating of fish. When they see fish they will dive toward the water. Just before the pelican hits the water it will straighten out its curved neck and hit the water straight in. As the mouth opens the pouch on the lower bill of the pelican will expand as the water is forced through it, and as the fish is scooped up The pelican comes back to the surface and the pouch returns to its normal size as the water drains out. The upper bill closes altogether; the fish is trapped inside and is swallowed whole. The pouch is not used to carry fish, only for catching them. I have stood and watched these creatures fish by the hour, and rarely do they come up empty.

The one to four young hatch from eggs after about 35 to 37 days of incubation, which both parents take part in. Both parents will also feed the young. These young will not be able to walk for about three weeks, and cannot fly for about two months.

Our text this morning is referring to the time when Moses was born. Pharaoh had ordered that all the male children be killed. Today also there is much evil going on because of sin. Thank God that He will never forsake you, because He loves you. Ask Him to be with you today.

SILK

I clothed thee also with broidered work, and shod thee with badgers' skin, and I girded thee about with fine linen, and I covered thee with silk. Ezekiel 16:10.

People have been making silk clothing and other goods for thousands of years. I don't know how the process was first discovered. For centuries the Chinese have been using silkworms to produce silk for them, and then it is processed and made into beautiful garments and tapestries. The Chinese are not the only leaders in the silk fabric business today. Japan, India, Russia, South Korea, Italy, Spain, and France are also involved in the silk fabric business. China is the largest producer of white silk fiber. India produces a golden silk.

Silk is the result of a caterpillar, not a worm. The silkworm caterpillar will eject a smooth, lustrous protein mixture that hardens with the exposure to air. Each silkworm caterpillar has two glands that are about three inches long, which produce this liquid silk. As the silk passes through the pink midsection of the gland it is coated with a sticky substance, which gives the cocoon cohesiveness. As these fibers hit the air, they harden, and the caterpillar wraps these around itself until it has a fine, tightly woven cocoon. These silk fibers may be 2,000 to 3,000 feet in length. The cocoons are harvested, soaked in hot water, and the silk strands unraveled. Five or six strands are used as a thread.

The cocoons that are used for silk are put into a hot room where the caterpillars are killed so they will not eat their way out of the cocoon as they turn into moths. When a pupa turns into a moth it emits a liquid that softens the cocoon, thus making it easy to come out. But that partially destroys the silk fibers. Naturally, some cocoons are allowed to mature and the adult moths come out to reproduce more caterpillars.

I thank God that He provided for our needs by creating such creatures as the silkworm. This morning I invite you to once again thank God for His creation, and that you have a part in enjoying and benefiting from it.

GROWING FOR 17 YEARS

And have put on the new man, which is renewed in knowledge after the image of him that created him. Colossians 3:10.

The female cicada uses her saw-toothed ovipositor, at the rear end of her body, to cut a slit in the branches of trees. There she will lay her eggs, 400 to 600 depending on her species. Shortly she drops from the branch and dies. The eggs hatch into nymphs and the nymphs develop into adults. That is the life cycle of the cicada.

Some people call the cicadas locusts. There are about 2,000 species of cicadas in the world. The dog-day cicada has a two-year life cycle, but the periodical cicadas have a 13-year or 17-year cycle.

The nymphs of the 17-year cicada, hatch from the eggs after a six- or seven-week period. They drop from the branch and burrow into the ground close to some nice tree roots. There they will set up their special little house where they will remain during the next 17 years, sucking liquid from the tree or shrub. During that time they will molt and change their body shell several times. Since it takes them so long to mature, and they stay in the nymph stage so long, there are some animals that dig down and eat them.

Once they have matured, the entire brood comes out of the ground. There may be millions of them. Many animals like to eat the cicadas, thus many of the adult cicadas will never take part in the great population explosion. Scientists have numbered the broods of the cicada. The 17-year broods carry the numbers I through XVII, and the 13-year broods numbers XVIII through XXX. In this way, scientists can keep track of the years and know which ones are about to come out.

Jesus promised to give us a new life if we will turn our life over to Him. We will remain in this sin-darkened world until the right time. Scientists do not know why the cicadas stay underground so long, but we know why we are here in this dark world so long. Ask God this morning to come soon and take you out of this world of darkness into the world of light.

BUSH BABY

But the angel of the Lord by night opened the prison doors, and brought them forth. Acts 5:19.

Most of us sleep at night and we have very little concept of what goes on in the world while we are asleep. The world is almost a different place at night, and I'm not talking about all of the people who stay up at night, some working to keep things going for the rest of us.

There are many of God's creatures that are nocturnal by nature. They sleep in the daytime and roam and hunt at night. In the rain forest belt of West Africa lives a nocturnal animal called the bush baby. This little creature is smaller than most house cats but it has as good or better eyesight than the house cat. It has a light-reflecting tapetum, located behind the retina of the eye, that aids the animal's vision at night as it makes its way through the trees.

These animals are basically insectivorous, but will eat a variety of fruits and nuts. During the nighttime hours the bush baby also looks for gum that flows out of the acacia trees. This gives them calcium that they don't get from eating small rodents and insects. The gum flows from the acacia trees when woodboring larvae of two kinds of beetles and one kind of moth form galleries in the branches of the trees. The gum is mobilized on exposure to oxygen; as it flows, the bush baby eats it. Once a "gum lick" is established, the bush baby will visit it frequently. One adult bush baby might visit up to 300 trees during a night looking for the gum.

The bush baby usually sleep in groups during the daylight hours; they hunt alone at night. The female bush baby will have two litters of young a year, usually with two in a litter. The gestation period is about 120 days.

God and His angels work at night as well as in the daytime. He opened the prison doors for His servants at night and Jesus wrestled with Jacob at night. He wants the best for us, and sometimes that must be done at night. Thank God that He is always on duty, day or night, watching out for your best good.

THE SHARP SHOOTER

Let thine eyes look right on, and let thine eyelids look straight before thee. Proverbs 4:25.

Have you ever been under the water at the beach or in a pool and tried looking at the sky or the shore? Without a mask or goggles things look distorted. As you look down into the water from above, the position of things is distorted, too. This is what is known as light refraction.

There is a kind of fish that is a tremendously sharp shooter with a stream of water. This fish is called the archerfish. God has given it a special optical system that allows it to adjust for distance and compensates in some unknown way for the bending of light rays by water. If the archerfish is within about four or five feet of a small object, it can shoot a stream of water under pressure that will knock the object right off its perch and into the water.

This is how it works. The archerfish has been so designed by God that it is able to form a canal with its tongue up against the groove in the roof of its mouth. With the pressure of closing the gills, it can shoot a stream of water through the canal for a distance of about five feet. As the archerfish sees a bug or something else on a branch hanging low over the water, it can come up to the surface and with just its snout sticking out of the water it takes aim, fires, and almost never misses. The bug falls into the water and bingo! it is eaten by the fish.

According to reports the archerfish does not have to depend on this method to eat. It can also go out into the coastal waters and survive. There are no low-hanging branches there to shoot bugs off of, so no doubt the archerfish has another method of obtaining food. Some researchers say they shoot their stream just for sport. What fun, eh?

Yes, God is a lover of the unique and unusual; He certainly proved that to me. Jesus tells us through the psalmist to keep looking at the way we are going and make sure that our eyesight is straight, not curved. We must have a straight view of God. Ask Him to help you have a straight view of His words today.

NEW ZEALAND'S SADDLEBACK BIRD

The Lord is my rock, and my fortress, and my deliverer.
2 Samuel 22:2.

Between the years A.D. 750 and 1300, a group of Polynesian settlers named Maori were the first to migrate to the island now called New Zealand, and settle there. They found the island heavily forested and rich in insects and birds. There were only two species of mammals there, both bats. So the Maoris began to import other animals onto the island.

They brought dogs, cats, pigs, goats, cattle, hedgehogs, ferrets, opossums, wallabies, and weasels. The opossums were brought in with the idea of starting a fur business, but it never materialized. As time went on, new settlers brought in even rats, hoping that with the dogs they would get rid of the wingless moa bird. They also cut down more than 70 percent of the trees to make room for agriculture. But this destroyed the habitats of some birds, one of them being the North Island saddleback, known to the Maori people as "tieke."

These birds are black with a reddish-brown saddle on their backs and have a fleshy, usually orange, wattle in the corner of their beak. According to a Maori legend, the god Maui and his brothers once snared the sun and beat it. They told the sun to move slower so as to give men a longer day. Maui was hot and thirsty and asked the tieke to bring him some water. The bird refused so Maui seized the bird and flung it away from him, leaving two scorched marks from his hot hands on the bird's back. The Moari believe this is how the saddleback got the two brownish marks which look like a saddle, on its back.

To save this and other birds from extinction the New Zealanders have set aside several nearby uninhabited islands as bird sanctuaries. The North Island saddlebacks have started to increase again, after being almost extinct. Some of these islands are nothing more than rock, but those rocks have saved the lives of many creatures.

Jesus is our rock and our salvation. We can depend on Him because He is solid and never changes. Put your trust in Jesus the solid Rock. You'll always have a firm foundation in your life and your life will always be safe.

355

ROSS ICE SHELF

Then the Lord opened the eyes of Balaam, and he saw the angel of the Lord standing in the way, and his sword drawn in his hand: and he bowed down his head, and fell flat on his face. Numbers 22:31.

In the Antarctic there is a large amount of ice. In fact, most of Antarctica is covered with ice. In the year 1841, a British explorer named James Clark Ross was searching for the South Magnetic Pole when he happened to come upon a very large ice pack. It was so large that he and his men spent many days and weeks trying to get around it, but they failed. Ross was not aware that this is the largest ice pack in the world, measuring about 500 miles wide, 200 feet high, and 600 miles long. It covers an area of about 200,000 square miles, or an area about the size of the State of Texas.

Many icebergs break off from this massive ice shelf. Some of these floating islands are about 20 to 30 miles long, some even longer. Despite the losses of these large icebergs, and there are many of them, the Ross Ice Shelf continues to stay about the same size. As the snow that falls in the Antarctic continues to pile up, this adds to the ice pack, so actually it does not lose any of its size. Some scientists say that the Ross Ice Shelf is moving toward the ocean at a speed of about six feet per day. Of course, the ice that gets into the warmer water or air begins to melt, and the icebergs are born.

The ice barrier stopped Ross but it helped Roald Amundsen and Robert F. Scott, the first two men to reach the South Pole. Today on this large ice shelf the countries of the United States and New Zealand have year-round research stations. They are located at the western end, on McMurdo Sound.

Balaam was stopped by an angel. The donkey saw the angel but Balaam did not. Balaam was going to do something that the Lord did not want done; that's why He stopped him. The Ross Ice Shelf stopped the British explorer, but others succeeded. In our Christian experience, we need to be stopped from doing some things and helped in doing others. We need to be sure that we are doing what God wants us to do; then we will succeed. Ask God to help you follow His will today, and you will succeed.

THE RHINE RIVER

Ye mountains of Israel, hear the word of the Lord God; Thus saith the Lord God to the mountains, and to the hills, to the rivers, and to the valleys; Behold, I, even I, will bring a sword upon you, and I will destroy your high places. Ezekiel 6:3.

The Rhine River is not the longest river in the world, but it is a very important river for the countries that it serves. It is probably the busiest river in the world, even busier than the Mississippi River. Like the Amazon River, the Rhine starts up in the mountains. The Swiss mountains provide the bulk of the water for the Rhine, but it picks up water from other rivers as it flows toward the North Sea. The Rhine is one of the few rivers that flow north; most rivers flow south. It is 820 miles long.

The Rhine begins in Switzerland under the name of *Rein*. As the two rivers, the Vorder Rhein and the Hinter Rhein, come together at the town of Reichenau, they form the upper Rhine. It passes through Austria and Liechtenstein and into the Lake of Constance. There it leaves the silt that has been brought from the mountains and goes on as a virtually clear river. By the time the river reaches Basel it has traveled only 233 miles and dropped 7,000 feet in elevation. In its final 600 miles the river drops only about 800 feet.

At Basel the Rhine heads north into the Black Forest area of Germany. Once past the town of Bingen, the river passes through the area of the castles of the old monarchs and other important people of days gone by. After leaving Bonn, the capital of West Germany, the river leaves the mountains and becomes darker in color and has many more ships on it. The river enters the North Sea at Rotterdam, Holland, which is a very deep seaport.

The Rhine is important in history for all of its charm and splendor. In the New Earth God will reestablish even more beautiful scenery for us. Pray that you will be able to enjoy the scenery that God is planning for you throughout all eternity. You'll not want to miss that.

SEA STACKS

And Moses wrote all the words of the Lord, and rose up early in the morning, and builded an altar under the hill, and twelve pillars, according to the twelve tribes of Israel. Exodus 24:4.

The oceans are often rough and always moving. In some areas this creates beaches and in some areas it creates cliffs or rocky shorelines. Almost always the coastal areas are beautiful.

Certain coastal areas are made of sandstone, and the constant battering of the waves wears away the rock. In some places the wash is so bad that the water has chewed the shoreline back for many hundreds of feet. The rock has crumbled and been washed away. As you drive along some coasts you will see some pillars out in the water. The constant washing of the waves has weakened the rock, certain boring creatures have made holes in the soft rock, and the combination of the two forces has caused the cliffs to deteriorate. Sometimes they leave pillars of stronger rock out in the water. These pillars are called sea stacks.

One of the most noted areas of sea stacks and cliffs is in Australia. It has been designated the Port Campbell National Park; there are about 20 miles of these sea stacks and cliffs. There are a number of arches also in this area. An arch that has a tower at each end has been named the London Bridge. At another spot, there are 12 sea stacks; they have been named after the 12 apostles.

There are sea stacks off the island of Bermuda. With the emerald water as a background, they are a striking sight. Stacks can also be found off the coasts of Oregon, California, Washington, the Hawaiian Islands, and elsewhere.

Moses built an altar under a hill with 12 pillars for the 12 tribes of Israel. In the walls of the New Jerusalem there will be 12 gates, one for each tribe. Thank God for His love today and for His preparations for you that will last forever.

KILLER CATERPILLARS

And the chief priests and scribes sought how they might kill him; for they feared the people. Luke 22:2.

The inchworm, or measuringworm, is known as the killer caterpillar. These caterpillars will eat flies. How can an inchworm caterpillar catch a fly? Is the caterpillar that fast? You probably have tried many times to catch a fly, and now you wonder how a slow-moving caterpillar can do it.

Mimicry is part of this caterpillar's hunting technique. It will bite off and spit out parts of a leaf. Then it will crawl into the hole it has made in the leaf and wait. As a fly approaches and lands on the leaf, the caterpillar will wait patiently, then all of a sudden it will swing around and with its six feet grab the fly. It may not eat all of the fly, but it will eat most of it. They mimic twigs, thorns, and scales.

Inchworms are just that, about an inch long. When the female lays her eggs, she will lay them individually, each one with a silk thread attached to it. She may lay up to 100 eggs, which hatch in about 14 days. The larvae will molt four times in their growing process. They split their tight skins, wiggle out, and in half an hour they are ready again to go after their prey. After the third molting, they spin a doilylike cocoon. About three weeks later they will molt for the fourth time, appearing as a moth.

These moths mimic the fern leaf. They appear in two colors, brown and green. Scientists are not quite sure how they get their color. Do they just molt into a color, or are they influenced by the environment? Another of God's interesting mysteries.

Jesus was once a victim of the priests. They didn't like the way He did things, for it challenged their traditional ways. Jesus didn't conform to tradition, He taught about the love of God in simple ways, and He went about helping people in their time of need. This made the priests jealous. Invite Jesus to come into your life today, and give your life over to Him. He loves, He does not kill.

KIWI

They have wandered as blind men in the streets, they have polluted themselves with blood, so that men could not touch their garments. Lamentations 4:14.

New Zealand is the only place where the kiwi bird is found. Therefore it has become the national symbol of New Zealand. Its picture is on New Zealand coins, stamps, clothing, and even on cans of shoe polish. It doesn't really look like a bird, but it is.

Kiwis don't have typical feathers like other birds, but they are coarse and furlike. They don't have wings, either. They have no enemies except man. Since they are the national symbol, they are now protected from slaughter by man.

The kiwi is about the size of a chicken. It has very poor eyesight. It can make out shadows, but objects must be very close if they are to be seen. The nose of the kiwi is at the tip of its bill. The kiwi comes out and hunts at night for its favorite meal, the earthworm. If it cannot find enough earthworms it will eat some snails or insects, and even some berries. There are some fine hairs at the base of the bill that are feelers for the kiwi. It is said that the kiwi has the keenest smell of any bird. Kiwis have a keen hearing also, and they will run at the slightest noise. They are fast runners and will run along like a spear thrower, with their nose straight out.

The kiwi lays a very large egg, one of the largest of any bird egg. It is about five inches long and weighs about one pound. The male will incubate the egg, not eating for a week at a time. It will take about 75 to 80 days for the one egg to hatch. When the chick hatches it is covered with a fuzzy down. In a few hours it is foraging for itself. The parents lay another egg and start another chick on its way.

God doesn't want us to wander around like the wicked, as though we were blind. He wants us to have good eyesight. The way to have that good spiritual eyesight is to continue to study the Word of God, which gives us the insights into our present and future life. Ask God to help you have good eyesight today.

GYPSUM

And spared not the old world, but saved Noah the eighth person, a preacher of righteousness, bringing in the flood upon the world of the ungodly. 2 Peter 2:5.

God told Noah what to do and what He would do if Noah was faithful. Noah was faithful, and God fulfilled His promise. The Flood came and Noah and his family were saved. Under the waters of that Flood great upheavals of earth occurred. Many natural resources were buried. Today many of those natural resources are being discovered. One of these resources is gypsum.

We depend a lot on gypsum, though we may not even realize it. There is gypsum in tooth paste. Gypsum is also used in matches; in molds to make sterling-silver handles for knives, forks, and spoons; in plaster of paris for splints and other uses; in the making of plates, saucers, cups, and other dishes to eat on; and in casts used by dentists in making dentures. Many of the houses that we live in have gypsum wallboard in one form or another. Gypsum wallboard is the biggest and most lucrative part of the gypsum business, which consumes more than 12 million tons a year, worth about $100 million.

Early inhabitants on this earth such as the Assyrians, Egyptians, and Greeks used gypsum in one form or another. The Assyrians used it in their cuneiform scripts and the Egyptians used it in making vessels, boxes, and sculptures. It was also used in constructing the Egyptian family pyramids. The Greek word for this substance is *gypsos*, meaning chalk. Gypsum in its natural state is white and chalky. It is soft and can be scratched easily.

Gypsum is the only product that can be softened with water and then when it is dry takes back its original hard form. This is why plaster of Paris is so good for casts—it dries quickly and gets hard.

God has a plan for everything that He does, and He gives us the wisdom to know how to use the natural resources He has provided. Thank God today for His foresight in your behalf. He is a God of love, so thank Him for that, too.

HORSETAILS

They did eat, they drank, they married wives, they were given in marriage, until the day that Noe entered into the ark, and the flood came, and destroyed them all. Luke 17:27.

In the coal layers under the earth, geologists have found fossil prints of the leaves of the plants that today we call horsetails. Apparently before the Flood they were very large bushes and are responsible for much of the coal that is mined today.

Horsetails are found on all continents except Australia. They will grow anywhere, and that is beneficial to mankind because they will cover areas where there is no other vegetation and keep back the erosion of soil. Horsetails grow up to about three feet tall in many areas, but the most common height is from eighteen inches to two feet.

The horsetail shoots up a stem that is jointed every so often; it is from these joints that the leaves grow. They have a glasslike deposit of silica in some of their cells that is suited for scouring pots and pans. The American Indians and early settlers in America used these weeds to scour their pans. Some researchers are wondering if there are still people in remote primitive areas who may still be using horsetails for that purpose.

There are 15 varieties of horsetails in North America, extending down into Northern Mexico. The aerial shoots of the plants are of two types: (1) vegetative branches that have tufts at the nodes, and (2) reproductive branches that have small cones on their tips. The cones release spores that have four attached threadlike elators, which coil and straighten rapidly, according to the moisture content of the air. These movements aid in the releasing of the spores, which reproduce new plants in June and July of each year.

Horsetails that have become coal are among the resources God has made for our use. Let us use them wisely. Ask God this morning to help you live a good life today and forever.

GEODES

Therefore thus saith the Lord God, Behold, I lay in Zion for a foundation a stone, a tried stone, a precious corner stone, a sure foundation: he that believeth shall not make haste. Isaiah 28:16.

Just by looking at a geode from the outside, it is difficult to imagine what a beautiful inside it has. But upon splitting the rock open, you can see some of the most beautiful sights in crystal formation.

There are certain places in the world where these geodes are found. A person going into the area of geodes needs to know what to look for. Rock hounds tell me that one cannot judge the beauty of a geode by the exterior appearance. To some they look like petrified cauliflower heads. However, one rock hound told me that when he sees an ugly rock he knows that there is going to be a beautiful crystal formation inside.

Geodes come in all sizes. One scientist said that his fellow scientists do not know definitely how geodes originated; their development and origin remain controversial. Some scientists believe that the geodes are still growing, through the process of evolution.

Geodes are formed by many types of crystals. In the State of Indiana, where a lot of geodes are found, 20 different minerals have been identified in geodes. Geodes are found in sedimentary rocks, such as limestone; rarely are they found in shale, siltstone, and sandstone.

Geodes are composed of a thin layer of a kind of quartz called chalcedony, which is very beautiful and named as one of the 12 foundation stones for the wall of the New Jerusalem.

While some people are trying to determine how the geodes are made, there are others who are trying to do away with the importance of the Cornerstone, Jesus. Christians know that Jesus is the true cornerstone upon whom we should build our life. Ask Jesus to help you build your life on Him today; He is the only sure foundation that will not crumble when everything else gives way. He is always there to hold you up.

GOATSBEARD

And ye are complete in him, which is the head of all principality and power. Colossians 2:10.

Goatsbeard—do you know what it is? "Sure, it's the beard on a goat." Wrong. "Oh, I know, it's a big dandelion." Wrong again. "Well, tell me what it is." You were on the right track when you thought that it looked like a dandelion, but it is much bigger than a dandelion and is not related.

Goatsbeard is a beautiful yellow flower that is found out in meadows and woods. It grows into quite a large flower, a little larger than dandelion flowers. It is not mistaken for a dandelion, as the flower is entirely different, having long pointed green bracts.

We are told that the goatsbeard comes from the Old World (somewhere in Europe or thereabouts). It is mostly a biennial herb, and is definitely a wildflower. The flower looks like an aster, sunflower and daisy, all in one composite. It has green leaves that sweep up from the base of the flower, which is composed of many little flowers at the center, surrounded by larger-petaled flowers on the outside. These are what are called "ray flowers."

I have seen these flowers beside the roadsides as I travel along, and I think they are beautiful. I am especially fond of them when the yellow flower has disappeared and they turn to a large white seedhead like the dandelion. This is why many people, at a quick glance, think that they are dandelions. The large pappus ball at the end of the stem is striking. It is very delicate in nature. Many people do not see the yellow flower because it closes at noon. Therefore it carries the nicknames of "sleep-at-noon," "noontide," "Jack-go-to-bed-at-noon," "meadow salsify," "Joseph's flower," "star of Jerusalem," "noonflower," and "bucksbeard."

Jesus has many names too. He is referred to as the "Morning Star," "Prince of Peace," "Counselor," "Lamb of God," "Son of man," "Son of God," "Lord of lords," "King of kings," and "Saviour." He truly is our Saviour and Lord, and we should thank Him this morning for what He did for us. Thank Jesus this morning that He is your Saviour and Lord. When you do this, you heed His voice.

MANTA RAY

These see the works of the Lord, and his wonders in the deep.
Psalm 107:24.

Manta rays are the largest of the ray family, which includes stingrays and eagle rays. The manta ray is a perfectly harmless creature with very small teeth and no stinging tail. It feeds on plankton and is very graceful as it swims in the ocean. It has big "wings" that flap in the water, and it can swim at up to 25 miles an hour by wafting its wings.

A group of divers and underwater photographers were filming underwater in the Sea of Cortes in Mexico when they saw a very large creature coming toward them. They discovered it to be a manta ray with a wingspan of about 18 feet across and a body about ten feet long. It measured three feet between the eyes.

The manta ray stopped right underneath one of the divers. He let go of the rope he was resting on and dropped to the back of the manta ray. As he grabbed hold of the ray's shoulders it surged forward. With the diver on his back the manta began to sail through the water to a depth of about 160 feet. The diver described it as "reality becoming fantasy and fantasy becoming real." He was able to see beautiful fan corals and other sea creatures, which made it a delightful trip.

Other divers had an opportunity to ride on the back of this large manta ray. They were ecstatic over this opportunity. They found a rope tied around its body and after several tries they finally got the rope cut loose. The rope had become embedded in the manta's skin. The manta seemed to want to say "Thank you," so it continued to come back for more riders.

Why some creatures act the way they do we won't know until we reach heaven. Some creatures almost seem human in their reaction to the treatment they receive. David said that those who went out to sea would see the wonderful works of the Lord. Certainly these divers saw them that day. What a wonderful privilege it will be to be able to see everything that God has created in its perfect form. Pray to God this morning, asking Him to help you be faithful so you will have that opportunity.

CORDILLERA BLANCA

And a man shall be as an hiding place from the wind, and a covert from the tempest; as rivers of water in a dry place, as the shadow of a great rock in a weary land. Isaiah 32:2.

The Cordillera Blanca is one of my favorite places. I have flown over it many times, and each time I took pictures. It was always a special part of my trip. The Cordillera Blanca are the "white mountains" in the Andes of Peru. They always have snow on them. There are more than thirty jagged peaks in this range; the highest one is Huascarán (waz-CAR-on), 22,205 feet high.

The Cordillera Blanca is about 125 miles long and is only about 100 miles from the Pacific Ocean. The western side of this range drops into the valley of the Rio Santa (holy river). On the eastern side, the streams flow into the Amazon River. Although the Cordillera Blanca is only a few hundred miles south of the equator, snow still remains on the peaks above 15,000 feet. It is sort of a perpetual ice cap; also, some glaciers are formed, which empty into some beautiful and picturesque lakes.

When I flew between Iquitos, on the Amazon, in the jungles of Peru, to Lima, the capital city, the plane always flew to the south of Huascarán. I wanted to see the north side. On one trip our airplane captain took us north of Huascarán. I was really excited and took some good pictures. I didn't know that a few years later an earthquake would take much of that side of Huascarán tumbling down into the valley below and destroy a city or two and many lives. I was saddened to hear the news of that event.

Many thought that Huascarán was a hiding place, only to find out that it was not a secure one. The prophet Isaiah told us that "a Man" would come who would be the hiding place for us. We can depend on this hiding place, because it is the Rock, Jesus. He will shelter and protect us forever, if we will allow Him to do so. Place your trust in Him this morning again and tell Him about your desire to be in His abiding care.

RED-SIDED GARTER SNAKE

But I fear, lest by any means, as the serpent beguiled Eve through his subtilty, so your minds should be corrupted from the simplicity that is in Christ. 2 Corinthians 11:3.

The province of Manitoba, Canada, is the place where one of the world's strangest displays of wildlife behavior is staged from April to May each year. It happens near the community of Inwood, about 60 miles north of the city of Winnipeg.

This bizarre event takes place in the lime pits, when the red-sided garter snakes come out of hibernation. Amidst the crawling, squirming mass of thousands of snakes, the mating ceremony takes place, involving all of the snakes. After the ceremony is completed the snakes leave the lime pits and crawl to their summer homes in the marshes and fields, up to ten miles away. There they spend the next three months living on frogs, leeches, worms, slugs, and occasionally small rodents.

In August the females give birth to the young. Shortly thereafter the young snakes disappear and are not seen for a year, when they return to the lime pits. Where they go no one seems to know for sure, but it is guessed that they live in abandoned anthills and rodent burrows—which may not have been abandoned until the snakes arrived.

The town of Inwood has many tales about these red-sided garter snakes. The people seem to be content with all of these snakes around. They do not want government health department officials coming around and inspecting their stores for fear that they will declare them "infested" and close them. Some people want to reactivate the lime pits for commercial purposes but the townspeople do not want their snakes harmed. They have learned to live with the red-sided garter snakes and enjoy them as part of their environment.

The markings are pretty on these snakes, and I sometimes wonder if that was not the case with the serpent that Satan used when he deceived Eve. The apostle Paul was concerned that God's people would be deceived in their minds, as Eve was. Only as we keep in close contact with Christ can this be avoided. Pray this morning, asking Jesus to occupy your mind today. Then the devil will not be able to get in and try to deceive you.

367

SEA UNICORNS

And we desire that every one of you do shew the same diligence to the full assurance of hope unto the end: that ye be not slothful, but followers of them who through faith and patience inherit the promises. Hebrews 6:11, 12.

Five sixths of Greenland, the world's largest island, is covered with ice. In many remote areas of the island, the people live on what they can hunt. Even in the northwest corner of the island, in an area called the Thule region, the native Eskimos eke out an existence.

When the ice melts, in a very short summer, the minerals suspended in the melting water help to produce much plankton (small sea life), which are eaten by the halibut fish. The halibut fish are the favorite food of the narwhal whale. The narwhal whales watch for the melt. Sometimes they are there ahead of the melt, and they patiently swim and wait, knowing they will be rewarded with halibut dinners.

When the narwhals arrive, the Eskimos get busy. The law allows the hunting of these whales only from kayaks. The kayaks, made of seal skin, are all in readiness, the hunting gear strapped to the top. At the sight of the narwhals, the hunters go into action to harpoon them. When they have killed one, which usually takes several men, the first harpooner gets the skin, called *muktuk*, and the tusk. The second harpooner gets the second largest share, and so on, but all get something for their help. The Eskimos store this muktuk for the winter in rock-lined holes in the ground.

The male narwhal has a left tooth that grows long, protruding from the front of the whale as much as ten feet. This tusk or tooth is straight but spirally grooved. A nice tusk will be sold for about $800, which is used to buy heating fuel and other necessities. The tusk makes the whale look like a unicorn, therefore the nickname "sea unicorn."

As these Eskimos await the narwhals, so we should await the promises of God. They will come to us, just at the right time, if we will wait patiently. God promised and He keeps His promises. Thank God for His promises today.

U.S. NATIONAL CHRISTMAS TREE

When thou shalt besiege a city a long time, in making war against it to take it, thou shalt not destroy the trees thereof by forcing an axe against them. Deuteronomy 20:19.

Trees can be a precious commodity, especially in areas where they are hard to grow. In the State of California, there are trees that are called redwoods or sequoias. These are very large trees.

The Sierra redwoods, which live only in California, are beautiful and graceful trees. In the King's Canyon National Park stands the second largest of these trees. It is called the General Grant. Back in the year 1924, Charles Lee, a resident of a nearby town, was looking up at the gigantic General Grant tree and admiring it. A little girl passed by and remarked, "What a wonderful Christmas tree that would be." Mr. Lee thought so too, so he wrote to the President, Calvin Coolidge. Within four months this tree was named the "official national Christmas tree."

A special Christmas celebration was held in 1926 at the tree, and has been repeated the second week of each December. One man who attended that first celebration has been there ever since. In 1971, because of a severe blizzard people did not go to celebrate, but this man and several rangers went through the snow to lay a wreath at the foot of the tree. He was only 71 years old then. He is still alive and attends the celebration.

The General Grant tree is 267 feet high and measures more than 100 feet around at the base. It is estimated that it contains more than 550,000 board feet of lumber and weighs about 5,000 tons. It is estimated to be about 3,500 years old.

God told the people in Bible times to save the trees. Today God is telling us to save the people. God loves trees but He loves people much more, because He created us in His image. Thank God this morning because He loves people. God is a people-oriented God.

BIRDS ON CHRISTMAS ISLAND

And the wild beasts of the islands shall cry in their desolate houses, and dragons in their pleasant palaces: and her time is near to come, and her days shall not be prolonged. Isaiah 13:22.

Christmas Island is a tiny island 1,334 miles south of the Hawaiian Islands. It is the largest coral atoll in the world, which means that the coral is like a horseshoe around a shallow lagoon. No one lived on this island until 1925. Then folks were brought here from the Gilbert Islands, which is about 2,500 miles west, to work in coconut plantations. During World War II the United States set up a military base there. During the 1950s and 1960s both the United States and Great Britain tested atomic bombs in the area, although no bombs were dropped directly on the island.

These atomic-bomb testings didn't seem to seriously affect the bird life on Christmas Island. There are about 18 different seabird species that congregate there, and it is the home for an estimated 16 million birds.

Several of the birds have unique habits. The fairy terns build no nest, but lay their eggs in a slight depression on the bare ground. The frigate birds catch fish. When one is carrying home his catch, the others try to take it away; they jockey in the air and clown around. The red-footed boobies build their nests in the branches of bushes. The blue-faced boobies, which have clownlike faces, lay two eggs but bother about only one. If the one hatches they forget the other. If the baby bird dies, the parents try to incubate the other egg. This extra egg is called the "insurance egg."

The tropic birds cannot walk but they are fantastic aerial acrobats. When they land they do so on a bush, then fall to the ground and shuffles along on its breast. They can hover, fly backward, and do many other startling maneuvers, but they cannot walk.

The islands of the seas are often wild, but beautiful, and full of all types of wildlife. God hears the cries of these creatures, and He will hear your cry for help. Turn to Him today and ask Him to help you with a problem you may have this morning.

INK

Write the things which thou hast seen, and the things which are, and the things which shall be hereafter. Revelation 1:19.

Have you ever wondered what people used to write with back in the Bible times? Did they make their own ink? John the revelator was told to write what he had seen. What did he use?

When I was a small boy in school, we had holes in our desks called inkwells. We would put a small ink bottle in the hole and from there we would get our ink to write with. We had straight pens and fountain pens. We dipped the straight pens into the ink bottle often, as the point didn't hold much ink, but the fountain pens had a rubber reservoir inside them, which would hold the ink until it was all used.

One day our teacher said that we would make our own ink. She went with us out into a field by the woods where our school was situated, and we picked pokeberries. The early American Indians used the pokeberries to dye cloth, and the soft shoots of the plant they cooked like asparagus. The roots and the seeds of the berries are poisonous.

After the berries were picked, they were put into a kettle and boiled and then they were put into a cheesecloth and squeezed. After the juice ran out, the berry pulp and seeds were discarded. The berry juice was cooked again for about half an hour, and the teacher told us that this was our inkwell, almost. She had to add some alum to keep the ink from fading. Alum is used by cooks in preparing some foods.

Our pokeberry ink had a crimson color. We learned that the more berries used, the darker would be the color of the ink. As soon as the ink cooled, the teacher allowed us to dip our pens into it and write. What fun we had drawing and writing with the ink we had made.

John wrote as he was instructed. Because he obeyed, we have the book of Revelation. It has much in it for us to study and understand today, and helps us know the reason for what is happening in the world. If we are obedient and follow the commands of Jesus, we will have a successful future as did John. Ask Jesus this morning to help you be obedient to His commands.

QUICK-CHANGE FLEA

Being then made free from sin, ye became the servants of righteousness. Romans 6:18.

How would you like to be born just for the purpose of being eaten as food? Such is the life of the quick-change flea. The water flea is not much bigger than a small grain of rice. It is a common resident of most of the ponds in North America. Its chief enemy is the young aquatic fly larva called a midge. If no midges are around, there is usually some other predator to eat the water flea. It seems that its only purpose is to be eaten. However, it does have a strong defensive strategy. As one scientist said of the quick-change fleas: "They don't take this whole matter lying down."

When the baby water fleas are born, they look quite different from their parents. In fact, some scientists have said that they look almost like a different species. According to the season of the year that they are born, their outer skin may be all armor. If they are born when the midge-fly larvae are active, the water fleas will come equipped with neck teeth or a special spine spike that makes them hard to eat.

It has been discovered that the midge larvae secrete some kind of a fluid as they swim around looking for their water-flea meal. When the female water flea detects the presence of the midge larvae, she is able to produce her young fleas with these defensive barbs; this cuts down the mortality rate by 50 percent. Researchers have also found that longer and warmer days cause the female water flea to produce her young with the special armor. The water flea is quite active and a fast swimmer; a quick sprint may keep it away from a midge larvae, and it may not make a meal for a while. But inevitably it is eaten sometime.

The one who has made his or her life right with God is no longer a prey of the devil, like the water flea is for the midge larvae. The Christian is a servant of God. We take on the armor by accepting Jesus as our personal Saviour and by studying the Bible to know His will. I invite you to accept Jesus into your life this morning and pray, asking Him to make you free from sin and help you to be His servant. You'll be glad you did.

THE SILVER DOME

The devil taketh him up into an exceeding high mountain, and sheweth him all the kingdoms of the world, and the glory of them. Matthew 4:8.

If the mountain the devil took Jesus to was in Palestine, it was not high as the world's mountains go. The Flood has left many high peaks and mountains.

In the country of Tanzania, on the African continent, stands Mount Kilimanjaro, a very famous mountain. It is the highest mountain in Africa. The highest peak of the mountain is called "Kibo"; it is 19,340 feet above sea level. The area around this peak is glacial. Because of the constant ice and snow, the early native Africans called the peak the Silver Dome, because as the bright African sun hit the ice caps and reflected down to where the people lived, it no doubt looked silver.

Kilimanjaro means "mountain of greatness" or "mountain of caravans," depending on which dialect you use. Kilimanjaro has three volcanoes within it, but only one, called the Kibo Crater, is the youngest. On a clear day Kilimanjaro can be seen for about 100 miles. It rises nearly four miles into the air and is located about 180 miles from the East African coast.

Although Kilimanjaro is so noticeable, the early explorers seemed to ignore it. Not until May of 1848 was it discovered by a German missionaries named Johannes Rebmann and Ludwig Krapf. Today people come from all over the world to climb Kilimanjaro. Although it is somewhat difficult to climb and the air at the top is very thin, there are rewards for those who conquer the climb. One can see much beautiful country round about.

Satan took Jesus up on a high mountain and showed Him all around and told Him that all would be His if He would worship him—the devil. I am thankful that Jesus didn't fall for the devil's bargain, and that He is our loving Saviour and Lord today. Thank Him for His love and His decision to reject the devil's invitation.

373

HOATZIN—THE WORLD'S
STRANGEST BIRD

For yet a little while, and the wicked shall not be: yea, thou shalt diligently consider his place, and it shall not be. Psalm 37:10.

One of the strangest, most interesting, and remarkable birds of today lives in the jungles of South America and is called the hoatzin (wahtssen) bird. These birds grow to about 25 inches long and weigh almost two pounds. The feathers are an olive brown barred with white on top and cream to rusty color below. The head is very small, with a strange-looking crest about four inches long. The eyes are scarlet red and surrounded with a light-blue skin with no feathers. The male and female look alike.

These hoatzins build a flat nest that is just a pile of sticks thrown together. The nest is usually built far out on a limb, four to fifteen feet above water, because their main enemies, the capuchin monkeys, are afraid to go out too far. Both parents will sit on the nest and incubate the eggs, which take about four weeks to hatch. The parents feed almost exclusively on leaves and fruit, another oddity for most birds, and the regurgitated food from the parents is necessary to keep them alive for three to four months, since the small hoatzins grow and develop slowly. When the chicks hatch, they have four clawed digits, two at each wing bend, which help them climb a branch or tree. When they are old enough to fly, the claws drop off.

When danger is near the nest, the chicks will drop to the water below and swim for quite a distance under the surface. When the danger is past, they swim back to the tree and climb back to their nest, using their claws. From one week old, hoatzin chicks are good swimmers. Adult hoatzins are not good flyers and do not fly more than about 500 feet from the nesting area. Only about 50 percent of the hoatzins have a clutch of chicks, and only half of the chicks live to be adult birds.

As the hoatzin chick escapes the wicked enemy, so may we, with the help of Jesus, escape the enemy, Satan. According to our Scripture today, it will not be much longer until Jesus will come and put an end to all the wicked. Pray today that you will be on Jesus' side and not be in the wicked group whom Jesus will destroy.

MOUNT EVEREST

And he carried me away in the spirit to a great and high mountain, and shewed me that great city, the holy Jerusalem, descending out of heaven from God. Revelation 21:10.

The highest mountain in the world, is Mount Everest, situated in the Himalayan Mountains on the China (Tibet)-Nepal border. This mountain was named after Sir George Everest, an early surveyor of India. Formerly it was known as Mountain XV. Its peak is 29,028 feet above sea level. The air is thin at the top, and the peak is virtually devoid of any wildlife. There are fierce winds and low temperatures, usually well below freezing.

This mountain peak has lured many climbers since the first ones in 1921 when a British expedition party, under the leadership of George Mallory, tried to climb it. They made it to the 22,900-foot mark and had to turn back. The next year seven of Mallory's men were killed in an attempt to climb the mountain. In 1924 Mallory and a friend were seen at the 28,126-foot mark, but were never seen nor heard from again. They were trying to climb the most treacherous east side, which was not attempted again until 1982. That team failed also, but a team of men did succeed in reaching the top by the east side on October 8, 1983. It took them five and a half weeks to make the climb.

The first climbers to reach the summit, as far as anyone knows, were Edmund Hillary and Sherpa, Tenzing Norgay, on May 29, 1953. Mount Everest has been a challenge to many climbers. Sixty-two of them have lost their lives trying to make the ascent. One hundred and forty-nine climbers, both men and women, have made the ascent successfully in 68 groups representing 21 nations. Truly this has been a challenge.

Climbers say the sight from the top of Mount Everest is beautiful. The revelator John saw the New Jerusalem from a high mountain and described it as beautiful, too. Tell God this morning how much you'd like to be in His New Jerusalem, and in 1987 try to live the kind of life that will please Him.

375

SCRIPTURAL INDEX

TOPICAL INDEX